# Unleashing Demons

*The Inside Story of Brexit*

## CRAIG OLIVER

HODDER &
STOUGHTON

First published in Great Britain in 2016 by Hodder & Stoughton
An Hachette UK company

4

Copyright © Craig Oliver 2016

The right of Craig Oliver to be identified as the Author of the Work
has been asserted by him in accordance with the
Copyright, Designs and Patents Act 1988.

A CIP catalogue record for this title is available from the British Library

Hardback ISBN 978 1 473 65245 3
Trade paperback ISBN 978 1 473 65246 0
Ebook ISBN 978 1 473 65247 7

Typeset in Bembo MT by Palimpsest Book Production Ltd, Falkirk, Stirlingshire

Printed and bound by Clays Ltd, St Ives plc

Hodder & Stoughton policy is to use papers that are natural, renewable
and recyclable products and made from wood grown in sustainable forests.
The logging and manufacturing processes are expected to conform to the
environmental regulations of the country of origin.

Hodder & Stoughton Ltd
Carmelite House
50 Victoria Embankment
London EC4Y 0DZ

www.hodder.co.uk

*You could unleash demons of which ye know not.*

David Cameron on being asked to sum
up the argument against a referendum


*Let go thy hold when a great wheel runs down a hill, lest it break
thy neck with following it.*

The Fool, *King Lear*, Act II, Scene IV


*So what was it about? People's emotions matter even when they
don't seem wholly rational . . . There is, among a section of the
population, a kind of hysteria, a contagious mourning of the kind
that I remember in 1997 after the death of the Princess of Wales.
It is not about the EU, of course . . .*

Boris Johnson, writing ten days after the referendum

For my daughters, Maya, Iona and Honor.

# Contents

## AFTER

# *Preface*

## Referendum Night

### 23 June 2016

IT IS 7 p.m. on the day of the EU referendum.

The Prime Minister's Press Secretary, Graeme Wilson, and I are trying to get from the Remain HQ back to No. 10 Downing Street.

The gates are half open at the entrance to Mansion House Tube station. We wander down to the barriers, but are told torrential rain has caused heavy flooding – and there won't be any trains for some time.

Back outside the station, I order an Uber cab. The world has turned monochrome, with swollen, grey clouds blotting out the sky. The air is heavy and it seems to take forever for the app to confirm a car is coming.

Both of us feel bruised by a brutal campaign. I have felt confident of victory all day, but am beginning to feel uneasy. Graeme has always been more cautious – telling me he'll believe it when he sees it.

A car arrives just as fat raindrops are beginning to fall again. We edge our way back to No. 10 through gridlocked traffic. Graeme points to some tweets showing thousands of people stuck at railway stations because of the flooding, struggling to get home. How many of them won't be able to vote?

As we reach the Embankment, I get a call from Chris Grayling, the Leader of the House of Commons, who, despite being pro-Brexit, has made a point of keeping lines open during the campaign.

He tells me very clearly he believes Leave has lost – and says he will have a key role in bringing the Conservative party back together again. He warns me that Iain Duncan Smith will be the first Leave supporter on the BBC at 10 p.m. and could criticise David Cameron and the way he ran the campaign. I text the Prime Minister to let him know. He calls back almost immediately, but there isn't much more to say.

It takes over an hour to crawl back to No. 10 – a journey that should take a quarter of that time.

When I arrive, Caroline Preston, the head of broadcasting, informs me that Theresa May, who has spent the campaign adopting a 'submarine strategy' of avoiding media where possible, is now keen to do the high-profile 8.10 a.m. slot on Radio 4's *Today*. We've already told the programme the Defence Secretary, Michael Fallon, is doing it, but her team is trying to set it up behind our back. I am clear we should not shift.

I walk upstairs to discover the staterooms are taken up with a variety of people from across No. 10.

I'm wearing a blue 'I'm In . . .' T-shirt. I've been wondering if it should have the words '. . . it up to my neck' on the back.

The doors sectioning off the Pillared Room, Terracotta Room and White Room have been opened up – and the wide No. 10 family has come together. Civil servants, special advisers and politicians mingle. A long table has been set up, laden with moussaka and lasagne. Wine and elderflower cordial are served.

I chat with a few people. The mood is good.

Jim Messina, who ran Obama's successful second campaign and is trying to do the same for Hillary Clinton, comes over for a chat. Always an interesting mix of the cool and the geeky, he's looking confident – telling me his model says it'll be around 52–48 for Remain. Close, but I'll take that. His prediction has extra force, because he was one of the few who called the general election right.

The Conservative party chairman, Andrew Feldman, comes over and says a lot of hedge funds have been running models, too – they are also confident of a Remain victory. That's reflected in the markets, with the pound buoyant.

As we chat, the PM comes over. He's looking relaxed in a casual, navy-blue shirt that isn't tucked in. Another poll comes through. It's 52–48 (on a sample size of 5,000) to us.

Samantha Cameron has some friends over. They want to know if I can get their children some Remain T-shirts.

There isn't a single indicator that suggests we should be worried.

I get a call from Faisal Islam, Sky's political editor. He's planning on breaking a story at 10 p.m. that Farage has already conceded defeat. I go into the dark street outside No. 10, with a phalanx of cameras behind silver crush barriers, and have a talk with him. He shows me the embargoed quote.

As we approach the closing of polls at 10 p.m., a couple of dozen of us, including the PM, gather around a TV in the Pillared Room. What looks like a dodgy cop drama lumbers its way to a conclusion before the results show comes on BBC1.

The Prime Minister's Parliamentary Private Secretary, Gavin Williamson, is showing everyone a letter coordinated by the MP Robert Syms. It's signed by eighty-four pro-Brexit MPs, and argues David Cameron should stay on whatever the circumstances.

The point is to show that those eager to get rid of the PM can't get the required fifty signatures. To me it simply shows there are dozens who wouldn't sign it.

The BBC programme struggles – hampered by the fact

there is no exit poll. After an hour of torture, I change into a suit and round up the press team to go to the Stronger In party.

We get in a cab that takes us a very long way round to the Festival Hall. The events team are glad to see us – standing outside the room, filling plastic bowls with some kind of stodgy rice dish. They warn it's a bit thin inside.

I walk in, avoiding the TV presenters Kay Burley and Julie Etchingham, and have a series of conversations with the great and the good of the campaign, all of whom think we've done enough.

This campaign has made for strange bedfellows and I'm happy to see Sir Brendan Barber, the straightforward and thoroughly decent former head of the TUC. I tell him the PM has been quoting him when he's been accused of Project Fear: 'If you see someone running towards a cliff, you're going to shout – and say some pretty rough things.'

The results are due to start coming in and I walk back to No. 10 across the pedestrian bridge linking the Festival Hall to the Embankment.

I decide to watch on my own in my office. I wrestle with a camp bed that's been put in there so I can get some sleep, knowing I will never use it.

One of the earliest results is Sunderland – and it isn't good. It was always expected to vote Leave, but 61 per cent to 39 per cent is worse than anyone was predicting

Sterling plummets.

I feel a wave of sickness wash through me.

I walk through to see Adam and Chewy, two of the brightest special advisers to the PM, who have been seconded to the campaign. There's nothing to say and we just pull excruciated faces.

A few more results trickle in. Newcastle is bad – but others offer hope the North East may be an outlier.

I text Ryan Coetzee, the campaign's Director of Strategy, 'What do you think?' He's with a team comparing each result to a model that imagines the outcome is precisely fifty–fifty in every area of the country. If one side gets higher than needed for that result, it's good for them. If they get less, it's bad.

Ryan replies: 'We're just very slightly behind the curve. By a point, basically . . . but we need more data from the south. It's looking too close to call. In fact, it's very fucking close.'

It's going to be a long night.

I doze for a few minutes and wake up to see a few results tumbling in. The lead is switching back and forth. I feel calm, but I'm urging us to safety with every result. Big London numbers come in, pulling us back – but then there are a series of smaller, bad results.

The BBC has designated the colour blue for Leave and yellow for Remain.

A pattern begins to emerge as results flash on the bottom of the screen: Blue. Blue. Blue. Blue. Blue.

Then we are pulled back by a massive Remain result.

Blue. Blue. Blue. Blue. Blue. Yellow. Blue. Blue. Blue. Blue. Blue. Yellow.

I resist calling Ryan for as long as I can. When I do, he tells me, 'We are just on course for a win – but it's going to be tiny.'

'How tiny?'

'The model is currently predicting we will win by thirty-two thousand votes, but obviously that could change.'

Christ . . .

I walk back through to see Adam and Chewy. Both say they are starting to feel pessimistic.

We desperately need more very big results in London and northern metropolitan cities. It's hard to see how that will happen.

David Cameron texts me: 'How worried should we be?'

I want to be able to tell him it will all be OK, but there's nothing I can think of. I reply that it's desperately close – and we just have to see.

The results start piling in at 3 a.m. The BBC screen says that it is precisely fifty–fifty.

The sensation is one of having been sure of my path, stepping into quicksand, and then being slowly but surely pulled under. I look around for something or someone to help pull me out. But there's nothing and no one.

The analysis is coming through from all sources that turnout in our areas just isn't good enough.

I call Stephen Gilbert, the Conservative party's former campaign chief, who has played a key role at Stronger In. I try to make it easy for him: 'It's not looking good is it?'

'I can't see us doing it now – no. The numbers we need in the cities are just too high.'

'Have you told the PM?'

'Not yet . . . no. I'm waiting until it's certain.'

Lucy Thomas calls me from the Stronger In party, close to tears as she tells me, 'ITV is going to call it for Leave.'

It's approaching 4 a.m. I walk through to see Adam and Chewy again. Graeme Wilson is now in the SpAds (Special Advisers) room. He slaps me on the back and says he is going to bed: 'It's over.'

I borrow his coat. I need some fresh air.

David Cameron is standing outside his private office. He looks tired. Resigned in every sense.

The Cabinet Office minister, Matt Hancock, and the Prime Minister's long-serving aide Liz Sugg are nearby. He waves us inside and slumps into the armchair he's used to chair thousands of meetings over the past six years.

He says he's been turning over in his mind if he should be less specific about when he goes – but doesn't think it will work. I say, 'I may be wrong, but I can't see how you can stay.'

I sit on a wooden chair. Liz sits on another next to me, Matt Hancock on the sofa.

David Cameron says, 'The trouble with all options other than going immediately is they collapse like a concertina. And the truth is, I wouldn't believe in it.'

Liz Sugg asks if – given that he told people he would stay on – resigning now will be seen as a betrayal of trust. Both David Cameron and I are touched by this – everyone knew it was a question he had to answer that way, but no one will really be shocked at the change. The simple fact is that he couldn't be responsible for delivering Brexit when he doesn't believe in it.

The PM says, 'It would be miserable. Every moment I was here, I'd be being prepared for the slaughterhouse – just waiting for the tap on the shoulder.'

The conversation goes round in circles – and he finds more ways to try and explain his decision, 'I'd be saying, "Come and punch me as hard as you like." And then I'd have to go.' He starts to move to the door. I give Liz and Matt a hug. Then I walk out into the corridor where he is pausing a moment. I can't think of anything other to do than slap him on the back. He says, 'Don't worry . . .'

I stop and watch him disappear down the corridor, with Liz Sugg beside him. It is obvious to me that this is over.

I walk out onto Whitehall. The street is deserted. My mind feels calm – but as I approach the memorial opposite the entrance to the Ministry of Defence, my body seems to go into spasm. I suddenly retch harder than I have done in my life. Nothing comes up. I retch again – so hard, it feels as if I'll turn inside out. Dots of light dance before my eyes. And then it is over. I spit. Tears are streaming down my face – not from sadness, but from the sheer physical exertion.

I clear my head and walk on.

Crossing the pedestrian bridge, I look out towards St Paul's and the City beyond. It has never seemed so beautiful as in this half-light.

I lean forward on the rail and take a deep breath, my thoughts already turning to what went wrong and why?

# Introduction

THE DEBATE OVER whether David Cameron should have called a referendum on membership of the European Union will rage down the years.

Those who say he could have avoided it are, I believe, denying what was political reality. The issue of whether we should remain in or leave the EU had been a slow train coming for years. It just happened to arrive in the station on David Cameron's watch.

A range of factors made it impossible for a Conservative prime minister to avoid. Scores of Tory MPs were rebelling on any and every issue that could possibly be linked to Europe; the right-wing press were full-throated in their demands; UKIP had become a significant force in British politics (eventually winning the 2014 European election); and over half the population indicated they wanted a say – with anyone under sixty never having been able to vote on the issue.

Those who declare we elect MPs to decide on such momentous things – and therefore shouldn't have had a referendum – forget that it was a central promise in the Conservative party's 2015 election manifesto. Had David Cameron not promised it then, the Conservative party, and consequently the country, would have become almost ungovernable. A great boulder would have been placed in the road, impossible to get round and stopping much else being done. Eventually his position would have become untenable.

In short, if he had not offered a referendum, it's likely someone else would have come along who was prepared to do it – and he would have been deposed.

In attempting to remove that boulder, David Cameron was well aware that he was risking his job and the fight would be bitter and divisive.

I sat with him in the back of his Jaguar on the way to a speech in 2015. Those journeys were always a tight squeeze, with the car's heavy armour plating and his red box placed between us minimising the space. He ran through the reasons for holding the referendum. I asked him if he could see the case against and he said instantly, 'You could unleash demons of which ye know not.' I thought it might be a quote from the Bible or Shakespeare, but when I looked it up, I couldn't find it.

Those words were prophetic. The demons were unleashed and he and his team faced betrayal, lies and political bloodletting on an epic scale.

All of this was filtered through the prism of an unbalanced media. The Remain campaign experienced the impact of a number of influential newspapers fighting for Leave with ruthless determination. Others, in favour of Remain, tended to be left-leaning and therefore lukewarm about the prospect of coming to the aid of a Conservative prime minister. Added to this was the frustration of the heavily regulated broadcast media, legally bound to provide balance, even when the other side were churning out stories that were at best deeply misleading and at worst, lies.

But it would be too easy to say that these were the only reasons Remain lost. We certainly made mistakes – and I was part of the team responsible.

All of the issues I have outlined above meant that we were swimming against the tide. But other factors meant we were doing it with one arm tied behind our back.

Our campaign was based on the simple proposition that

electorates don't vote against their own pockets. That view is summed up best in the closest thing to an iron law in politics, James Carville's realisation when running the first Clinton presidential campaign, 'It's the economy, stupid!' The view that the economy would trump immigration as the primary concern of voters was backed up by plenty of solid polling evidence, as well as the pattern of how electorates had behaved going back over a century. It was wrong – and devastatingly so when we did not have enough of an answer on freedom of movement.

More to the point, we assumed that an army of nearly three million people who had become so disengaged and disillusioned that they did not vote in the 2015 general election – and probably for some time before that – would not vote. When polled, that group said they did not trust the opinions of politicians, businesses, economists or experts, making them almost unreachable to a campaign arguing for the status quo. That group was susceptible to claims of an establishment conspiracy against them, with politicians ignoring or betraying them for too long, something Leave understood and exploited. They voted in numbers great enough to ensure the country voted 'Out'. We realised too late – and didn't do enough to combat it.

It's a cliché to say that history is written by the winners. This book tells the story of those who lost and how – as the Remain campaign pollster, Andrew Cooper, put it – we struggled to communicate a complex truth in the face of simple lies.

# JANUARY

# Chapter 1

## We Are All Just Prisoners Here

IT IS THE first day of 2016 and George Osborne is sounding the alarm bell.

He sends an email revealing he's anxious that the Leave campaign has managed to 'out-gun' the Remain campaign in the newspapers. He thinks they are doing a great job 'keeping the papers fed and creating a sense of momentum,' going on to ask, 'Where is the Remain campaign's equivalent? I literally cannot remember a single thing they have done since the not very successful launch months ago.' He mocks the fact that their big new-year initiative is a single newsletter and concludes, 'I'm sorry to be so blunt – but we've put up with this for too long and nothing is happening, and we have got to sort it out.'

He wants No. 10 either to take over the Remain campaign with people he knows and trusts – or for us to consider setting up something entirely different.

Others agree the campaign is 'listless and drifting'.

But Stephen Gilbert, the Conservative party's long-serving campaign director, who has had more contact with them than any of us, believes this is grossly unfair and they are doing what is necessary to set up an effective campaign.

There's no point saying it, but I'm reminded of the line in the song 'Hotel California', by the Eagles: 'We are all just prisoners here, of our own device.' As the Government, we are in the middle of a renegotiation with the European Union aimed at giving the UK a 'special relationship' within it. Until that deal is done, how can the Government campaign effectively? David Cameron has said explicitly, 'I rule nothing out,' on being asked what happens if the outcome of his renegotiation is not satisfactory. That means he could recommend leaving.

So, instead of relaxing on the first day of the year, inboxes fill with plans of action. It's suggested Stephen be seconded to the Remain campaign; there should be a beefed-up grid of EU stories, rolled out daily; Cabinet members are to be encouraged to speak up for the renegotiation, starting with a speech by Liz Truss, the Secretary of State for the Environment, Food and Rural Affairs.

No. 10's Director of Strategy, Ameet Gill, points out we are in danger of tying ourselves in knots – creating stories that suggest the renegotiation is crucial, while also hinting we are probably stronger in Europe regardless. He and I agree that the most effective way we can use the next six weeks is to demonstrate how hard we are fighting for Britain; and then sell the deal if and when we get it.

Everyone keeps saying this will be the biggest decision for the country since the Second World War, so I have decided to keep a diary. At the end of a long day, I note, 'If I have to call it – we will win this referendum, but it'll be bloody and dark, and the victory could well be Pyrrhic.' We are beginning the year looking forward to civil war in the Conservative party – the future desperately uncertain.

It is dark and almost unnervingly warm as I enter Downing Street after the Christmas break. The policeman who opens the gate greets me by saying, 'Happy new year! It's like you've never been away!'

I haven't, I think, as I smile and return the greeting.

I have always known this would be the year of Europe, but what I wasn't expecting was that there'd be no hiding place from the off. After a brief 8.30 meeting followed by a small group discussion on a Daesh/ISIL video involving a man trying to set himself up as the new 'Jihadi John' next to a five-year-old child – both, shockingly, with British accents – the PM has a quick private meeting with Chris Grayling, the Leader of the House of Commons.

There's been a bit in the papers suggesting he and the Northern Ireland Minister Theresa Villiers might announce they are going to campaign to leave the EU before the end of the renegotiation. That would mean a breach of collective responsibility, the convention that members of the Cabinet must publicly support all governmental decisions made in Cabinet, even if they do not privately agree with them. It raises the question of whether they should be fired for doing so.

The PM sees him one on one. After fifteen minutes Chris emerges pale and with a tall man's stoop, asking to have a discussion with the Chief of Staff at No. 10, Ed Llewellyn. Kate Fall, who is Deputy Chief of Staff – and who I have come to see as one of the shrewdest and most emotionally intelligent people in politics – goes in to see the PM with me. He says it was as we thought: Chris does want to campaign for out, but ideally while remaining in the Cabinet.

The PM is already clear in his mind – that can't happen. It would look as if he was being pushed around. He says he laid it on thick, telling him it would spread disunity. His mind is already turning to the prospect of a reshuffle, considering people who could replace Chris Grayling.

One argument that was tried on him was, 'What is the point of doing it now? The renegotiation is supposed to be sorted in six or seven weeks.'

The PM believes Chris's logic is that the Leave campaign is in a total mess and needs rescuing. It's being run by Dominic Cummings, whom the Prime Minister once referred to as a 'career psychopath'. He had become convinced that Cummings had been briefing against the Government he supposedly represented as a special adviser at the Department for Education. My predecessor,

Andy Coulson, had refused to allow Michael Gove to have Cummings as a special adviser, believing him to be trouble. Gove had used the period between him going and me arriving to plead Cummings' case and he had been re-employed.

Briefings against No. 10 became frequent. Suspecting Cummings, the PM decided to haul him and Gove in to clear the air. Offered the opportunity to explain whether he had a problem or not, Cummings was unprepared to say to the PM's face what many suspected he was saying privately. Incredibly, his tone was meek and mild – actually praising the Prime Minister for his leadership.

Eventually Cummings left Government – managing to keep himself in the Westminster limelight occasionally with an eccentric blog that led some to accuse him of flirting with eugenics, something he denies. His Twitter feed was named 'The Odyssean Project' and claimed to be based on the thinking of the physicist Murray Gell-Mann, who said we need an 'Odyssean' education, 'integrative thinkers' who can take 'a crude look at the whole'. He had always struggled to explain why this was the case.

Despite Cummings' academic bent, I believed his great flaw was to personalise everything – adopting a scorched-earth policy towards those he clashed with, most famously Iain Duncan Smith, whom he described as incompetent.

Now Cummings is very much back and at the centre of the Leave campaign.

Chris clearly thinks the Leave campaign needs a bit of leadership – and he's the man to sort them out. He's a decent man, who always wants to be above board, but I suspect he's told a lot of people what he's doing, hence the hints in the morning papers, and will find it hard to back down from that. He's planning to write an Op-Ed piece for the *Telegraph* expressing his views – something we all agree would mean he had broken collective responsibility. It would be unsustainable for him to stay in his job. That in turn would be reported as the first 'Referendum Crisis', and would not augur well.

One suggestion is that we accept Chris Grayling's resignation, but make clear that at the end of the renegotiation there would be a suspension of collective responsibility for the rest of the Cabinet. The PM likes the idea, because it could cauterise the situation. But would it work, or just fire the starting gun on chaos? I wonder, 'What will the average, self-interested Cabinet minister do?'

I sit down my deputy, Graeme Wilson, and the Prime Minister's official spokeswoman, Helen Bower, at the old wooden table where I chair most of my office meetings. They're shocked we could be facing a reshuffle today. Both can't fathom Grayling's thinking – but my theory is that it's beneficial for the less well-known 'Outers' to stamp themselves as a leader of the campaign; doing it later will mean they're just another foot soldier.

By now Theresa Villiers has arrived to see the PM and is in his office. I wait outside – and she's out within a couple of minutes. She's smiley and chatty, as pleasant as ever, looking unusually relaxed. I chew the fat for a bit, before going in to see the PM. He tells me her concern was simple; she was going to have to resign because Government policy would be to stay in the EU after the renegotiation. She's been reassured by the PM there's no need to do anything now – he will drop collective responsibility on this issue when the renegotiation is complete.

The PM is relieved as we walk through to the front of house over the brand-new carpets that have been laid during Christmas break. The fear that Grayling and Villiers had been working as a kind of tag team, the first softening the PM up, the second magnifying the problem, is evaporating.

After a couple of hours in Barking with the Conservative London Mayoral candidate, Zac Goldsmith, doing a lot of supporting media, the PM and I get back in the car to No. 10. A paper bag full of Pret a Manger sandwiches and fruit salad has been left on the back seat – the classic snatched lunch for the PM on a visit.

He tells me about the Christmas break, including having Michael Gove and his family to stay at Chequers. The question of whether Michael would be 'In' or 'Out' hung heavy in the air. DC says he had several conversations with Sarah Vine – during each of which she told him she was sure Michael would support him. It was clearly emphatic enough to assure DC that would be the case.

We begin to talk about the Grayling situation. My view is there's no fudge here, 'You can't be half-pregnant. Either Chris is going to breach collective responsibility or he isn't.' If Grayling goes now and says we must leave Europe before the end of the renegotiation, we're in an impossible bind. If the PM fires him, it looks chaotic. If he doesn't, he appears weak.

The aim must be to persuade him to pull back.

The PM is concerned about everything unravelling, fearful over how the wider Conservative party is reacting to this. His analysis is that everyone, including him, has traded on having a go at 'Europe' for years. He describes it as a kind of displacement activity, 'using it to soothe our fevered brow'. The issue has reached fever pitch now that MPs and Cabinet ministers are going to be confronted by the reality of a decision. It also means the EU's reputation is in tatters – with no one having done any positive public relations for it, and most openly attacking it, for decades.

As we glide through traffic, I tell him I have come to the conclusion that if the UK votes to leave the EU it will set off a chain of events:

- He will have to resign.
- The SNP will push for – and likely get – a second independence referendum.
- There'll be a massive reassessment of Britain's role in the world, with a struggle to assert ourselves as a front-rank player.

Back in Downing Street, the Chief Whip, Mark Harper, has gathered with Ed Llewellyn and Kate Fall. All are agreed – there's not much chance of finessing this issue, unless Chris is prepared to compromise. Allowing him to write an article saying he's given up on Europe while staying in the Cabinet before the conclusion of the renegotiation just doesn't work.

The PM has asked Chris to see him again and he ushers him into his office. Chris emerges a few minutes later, looking even more uncertain. DC's pitch has been, 'I try to be a pretty flexible captain – but like every captain I've got to have some rules.' He's explained that he will suspend collective responsibility, but crucially, not until after the renegotiation.

Chris is now going for a walk to think about his position.

It feels to us as though he has walked into the headmaster's office with a plan that he hasn't thought through.

An hour later, word comes back from Chris that he won't resign, but that he wants the PM to confirm he will be suspending collective responsibility. He also plans to give an interview announcing that he will be campaigning for Leave. Neither of these things is ideal. But I guess it's better than dealing with a resignation on the first day back.

I wander back through to my office and tell Ameet of my fear that this is going to be typical of the next few months – a lot of screwing around all day, with little gain at the end of it.

# Chapter 2

## Famous Last Words

THE NEXT DAY there is a discussion about what the PM will say when he announces all of this in the House of Commons. Essentially, it's agreed that collective responsibility will be suspended, but only after the renegotiation – and crucially, there will be an official Government position on whether we should stay in the EU or Leave – though Cabinet ministers will be able to campaign on whichever side they want.

Within minutes of the end of the meeting, the BBC journalist John Pienaar calls me to say he understands the PM will today clarify that collective responsibility will be suspended. It has obviously come from Chris telling everyone. David Cameron rolls his eyes at the news – and we agree to walk into it, looking relaxed and reminding people that *The Times* had floated the idea over Christmas, so it's hardly big news.

Serious issues with the Cabinet aren't our only problems. There are deep concerns the renegotiation is going off track. For months now, civil servants – and often the PM himself – have been engaged in working out a new settlement for the UK in the European Union. Ideally, we will be able to demonstrate that significant concessions have been made and we have even more of a special status within the EU. Progress is slow and there are plenty of hurdles.

In the movie *The Big Short* they get round the issue of how dull concepts like 'sub-prime mortgages' are with the slightly dubious device of getting the actress and model, Margot Robbie, to explain them while reclining in a bubble bath. No such narrative devices are available to help us get round how mind-bending some of the renegotiation was, with Euro wonks trying to make it palatable.

The PM worries there isn't enough progress on curbing welfare for migrants – the idea being that fewer benefits and less money will mean a smaller 'pull factor' for migrants, reducing the number coming. He's determined to deliver more on this.

The EU wonks have sent a paper saying we should explore Angela Merkel's idea of redefining what is a worker. Mats Persson, who is the expert on all things EU, says it has the problem of being 'discriminatory', a big no-no in Europe, but Germany seems prepared to run with it. Experts gather in the PM's study and my head aches at the end, just about grasping it.

We have been asking for a four-year ban on migrants to the EU getting benefits. That seems to be a non-starter. Instead:

- Merkel suggests we could redefine what a 'worker' is under EU law to say that they would have to be self-sufficient when moving to another country.
- That means the definition of 'self-sufficient' is crucial . . . too low and it wouldn't make any difference to migrants arriving.
- Say it was set at £20k, that would mean anyone earning under that would not be considered self-sufficient and would not be allowed to come to the UK.
- If someone could show they could earn more than that figure, they could come.

After working it out, and listening to a lot of negativity, I say, 'Hold on a minute. Isn't this too good to be true? If you look at it through the other end of the telescope, we would have achieved a major shift in EU policy – changing the concept of freedom of movement. Surely that means it won't happen?'

Others nod hard. It feels like another wild goose chase.

David Cameron agrees. But he's convinced we need something

in this space. He wraps the meeting up, 'So we've got three things to be going at: an emergency brake on the number of migrants; a brake on the welfare payments they are allowed; and the redefinition of what a worker is.'

My worry is how complex all of this is becoming. We are dealing in concepts that are not easily grasped or translated – even to people who are at the centre of things.

Everyone looks nervous, wondering how the hell they'll land any of this before the next European Council in just a few weeks. As of early January, it looks increasingly likely we won't reach a deal by then. There's a very real prospect of this dragging on – and that isn't an attractive prospect for a number of reasons:

- there's a danger this process would clog up the arteries of government, making it the dominant, almost the only issue for months, perhaps even until the end of 2017 (the last date there can be a referendum).
- there's no evidence that holding out for longer would get a better deal; more likely Europe will think we are not serious. There are already signals from some Governments that they think we have given up anyway and are just time-wasting on the way out of the EU.
- there could be another summer migration crisis.
- and in politics, it's always better to go when you have as clear an understanding of the landscape facing you as possible. Who knows where we will be at the end of 2017? The economy could be in recession, the Government facing a severe bout of mid-term blues, and the Eurozone back in crisis.

Today is becoming one long rolling headache of a Europe meeting. The cast changes, but the location – the PM's office – doesn't.

Next up is a discussion including the Chancellor about whether Liz Sugg, No. 10's Director of Events (viewed by me as our secret weapon, because of her skill at organising events involving the PM with creativity and precision), Ameet Gill and I should be going to meetings with the 'In' campaign. Kate Fall worries that the PM will be criticised for pre-judging the re-negotiation when it inevitably gets out. It's putting a lot of trust in people we don't know.

I take her point – but if everyone wants us to input into the campaign, there's no way of doing it without being there. We'll just have to take the consequences.

At this point George Osborne takes a deep breath and delivers a long speech beginning, 'I've never met Will Straw, I've never met Ryan Coetzee, and I don't even know the surnames of their media team . . . What I do know is they have never won anything in their lives.' His point is they may be great – but he wants to be sure they are on the case, chasing things down aggressively, sorting the grid, deciding who's going to go on the radio and TV. Essentially, these people do not traditionally wish us well in politics – how can we be sure we can work with them?

This sparks questions about whether we should set up a completely different campaign. I wince at this and say, 'I understand the frustration, but the reason we can't do things better is we are stuck in this crazy bind with the renegotiation. As far as I can work out – the Stronger In team are desperate for us to join forces. We're starting to make inroads – and we'll be able to do more.' George seems to accept this, but spells out again that he wants people he can trust in there.

Without saying so, we have effectively decided to back the Stronger In campaign and given up on setting up an alternative.

Wednesday 6 and Thursday 7 January are spent debating the Prime Minister's advice to Cabinet on the issue of collective responsibility during the referendum.

Some have gone back and read the 1975 Cabinet minutes on the Government's plan for a referendum on the predecessor to the EU – the Common Market. What is striking (apart from the fact that the country seemed to be in a disastrous mess) is how concerned they were with the detail of it all – who was allowed to use the department copier, etc.

Today's Cabinet Secretary, Sir Jeremy Heywood, is clear these issues are just as relevant today. He says the first point to be made is obvious, that people will be expected to show good manners to each other.

Famous last words.

Twitter is alive with a question I expect to be cleared up very quickly: what is our position on Cabinet ministers who want to 'Leave' giving speeches in the Commons? Do they have to move from the frontbench to the backbenches to do so?

The PM is in no doubt – ministers should not be allowed to give Leave speeches in the Commons.

I didn't expect that. 'But hold on – you've just said you'll suspend collective responsibility on this issue.'

George Osborne also believes we must not allow ministers freedom on this in the Commons. Anything else will be chaos. Someone describes this as the 'Victorian father' approach.

My concern is, will this approach survive contact with reality? 'You're creating a problem – but if your posture is relaxed, it will have far less impact if someone causes trouble.'

The PM's view is that we need to be flexible. He describes the Commons as being like a pressure cooker: 'We allow steam to build and then we let it off.' Perhaps, but doesn't that some-times mean us looking weak and pushed around?

Various drafts of the letter go back and forth – with two areas of discomfort: what do we say about special advisers?; and the issue of whether ministers will be allowed to speak from the backbenches.

The PM flies to Germany and the Chancellor is out delivering a speech on the economy. Both now agree we need to take a tough line. Others are nervous that we're in danger of igniting a massive process row.

It's agreed there'll be a conference call with the PM.

He comes on a distant and crackly line, explaining he's using the speakerphone on Ed Llewellyn's BlackBerry. He's just delivered a speech to Angela Merkel's party and starts by saying, 'Well, if the CSU were the only people we were negotiating with, we'd be home free.' He confirms he's hardened his line: we should be tough on special advisers campaigning and tough on ministers speaking in Parliament. He'll explain this when he chairs political cabinet next week, which is when party political matters are discussed without civil servants being present.

Kate Fall wonders why we need to do any of this now. The PM agrees we could just leave it until the European Council on 17 February and hope it will be swept away by people declaring their positions while campaigning, but he suspects they won't let it drop now.

I disagree with the position, but accept it, providing he doesn't cave in on it. He says there may be a time when we need to let off steam. I wince a little, but stay silent.

The conversation moves on to Special Advisers – or SpAds – the political operatives employed by Cabinet ministers to do their bidding. Typically each has a couple – one to work on policy, one on the media. The PM says SpAds working for Leave ministers should only campaign in their spare time – whereas the rest can do what they want, because the Government position is likely to be to Remain. I reach for an analogy to show why this seems unnecessarily rigid to me, 'Aren't you in danger of sounding like the sheriff of Chinatown who says he won't tolerate gambling and prostitution, when he knows it'll be happening under his nose and he can't do a thing about it?'

Others agree – we are likely to succumb on this if they get on their high horses and cry foul.

The PM goes back to his pressure cooker point – allow pressure to build, then let off steam. A couple of us have one more push, and ask, 'Are you really comfortable with that? We stood firm on Purdah and relented. We stood firm on collective responsibility and relented . . . now this. We'll look weak if we set things out and then back down.'

I half expect the PM to snap at us, but he understands we're trying to chart a course through impossible waters, and finally rules, 'Look – I recognise we are being tough – but we are doing it at a time when we have made a concession, so we look reasonable. This is about the Government not looking like a total mess.'

There is a long pause.

'Okay,' I say.

There is another long pause.

'Okay,' Kate says.

The PM ends the call – our course is set.

The truism that politics makes for strange bedfellows becomes abundantly clear that weekend. Peter Mandelson calls me for a conversation that lasts ninety minutes. I discover he's the kind of person who wants to explore issues at length – sometimes interrupting his long monologues to ask someone in the background to bring in a heater or some other comfort. I'm happy to hear him talk – occasionally chipping in with a thought or two.

I ask him about the article he's written for *Newsweek*, which was reprinted in that morning's *Times*. It's another reminder of how Corbyn is destroying the Labour party. His view is that the group running Labour aren't interested in power in the short term – they want to ensure the Left secures its grasp, purging the party of Blairites like him. He suggests the question is not: should Jeremy Corbyn have Hilary Benn in his shadow cabinet? But: why is Hilary Benn having anything to do with Jeremy Corbyn?

Only then does he go on to talk about the Stronger In campaign. He believes it is a rudimentary cheerleader for Europe (held back while the renegotiation is going on) with a good core team. His main concern is the lack of someone who can liaise directly with No. 10 and the Conservative party. Without saying it, he's asking me to think about how we make it happen.

He reassures me the Labour party will be on board, but the one block is that they fear the renegotiation will do a lot of damage to what they call 'Social Europe', the protection rights for workers.

Finally he set out three worries:

1. The docking of the Government and the campaign (again asking how this would happen and which big figure would be on board).
2. Immigration – the campaign has no core script on this and is not confident in its talking points.
3. The concern that the terror attacks on Paris, and the outrage over women being attacked in Cologne by immigrants, have the effect of making people fear that Europe is becoming a funnel for terrorism.

I assure him that Ameet, Liz and I will be engaging more.

Finally he talks with fascination about who from the Cabinet would be In – and who would be Out. He says if the Outers are limited to IDS (Iain Duncan Smith), Grayling, Villiers and Whittingdale, it will be a great thing.

It has become a tradition to start the New Year with an interview on *The Andrew Marr Show* on BBC1. That means getting up at an ungodly hour on a Sunday morning to ensure I have combed through the newspapers for any issues that might trouble the PM.

We have announced a plan on regenerating housing estates, which is leading the news – it's a good demonstration that the Government will be about more than the referendum this year.

I feel reassured that after months of crap about us being on the back foot, the Out campaign is seen as being in trouble. The polling guru John Curtice says that at this stage they should be dramatically ahead because of the inevitable late squeeze. They are at best level in the polls. It's exactly the kind of statement that gives us reassurance about how people will act.

The papers have spotted the chronic lack of leadership on the Leave side. On the one hand it could be a golden opportunity for someone to step in and give their career booster rockets, but on the other, it could be a disastrous choice. I can imagine the calculations going on for some – it's a high-risk bet: backing Leave could see them achieve glory that might not come their way otherwise, or see their career destroyed.

Arriving at No. 10, I text the PM to let him know I'm downstairs. I take a few moments to consider the historic cartoons that Chancellors have chosen to line the stairs running up to the PM's flat.

Most of them are fairly weak, using heavy-handed metaphors and a buzz phrase of the day. I note Norman Lamont holding a watering can as he tends the green shoots of recovery – while a workman behind sharpens a scythe labelled 'Public Sector Deficit'. Another is of Nigel Lawson reclining against a huge pile of fish as he lazily watches his line, taut with another fish on the end.

The PM comes bounding down the stairs carrying a large tennis bag, ready for a match with Boris Johnson later on the American ambassador's court.

We go into his private office and he makes me an espresso from his private machine as I take him through a few things, including ensuring that he uses the phrase 'a real prize is within our grasp' when talking about the renegotiation.

The papers have a little on how the Home Secretary, Theresa May, is flirting with leading the Out campaign and we talk about how to handle it if it comes up. We decide he should point out she has a long record of defending the European Union.

We continue the briefing in the back of the car to Broadcasting House. When we arrive, DC suddenly realises he is wearing an old suit, which has worn through at the knee. We have to send for another one that is smarter.

The show is on air when one of the support team turns up with a choice of three suits. DC isn't thinking and immediately takes off his trousers in front of us both. The poor breathless lady shoots me a surprised look before turning away.

The interview is a relative breeze. The first half on Europe including possible dates for a referendum; then what's happening with the renegotiation; finally, the smart will have spotted him dropping a heavy hint that he may be prepared to give parliamentary sovereignty a boost – a way of filling out the final renegotiation package.

At the end of the programme, Marr tackles the issue of whether DC will stay on if we lose. There's been a lot of discussion about this in prep. Ameet thinks he should make clear he would go – because people will realise just how tempestuous things will become by voting Leave, and that they are losing a good PM. DC believes that view is kind, but in reality it will mean the referendum is on the Government and him. We can't let that happen. In the Scottish referendum, he famously asked people not to vote for independence just because it was 'an opportunity to kick the effing Tories'.

My feeling is that if we lose the referendum our feet will not touch the floor as we are ejected from No. 10.

When asked, he says that he would stay on, though in his heart he knows there are almost no circumstances in which he would stay. His answer is about attempting to protect the campaign from turning into a referendum on him – and because he should not box himself in completely. We can't be certain of the circumstances, whatever the outcome on 24 June.

The show is played out by Squeeze, singing a song called 'From Cradle to Grave' from their new album. When they are done, the PM applauds and the show is over. I think the band seem remarkably frosty to him – though Glen Tilbrook laughs as I tell him I saw him perform at Jeremy Vine's fiftieth birthday party.

It soon emerges they've changed the lyrics of the song to complain about the destruction of the welfare state and council houses. I tell the PM this as he calls after his match with Boris. 'Of course, all of them live in council houses,' he says sarcastically. It's a wilful misinterpretation of what we're doing, which will actually improve lives, but I tell the media team to just shrug it off.

DC is in a good mood after beating Boris at tennis. After the match he speaks to him about Europe. Boris has hoped the President of the United States might want to visit one of his big London legacy projects. He's reminded, 'He's not going to do that if you want to leave Europe.'

Boris has been flirting with Brexit, but clearly isn't sure. We're in for a tortuous wait before he finally shows his hand.

# Chapter 3

## Remind Me Whose Idea This Was?

A MAJOR FOCUS OF the week beginning 11 January is who will be 'In' (with the PM) and who will be 'Out' (against him) in the event of a successful renegotiation.

Conversations keep circling back to what Theresa May will do. Some feel her past speeches will make it hard for her to go for Out. The PM believes authenticity would be a problem for her, so he thinks that she won't – if you take a position that isn't where your instincts lie, there's a real prospect of being 'smoked out'. He goes on to give a few more details of his meeting with Boris after tennis, saying he believes he can be brought on board by the prospect of a bill detailing that the UK Parliament is sovereign.

Coming into Downing Street just before 8 a.m. on 12 January, I spot Boris bumbling around, iPhone in hand. He looks even more of a mess than usual, with his hair particularly unruly and wearing a scruffy anorak.

I say, 'Hello,' and as we walk towards the front door he tells me he's made the mistake of arriving half an hour early for political cabinet. Just before we get there and with the snappers and journalists within earshot, he suddenly raises his voice and says, 'Now come on then, Oliver. Surely you admit we have to go for Brexit?'

The joke dispatched, he doesn't even look at me before moving on to his next trick, staring at his phone and saying to an email or text he has apparently found there, 'No, I do not want to write a piece on leaving Europe.'

It's classic Boris, funny, not worried about who he embarrasses, and attention seeking.

As we go inside, I decide to tease him back on the subject of how his tennis game with the PM went. He says, 'He needs to sink a few thousand into his backhand!' I note how he's skilfully had a go at the PM, without revealing that he was beaten by him. He settles down in the Thatcher Room and I ask one of the team who are setting up for the day if they mind bringing him a cup of coffee.

Political cabinet begins with a presentation by me on the current state of the Labour party and how we should handle them. I'm under no illusion that it's been stuck in there as a filler, so the letter giving advice on collective responsibility isn't the only topic of conversation.

It feels like a crunching gear change as the PM moves to the main discussion. I have a good look round the table – everyone still as a statue, recognising this could be an awkward moment. The PM sets out his argument for collective responsibility, before concluding: 'We can't look like a rabble that's attacking each other in Parliament . . . If we can't do it by being civilised, we'll be letting ourselves down.'

At that point, the series of ministers pile in. The quietly authoritative Patrick McLoughlin, the Secretary of State for Transport, gives a stern lecture on how the party owes a huge amount to the PM, dragging it back to electability.

After a few others have chipped in, Chris Grayling says what the PM has set out is 'perfectly reasonable and sensible'. Iain Duncan Smith is cooperative, too, saying that having been leader at a time when the party was more interested in tearing chunks out of itself, he thought it important we do not allow ourselves to get personal: 'It'll be a ferocious debate. The idea we can finesse that is ludicrous. It'll be a little bit about the head – and a lot about the heart.' I find myself thinking that is precisely the wrong way round, but he's probably right. He then tries to push for the referendum to be later than June, suggesting it will get in the way of some really important local elections.

Only Michael Gove seems to misstep, making a Pollyanna-ish, but oxymoronic speech about allowing ourselves to be a truly national party, because we will have people arguing both sides of the case. One of my team leans over to me and whispers, 'Try schizophrenic.'

In a way, the meeting is more interesting for the people who did not speak – Theresa May and Sajid Javid, both of whom are playing their cards very close to their chests.

After it, some of the team want to discuss Theresa May. Her sphinx-like approach is becoming difficult, with the press really questioning which way she will jump. I suspect anything we do to try and bounce her could prove counterproductive. We go for a cup of tea in the No. 10 canteen. I am trying to have a healthy new year and ask for peppermint tea. Marge and Alison, who run the tiny canteen, look in a cupboard under the urn and come out with an old shoebox full of herbal teas from God knows when. No peppermint. I have camomile and ginger, which tastes like diluted dust. The conversation turns around this being the biggest thing the PM has faced and him not even knowing if the Home Secretary is backing him or not.

Apparently DC is worried that she does not realise she would be a central figure in any future Government of his – and wants to communicate that to her.

Theresa isn't the only cause for concern. The next day an obscure report, buried on page two of the *Daily Express*, sets the cat among the pigeons. 'Friends of Boris' (journalistic code for him or someone very close to him) are reported as saying he has no intention of leading the Out campaign. The PM asks to see a copy, hoping he can spot any telling Boris phrases. He suspects 'The trouble is I'm not an outer' is one of them. If he isn't up for it, it's a major blow for those who want to Leave, and a boost for us.

But there's a swift counter-briefing from Boris' team, this time hinting he might be Out.

The day turns into another rolling Europe meeting, culminating in a big session with the PM and Chancellor. The big debate is if we should push for 23 June. Normally, Parliament's 'statutory instruments' would have to be put in place around now. The problem is it will look like the whole renegotiation is a stitch-up and we're going for a big bounce.

The conversation turns to how Parliament would react. The working assumption is there would be well over a hundred Out MPs. What is striking is how lukewarm Jeremy Corbyn is on remaining in the EU. The suspicion is that the only thing stopping him going for Out is that he doesn't want to completely split his party. He is vital to the Remain cause, because he is capable of mobilising an army of supporters to our side – supporters who are not well disposed to David Cameron.

The PM says he doesn't think too many people would object to June. Stephen Gilbert says the campaign's preferred date for a referendum would be November – so that they could have plenty of time to do their segmentation of the electorate and to target it properly.

From an 'air war' (the term given to the media side of the campaign) perspective we want this done quickly. I believe the debate will be out of control from the moment we come back from Brussels with a deal – the best approach in that circumstance is complete shock and awe, which there is no way we can sustain until November.

The conversation concludes there are three options: June, September or November. June might not work. November would mean we had to go through the nightmare Tory conference with all the Europe posturing that would involve. September could be after a summer of migration problems. We settle on a clear order of preference: June, November, September.

News comes through from Brussels that is extremely significant.

Tom Scholar, our super-bright and worldly-wise negotiator, warns that the Commission 'will issue a draft proposal at the very beginning of February', with 'sherpa meetings' (involving top civil servants representing each Government) on 5 and 11 February. He wants to complain in the strongest possible terms, as it will look like we are being bounced.

The reason he's so concerned is that the renegotiation is supposed to be coming to a head in mid-February. If a text is out there from the beginning of February, it risks the Outers being able to shred it, without us being able to defend it, attack it, or sign up to it. It'll merely have the status of a proposal, but not in the eyes of the media. Moreover, it's perfectly possible that what they issue could be the high-water mark, with the final document even worse than what was originally published.

Liz Sugg, Ameet Gill and I walk over to the Conrad Hotel opposite St James's Park Tube station. It's been picked for our first official meeting with Will Straw, who is leading the Remain campaign, by Stephen Gilbert, who says, 'It's nearby and full of American tourists.' In other words, we won't be spotted, although he urges us to go in through the lobby and not the main entrance. Stephen has now resigned from the Conservative party and set himself up as a consultant.

We go down into a basement filled with windowless meeting rooms. In ours, sandwiches, salads and cake that look like they have emerged from a 3D printer await us.

Will is bright and amiable, eager to be collegiate. I recognise him from a press photo in which he is leading a march in the pouring rain. He is tall, lean and smartly dressed. I wonder what it must be like for him, having set up the campaign as a bright young thing in the Labour party – only for the Tory government machine to heave into view.

On the way over, I tell everyone it's important for us to be helpful and diplomatic, but the truth is, we hold all the cards here. If the meeting goes badly, the recommendation will be to revisit the assumption that we are backing them and reconsider setting up our own campaign.

We talk about when the referendum should be held. Will explains that November would be best for them. I make arguments for June – and am surprised when Stephen says, 'So my understanding is that it's the strong view it should be June.' I couldn't work out if he was being heavy-handed, or if he hadn't really understood what Will was saying.

We run through our thinking – about how a deal in February is more likely than not now, but by no means certain. Also, how when the deal is done, we need a blitzkrieg of activity. Will offers up a series of thoughts, including a suggestion that Tony Blair and Peter Mandelson should go out and sell the case. I make a mental note that this should not happen. Not because they aren't talented politicians, but because they were ultra-Europhiles, having both wanted to join the Euro – and that would not help our cause.

I hang back at the end to talk with Will about the best way to ensure we dock with the campaign in terms of communications staff. They need a Tory now, finding they are struggling to get any traction with the newspapers. I see the point, but again we're trapped. If someone from No. 10 is arguing the case for the EU before the renegotiation is complete, it will look bad.

Later I sit down with Stephen Gilbert to discuss our view. Despite it all, I am impressed by Will, who comes across as someone we can do business with, setting aside party differences in a common cause. The inevitability of my involvement in the campaign feels hideously real. I comforted myself after the general election that I'd never have to go through the torment of a full-scale campaign again. Last May looks fun compared to this – a relentless slog, with the added complication of the blood and guts of an all-out Tory war. None of it seems appealing.

★　★　★

By mid-January, the papers are full of theories about the shape of any deal we'd do with Europe. One is about the German redefinition of the concept of the worker. They have it wrong – claiming Brits will be affected, too. I call the PM to talk about it as he is on his way to the constituency. He says I should leave it: 'There's a lot of crap out there . . . It's not bad if people are confused.'

I ask him how his chat with Theresa May went. The line is crackly, but I can tell he is frustrated. It sounds like she refused to come off the fence. I feel irritation on his behalf. Of course, looking at it purely from her point of view, it's a smart strategy – allowing her to have her cake and eat it – but it doesn't seem fair on David Cameron, who has treated her well. I notice the Outers are equally frustrated by her, claiming in newspaper briefings that she has 'marched them to the top of the hill' and left them waiting.

But if our problems seem bad, they are nothing compared to Labour's. Watching Jeremy Corbyn's interview on *Marr* is a strange experience. With the sound turned down, he looks reasonable enough, but what he's saying is electorally disastrous. He starts by wanting to open talks with Argentina about the Falklands, before moving on to putting Trident submarines to sea without nuclear warheads, and then concluding he'd like to reintroduce secondary picketing. It's as if he will jump willingly into all the elephant traps being laid out for him.

Janan Ganesh tweets: 'Imagine giving a TV interview in which your proposal to bring back secondary strikes was not the worst or second-worst idea.'

The next day, DC's inner circle has dinner with Lynton Crosby, his 2015 election campaign director, in the dining room at No. 11. The table is set for seven, with the PM sitting at the top. Lynton sits to his right. George says he's done everything to warm the place up – with portable heaters dotted around the walls.

The food is pretty basic – a watery beef stew with rice, and a bowlful of overcooked carrots and peas. The stew is tasteless and everyone adds a lot of salt. It is all made worse by the fact I'm having a dry January.

Lynton has made it plain he is going to be studiously neutral in this referendum, but he's happy to talk, as he regularly has done since the election.

Top of the agenda is whether we are right to push for June. Everyone agrees it is the right date. George wonders what the SNP will do. Most believe they'll say overtly they are all for In, while doing little to campaign for it. They've already refused any attempts to have cross-party working.

The next item is: What do we need to bring home on welfare/immigration? George says that in his conversation with Jean-Claude Juncker, the President of the European Commission, it was clear they were alive to the politics of this, with Juncker saying, 'DC must have something with four years in it, because that was what he argued for in his manifesto.'

The next subject is 'key messages'. There's been a bit of a question about whether we were wise to emphasise security. When we did, the journalist Dominic Lawson pointed out that the EU isn't about security; that's down to NATO, etc. Lynton says we need to make a bigger argument: 'Now is not the time for the West to divide . . . strength in numbers, etc.'

He's also sure that the PM should not race ahead with making pro-EU arguments – he needs to demonstrate just how hard he is working for a deal. He adds that we shouldn't be going for a big-bang budget either: 'Nothing that will scare the voters.' The Chancellor says that should be a principle at all times.

Much of the discussion is about getting our heads around how different all of this is going to be. George sums it up best: 'We're fighting our own here. Hopefully with the end result we won't destroy each other.'

All through the evening, DC seems a little distant. He lets us know what's distracting him at the end of the meal with the joke, 'Remind me whose idea this was?'

★   ★   ★

The screw is turning as we approach the now crucial beginning of February, needing to explain what we can expect from the renegotiation. Reports from the frontline in Brussels are concerning. The crucial issue of what would happen on curbing benefits to stop migration appears to be getting nowhere.

The feeling is, if a document is leaked without satisfactory progress in this area at the beginning of February, we will be promptly torn to shreds – even though the renegotiation is not over. We needed to ensure that whatever is sent out looks credible.

During this period, I have regular meetings with Andrew Cooper, the pollster for Remain. Andrew and I struck up a firm friendship while he was Director of Strategy at No. 10 and I could always rely on him to tell it to me straight. I tell him things are looking superficially good for us in the media. There are two Leave campaigns tearing lumps out of each other as they fight to get the official stamp of approval, with all the funding and recognition that comes with that. *The Times* has a spread lamenting the chaos on the Out side – with it really appearing like Monty Python's 'People's Front of Judea' versus the 'Judean People's Front'. The expectation is that on our side the Government will dock neatly with Britain Stronger In Europe, with everyone appearing grown-up. I warn him that this sense of calm is likely to be shattered after the renegotiation.

Andrew tells me the online polls, which haven't had their methodology changed much since the disaster of the general election, put us ahead 51–49 (with the odd outlier putting Leave ahead). However, 'more reliable' phone polls put us ahead 60–40.

He has done some work that is vital to understanding the electorate – and therefore how the campaign will be fought. There are three groups who will essentially vote to Remain in the EU come what may:

Ardent internationalists: 10% of the population
Comfortable Europhiles: 22%
Engaged Metropolitans: 4%

Then there are two groups who won't do anything other than vote to Leave:

Strong Sceptics: 19%
EU hostiles: 10%

That leaves just over a third of people in the middle:

Hearts *vs* Heads (people wanting to leave in their hearts, but having intellectual doubts about it): 14%
Disengaged Middle (people who struggle to care one way or another): 21%

Andrew says that the last two groups are 'in play' and could go either way. They will be targeted by Remain and Leave. It is common to hear from Europhiles that we should sing the praises of the EU. But Andrew is clear this is a mistake. These people are vociferous in their dislike of the EU, but what will sway them is if their pocket is likely to be hit.

Perhaps the most interesting debate in these groups is on the issue of security. I've heard a number of people in No. 10 egg each other on to the view that the national security argument is central. According to Andrew's research, it holds little sway. I've always felt it sounds a bit bogus to suggest we'd be less safe if we left; surely we'd be cooperating on this stuff anyway? This is not the view of the recent heads of the security services, who believe it's vital we are in the room when things are decided.

It seems that I was right to be worried by how complicated some of our messages are.

We have called the referendum on a complex subject and given ourselves only four short months to educate people on the crucial link between Europe and the economy – amid the white noise of a frenzied argument.

# Chapter 4

## She Could Be PM in Six Months

THE NEXT BIG moment on Europe is Davos – that annual networking jamboree in the Swiss mountains. Our convoy races out of the Parliamentary estate immediately after Prime Minister's Questions. My car gets stuck behind a laundry lorry moving incredibly slowly. There then follows a chaotic chase for the next couple of miles as Sean, the driver, attempts to catch up with the PM's car carving its way through London traffic with the aid of motorbike outriders. He flicks on his blue light and starts madly overtaking people while honking his horn. Finally we catch up.

We arrive in Davos in darkness. The town is coated in a thick layer of snow and has a real holiday feel, with tourist-brochure buildings, and forests of giant pine trees stretching towards the mountains.

I take a few minutes to go for a walk after dumping my bags and run into Christine Lagarde, the Head of the International Monetary Fund, and her entourage. It's the classic Davos cliché – encountering some of the biggest hitters on the planet as you wander down the street.

I find myself lugging the PM's red box out into the snow as we head to a restaurant called Pot au Feu, which has animal skins draped all over the walls. It's roasting inside, the temperature pumped up to an absurdly high level. The dinner starts on a low note. It's become evident that tomorrow's papers will be full of Europe suggesting an end to the Dublin agreement, which says asylum seekers can be returned to the first country they arrive in. It's been a crucial line of defence for us. If we can't say they can be sent back, it will create another stick with which to beat us for the Brexiteers.

DC looks at me and says, 'They are not making it easy for us . . .'

The next morning I wake up dehydrated, despite having a dry January. The moment I open my eyes, the phone goes. It's the BBC's Norman Smith – he's only doing his job, but I yearn for the time when answering difficult political questions cold and at an ungodly hour is not the first task of every day. Apparently, anonymous Cabinet ministers have been briefing that they fear the PM will be in campaign mode from the moment the renegotiation is done, while they will be held to collective responsibility. They want a Cabinet meeting the weekend he arrives back with a deal so they can be free to speak out. They show no recognition of the fact that the PM is already doing something extraordinary by allowing some ministers to take an opposing view to the Government, while still remaining in the Cabinet.

I don't want to set any hares running, just saying the PM will hold a Cabinet 'soon and in good order' after the renegotiation. Despite that, Norman Smith thinks we will have to relent – and the next bulletin reflects that.

When I brief the PM, he's clearly worried by this. He wants to say there are only Cabinets on a weekend in a national emergency – and this won't be a national emergency. He is working in the lounge of his suite, with great views of snowy mountains all around. I persuade him there's no need to box himself in now.

Most of the European Commissioners are in Davos and the PM is keen to grab Jonathan Hill, the British Commissioner responsible for Financial Stability and Financial Services, to get his take on what is going on.

Jonathan sweeps in wearing a heavily patterned scarf and the PM offers him a coffee. I'm the only one who seems to be able to work the fiendishly complex capsule machine in the corner, so it's left to me to make him one.

Jonathan doesn't varnish the truth. His view is that: 'They [the Commission] are shitting themselves.' He says they are scared to death about the migration crisis. He believes they've had a disastrous last year, and 2016 could be even worse. He says, 'They want to have a quick win, taking our thorny issue off the table.' He thinks they believe we are desperate to do a deal and are consequently 'low-balling' us in their offers. He also thinks what they are offering on welfare is nigh-on incomprehensible. 'We need to get them to the politics of this. At the moment it's all too techy. They need to understand that if they don't get this right, the whole thing could unravel – with Britain leaving the EU.'

DC says the briefing has 'hardened his heart' and that with the polls tight, the one chance we have of a 'game changer' is coming back with a strong deal. We agree he will use his Europe speech this afternoon not only to call for business to speak out, but also to say he will walk away from the February Council without a deal if it isn't good enough.

The pause button could be pressed. This is big news. If there's no deal in February, June would be out of the window for a referendum and the next suitable date could be November. We are all worried about September because it will probably have been after a summer of 'Migration Crisis 2'. I worry about having it after a Conservative party conference – but that is a discussion for another day.

We make our way to the conference centre. The weather is cold, but it's a clean, bright day. Inside it's all thick carpets and café bars. Delegates from around the world sip lattes and hammer away at their laptops. 'What are they all getting out of this?' I wonder. The common answer is: you can set up the number of meetings you normally have in a month in a single day. But no one seems to be doing much.

We go to a tiny prep room for the PM's speech. He's started to think he shouldn't be doing it off the cuff, as he needs to land two key points: challenging business to speak out over the referendum, and saying that if the right deal isn't on offer in February, he'll walk away.

Before he goes on, Mark Rutte, the Dutch Prime Minister, drops in. Gordon Brown is on mute on the conference TV channel, and I imagine his dour, apocalyptic tones.

Inevitably the renegotiation comes up. Rutte looks spry and self-confident, leaning back on the oatmeal sofa in the dimly lit room. He says he's been told the British people are too conservative to leave – and they'll end up coming on board, just like in Scotland. All of us think it is a dangerously complacent view and realise European leaders need a jolt of electricity to make them wake up.

We head into the hall as it is filling up and I sit in the front row. DC arrives on stage, laying his notes on a high table to the side, but doesn't refer to them once. As ever, he's a class act, looking confident and in control – effortlessly making his case for reform and getting in the two key news points.

I check social media as he gets to the Q&A. Tim Montgomerie, a leading Brexit journalist, is already tweeting that IDS, Chris Grayling and Theresa Villiers should resign from the Cabinet immediately, because the PM is campaigning flagrantly and they are not.

When it's over, we do a couple of interviews. First with Robert Peston and then TF1 – a French TV station. The reporter reads from a sheet of paper, saying she plans to ask the questions in English, but that she won't be able to understand his answers. We joke that it sounds like the ideal interview, but inevitably there's a screw-up. She asks him if he considers himself a European. He responds with a fulsome, 'Yes.' Of course, he should have said he considers himself British first. The front-page splashes of tomorrow's *Mail* and *Sun* form in my mind within moments of him saying it. It's a rare mistake from him and probably our fault for putting him in such a bizarre situation.

My phone then comes alive with texts from London. Theresa May has been seen lunching with the leading 'Outer' Liam Fox at Quirinale. The hacks say it's the kind of restaurant you go to if you want to be seen – and feel she is playing games. I ignore attempts to get us to comment.

The next few hours are like a strange Davos dream, where I encounter Sheryl Sandberg, the CEO of Facebook, as well as Bono, Kevin Spacey, David Miliband, Tony Blair and Richard Curtis – most of them in a former asylum where an international aid event is being held.

We then depart for a private dinner. Kate Fall has assembled an eclectic group including the historian Niall Ferguson, Anna Botin, the CEO of Santander, the Chancellor, the Director of BBC News, James Harding, and the Governor of the Bank of England, Mark Carney, whom I sit next to.

The conversation at my end of the table turns, inevitably, to Europe. I'm curious to see where Niall Ferguson stands on it. It turns out he's a firm Remainer, saying it's better to be in meeting rooms than in trenches. He believes the atavistic senti-ments that plagued the continent in the first half of the twentieth century are strong undercurrents now, and the EU plays a benevolent role in calming them.

James Harding asks why we aren't more enthusiastically pro-European. I explain as gently as I can why that approach is dead wrong – the key 'in play' groups being the 'Hearts *vs* Heads' and 'Disengaged Middle', who are deeply cynical about the project, especially now it is plagued by an immigration crisis.

As the drink flows, I get drawn into a conversation with James Harding and George about whether Theresa May will make a bid to lead the Out campaign. George says he doesn't think she would take the risk as she's been too pro-European in the past. I volunteer the one line I think she can utter that will give her credibility, 'When the facts change, I change – and there has been a step change in the issue of migration, which means I can no longer support our membership.' That and the *Mail* and *Sun* cheering her on could ease her in.

I run into Richard Curtis, the film director and leading figure in Comic Relief, at a late party hosted by the public relations guru, Matthew Freud. We walk back to our hotels. He's one of the most charming yet insightful people I have met in this job. He's spotted a key problem – hardly anyone has much concept of the European Union, or how it impacts on their lives. We agree there needs to be a re-education programme, but I'm also not sure a lot of people will take the word of key figures, or more to the point, if there's the time available. It's increasingly apparent to me that no one has done the EU's public relations very well in the last forty years. With that, he bids me farewell and disappears into his room in the converted asylum.

I take the funicular down the mountain. I find myself wondering – should that PR have started properly in 2013, when the referendum pledge was made? An organisation could have been set up way back then, designed to explain the benefits of the EU and why it's crucial to our economy. At the moment, it looks like something won't really get moving until after the renegotiation ends – probably next month.

The next morning the PM wants to know if I have partied the night away. I report back on the Freud party, including having run into Tony Blair there. DC tells me he arrived back at his suite to discover Blair had used it to meet someone for a nightcap. He is understandably bemused, but we think Blair had thought it was OK because it was a British Government resource. I joke that I'm sure he didn't need to worry too much, 'though I'm sure he took time and found comfort in the loo.' This is a peculiar line from Blair's autobiography, which both of us periodically joke about. DC laughs and winces, 'No . . . please . . .'

As we wander around Davos on our way to a meeting on our final morning, I consider how this is a place the Brexiteers would hate – with car parks filled with the same model of black Audi, and the sense that everywhere you might run into some of the most famous and powerful people on earth. They see this, with some justification, as the ultimate expression of the gilded elite being literally out of touch – up a mountain in an exclusive ski resort – ultra-European and in complete denial.

As if to prove the point, a Swiss army helicopter transports us back over a winter wonderland: trees coated in ice crystals protrude dark and jagged from the mountains, like whiskers on the face of a giant. There's no sign of life, save for the occasional chalet apparently dumped in the middle of nowhere, with no obvious link to the outside world.

On Monday 25 January, I find myself scribbling in my notebook: Is there anything but Europe?

DC clears out the 8.30 a.m. meeting and tells a much smaller group, 'I'm worried about the state of the renegotiation.' He says he thinks we need to shock everyone into realising we really could walk away in February.

Senior civil servants say they were in Brussels yesterday and all the mood music was that they understood they would have to do a deal that will work for us.

The PM seems to be giving up on February – meaning he is giving up on a June referendum. He describes this as 'not the end of the world'. Of course it isn't, but it means we are opening up another six months of Europe, almost certainly having to go in November – after a divisive party conference.

Other irritating things are happening on Europe. Stuart Rose, the former boss of M&S and Chair of the Stronger In campaign, goes on the *Today* programme and gets embroiled in a row about whether it is right to claim people will lose £3,000 if we leave the EU. Instead of constantly pivoting out of the question and pointing to his key messages, he just argues. The result – a missed opportunity.

Then there are stories about the likes of Unilever, apparently saying that leaving the EU wouldn't impact on their business. It seems to me they are being naive by saying they wouldn't shut factories to journalists, who then print it without going into the nuance of the position, that it would have an impact on jobs and investment in the medium to long term.

When DC hears, he says, 'For God's sake, Unilever's Chief Exec is one of the biggest pro-Europeans I know!'

The next part of the meeting is spent crawling through where we are on each of the four areas of renegotiation:

1. Getting us out of 'ever closer union' (the sense we'd be drawn more and more into a politically united Europe).
2. Reducing bureaucracy.
3. Stopping members of the Euro dominating countries (like the UK) who have their own currency.
4. Dealing with the pressures caused by freedom of movement (migration).

The sense from the negotiating team is that we are delivering on the first three – but there's more to do on the crucial fourth area.

After a press conference with Enda Kenny, the Irish Taoiseach, DC calls Angela Merkel. She begins, 'Allo. These are demanding times. Everything is so far OK. I have my health . . .' It seems an odd thing to say – basically an oblique way of hinting she is facing endless pressure on migration in her own country.

The conversation turns quickly to our area, with DC saying, 'I'll be very frank. There's a lot of good will, but where we've got to on immigration and welfare is hopeless. If we let the official process grind on, it will be a car crash in February.'

Merkel agrees, 'It certainly looks like a typical European solution.'

DC says, 'Yes, too small and too complicated. If there's a real deal, I can take it. But if there isn't, I can't, because we will lose.'

Merkel is definitely in a mood to be helpful. At one point she starts floating the idea of what an acceptable limit would be on migration. She asks if we have a minimum wage and what it works out at a year. £13k a year, comes the reply.

It's Burns Night and there's a special dinner at the Scottish Office. David Mundell hosts a great evening of poetry, questionable food and speeches. My favourite moment is the German Ambassador telling me and Michael Gove of his plan to send envoys to the UK to explain to us just how bad it would be if we left the EU. Both of us explain – awkwardly – why that might be counterproductive.

The next day the 8.30 a.m. meeting is cancelled, which is usually a sign something is up. I walk through to find the whole Europe negotiating team talking to the PM. They have it on good authority what the first draft of the renegotiation document to be sent round in a few days will look like.

The welfare/migration section will apparently accept there should be no 'unjustified direct or indirect discrimination', which means there is an acceptance that there could be 'justified discrimination'. After all the 'No discrimination' shouting, this seems a major breakthrough. There are other encouraging sentences that build on this, but the rest is pretty mushy . . . certainly not enough detail that could lead us to saying we have a deal.

On an easier note – there's a piece in *The Times* saying the leading Leave MP Bernard Jenkin botched an attempt to get Dominic Cummings fired from their campaign. Apparently he'd wanted it to happen at a board meeting, but Cummings got wind and rallied support.

There seem to be two bones of contention:

- Cummings' abrasive tone, slagging everyone off.
- His hare-brained scheme to campaign for two referendums. His colleagues appear to have worked out that they may not be chosen by the Electoral Commission to be the official Leave campaign, because they could come across as not really wanting to go. This is crucial in the competing 'People's Front of Judea' and 'Judean People's Front' world of the Outers.

This is a morale boost as the In campaign meet in the Churchill Room in the basement of the Conrad Hotel. I run them through a variety of thoughts, including the PM doing a national address if there is a successful renegotiation.

We are being approached about debates by the BBC, who are desperate to have a 'bear pit' format, where 12,000 people are in an arena. They also like the idea of Conservative 'Inners' facing Conservative 'Outers'. After all the crap we went through in the election, I'm certain they need to revise those ideas now.

Lynton's right-hand man, Mark Textor, who is on a rare visit from Australia, is waiting for me back in my office. It's always good to see him – total clarity of thought, reminding me of the 'keep it simple and clear' approach when it comes to the referendum: 'It's better to have one strategy that's seventy percent right, rather than ten that are one hundred percent right.' One team – all pulling in the same direction. That requires discipline and egos to be put in check. How that is possible with a coalition stretching from the Government to the Greens is going to be some task.

He moves on to the mess that is Corbyn. I roar with laughter at his turn of phrase, 'Oh yeah . . . we've been following all that on the news – the guy's now an international superstar of fuckwittery.'

Sajid Javid is due to go on *Marr*, ostensibly to talk about some

BME proposals. George gets wind of it and is nervous that the gap between him and the PM on Europe will be obvious.

I call Sajid to have a frank conversation.

He's very straightforward. Everything is meat and potatoes with him. He tells me, 'I'll sit on the fence and tell him I'll wait for the deal.' I tell him that worries me – he needs to sound much more like he's behind the PM. I suggest he says, 'The PM is fighting for Britain. This is a poker game – people are going to take positions. I have every faith in his ability to sort it out.' He also doesn't need to answer hypotheticals, simply saying, 'I'm totally united with the PM. I expect a deal. But I rule nothing out.' He seems to take this, but I suspect a few more calls will be needed.

On Friday 29 January, we take a circuitous route to Brussels. Up at 5 a.m. and arriving at Northolt forty-five minutes later, with the aim of meeting the PM in Aberdeen – before turning back to Belgium.

When I get on the plane, the RAF flight attendant informs us that flying conditions will be 'bumpy and challenging' and because Storm Gertrude is so torrid, nothing is getting in or out of Aberdeen. We have to meet the PM in Edinburgh.

The flight attendant wasn't kidding. The whole trip is a rollercoaster ride: notebooks and crockery flying around, grasping the table in front of me just to keep steady.

I go through the papers in these conditions – teasing the negotiating team with lines from Richard Littlejohn's column in the *Daily Mail*, that the whole renegotiation exercise is a 'dishonest, intelligence-insulting charade'.

The Commission has been briefing hard – saying they are closing in on a deal. The idea seems to be that they want to box us in. The PM is doing BBC Scotland in the car down from Aberdeen. I advise him to say there are grounds for optimism, but there's still a long way to go.

DC arrives on the plane in Edinburgh looking windswept. He's had a two hour and forty minute journey from Aberdeen, seeing overturned lorries and uprooted trees along the way. The metaphors seem obvious.

We go through the Commission briefing and spell out what we need to do to shift it.

The conversation turns to the fact the Home Secretary still hasn't told us where she is going – leading the Out campaign, or sticking with us. Just before take-off, DC looks wistfully out of the window and says, 'Well, it may work for her. She could be PM in six months' time.'

Meanwhile texts are flying in from panicky people – one from Nick Boles, a minister in the Business Department, saying the emergency brake isn't enough.

We take off with an extraordinary amount of thrust into the wind.

Having landed in Brussels, we are whizzed into the characterless UKREP, where Jonathan Hill is waiting for us, having just seen Jean-Claude Juncker, the President of the European Commission. Coffee is brought to us in two giant cafetières. It tastes disgusting and everyone winces. He leans over to me and says, 'I think that's instant coffee that they've just stuck in there . . .'

He briefs the PM, saying he started by telling Juncker, and Martin Selmayr, his chief of staff who is seen by many as the power behind the throne, that all of the blabbing to the press is completely unhelpful. Apparently Selmayr agreed, saying, 'Yes. The British must stop this.' Everyone took a moment to process the fact that he could be so brazen.

Despite all the issues, Jonathan Hill is confident we can do a good deal: 'They just want to take one of their problems off the table.'

While DC disappears into a lunch with Juncker and the negotiating teams, Helen Bower and I go to talk to the Brussels press pack. So many of their questions are crawling through the minutiae. I really don't envy them – writing about stuff most people aren't even aware of, let alone care about.

When we link up with the PM again, he says, 'That went well!', telling us everything is going in our direction, not least that they appear to have accepted that the emergency brake on welfare would apply now.

All weekend, in London and in Brussels, the negotiating team work on the first version of the draft document that's about to be released.

Come Sunday afternoon we sit round the oak table in the Thatcher Room in No. 10 to be talked through it, under the glare of the Iron Lady's portrait. The conversation turns to the emergency brake on welfare. It goes round and round so much that everyone is relieved when the PM says, 'You're confusing everyone, break it down.'

They do:

- We want it triggered now.
- It needs to be renewable.
- It should apply for a minimum of seven years.

The Prime Minister goes into a meeting with Theresa May, Philip Hammond and George Osborne in his study. While they are in there, various people try to read the runes on where Theresa May is going to land in terms of Remain or Leave. Some think she is heading out; others that she simply relishes keeping us guessing; others that she simply can't make up her mind. My guess is she sees her strategy as setting herself apart – trying to demonstrate she is her own person.

Donald Tusk, the President of the European Council, arrives and DC goes into dinner with him. A few of us eat the same food in the state dining room. Silver-service waiters give us gravadlax, roast beef and pear crumble. The wine is excellent and we're all enjoying it a bit too much, when after only ninety minutes, dinner breaks up.

We rush down to the study – where DC can hardly wait to get away. I ask him to hold his horses to get the headlines. It's been agreed that there will be another twenty-four hours of negotiation on the text – this is a good sign as it means we can get more. It's also been agreed that an emergency brake on welfare would apply in the current circumstances. It means we have got our four-year ban on benefits for migrants, though the details on whether it is temporary or renewable aren't clear.

The meeting breaks up and I have a separate discussion with the comms team in my office. While we are talking it emerges that Tusk was asked if there had been a deal walking out the front door. He responded rather brusquely, 'No deal.'

The media is confused – is it all falling apart? We then sweep in to tell them it's going to plan. They aren't quite sure what's up and what's down.

# FEBRUARY

# Chapter 5

## Who Do EU Think You Are Kidding?

A S FEBRUARY BEGINS, we are racing towards the first draft of the negotiated settlement with the EU being released and the prospect of a full deal in a fortnight. That means we'll be calling for a June referendum. It's by no means certain we can get the bill to make that happen through Parliament. We will be relying on Labour. DC says he normally doesn't like going for a vote without a clear idea of where he'll land, but he's prepared to do so in this case.

The next big question is posed by the civil service: 'Is Chris Grayling going to be expected to defend the Government's position on this draft deal before collective responsibility on Europe has ended?' We are holding the line that collective responsibility applies right up to a decision in the Cabinet after the council. What no one seems to want to admit is, in reality, we are campaigning now. No one seriously thinks we're going to suggest anything other than to stay in. The 'I rule nothing out' line is increasingly threadbare. We're planning a major speech at the Siemens factory in Chippenham tomorrow, which will be a signpost that we believe we are well on the way to a deal and suggesting that, with an enhanced special status, we should remain in the EU.

We talk about how we will use key moments to explain what we are up to and how we will try to get the PM to educate about Europe. DC says, 'My approach has not been to overturn the table and shout – I've patiently explained and worked with people.' It's agreed he'll say that publicly, demonstrating that he is the patient grown-up, '[who] doesn't believe in more uncertainty at a time of uncertainty.'

We also agree we need to use the advantage of being in Government to release a steady stream of stories showing progress. We create a grid to claim various successes in the renegotiation, including getting an agreement that if fifty-five per cent of parliaments are agreed, they can wave a red flag to any European legislation. We hope to create momentum, while the Outers have to react to us.

I have a hilarious meeting with the Home Office SpAds. We wend our way through the key items in their in-tray. I use the 'Any other business' item at the end of the agenda to tease them a little. I say if we get a deal at the February Council, it will be a key moment for the negotiating team, in which Theresa has been a central figure, to make the case for remaining. One of them blurts out, 'Theresa will be away that week!'

'Yes, but she'll be back on the day . . . We'll need to get lots of voices out.'

'She's going away that weekend with Philip!' is the rushed response after a couple of seconds of thinking time.

'Yes. But she'll be back on the Monday, and that will be a crucial time,' I continue patiently. They assure me they're more than willing to help and will get back to me.

The front page of *The Times* the next day looks briefed by people close to Theresa May. It says DC 'faces last-minute opposition from her to a compromise on migration'. She wants, among other things, Brussels to close a back-door route into Britain that's being used by migrants from outside the EU.

It says it's leading to fears in No. 10 that she could refuse to back the reform deal.

Everyone takes a deep breath and reminds themselves the concerns being briefed are all being dealt with in the document. In other words, they can't be used to say the deal is weak.

There's another, bigger problem. The word 'phasing' hasn't cropped up in any discussion we've had in the renegotiation. We've been pushing for a simple four-year migrant benefits ban. Now it emerges the document will say in-work benefits will start at zero and be 'graduated' or increased over time. What does that mean? Does it neuter it?

Cabinet involves a section where the PM takes everyone through where we are on the renegotiation. There's a moment where Chris Grayling points out that the argument is being had now, so can people be allowed to speak out now? The PM tries to sound emollient, saying, 'The Government's position has got to be that we keep good order while the negotiation is ongoing.' But his message is clear: collective responsibility pertains until a deal is done and Cabinet has met.

Looking round the room I can see that people are sitting forward, their attention heightened. No one fights back, though. The point is, the PM wrote a letter to them spelling this out a few weeks ago – they didn't complain then, so they can hardly complain now. It's not long after Cabinet has broken up before I get calls suggesting the PM has said we can be relaxed about people blurring the lines. Some ministers have clearly been briefing journalists. I'm hardline – that is certainly not what he said.

With journalists I trust a little more, I plant the seed, 'People feel strongly about this. If they want to speak out, they have another option.' In other words: if they feel that strongly, they can always resign on principle. No one does.

With Cabinet done, we knock off a clip for the lunchtime news and get the train to Chippenham for the big speech. My view is that the PM needs to look utterly confident – constantly pulling back to the big picture, while everyone else tries to drag him into the weeds. You wanted me to end migrants getting welfare benefits for doing nothing? I'm doing it. You said it would be impossible for me to get a four-year benefit ban? Well, it's happening.

He sits in First Class with a black marker gathering his thoughts on a sheet of A4. He is visibly wound up by the *Times* front page. Suddenly he picks up his mobile and is calling Theresa May, asking her to make clear we have been victorious in our plan to crack down on 'swindlers and fiddlers' attempting to come into the UK. When he hangs up, DC seems to think he's made an impact.

The Siemens factory in Chippenham looks like it could do with a makeover. DC wants to do his speech 'sleeves rolled up'. I think this is a moment for him in a suit and tie. He says, 'I always think you look like a bit of a fool in a factory in a suit and tie.' We compromise on him doing it with his jacket off.

He gives it some welly. The workers hear him in respectful silence − rewarding him with a round of applause. DC feels he 'made it simple', essentially making the case for why Britain should stay in a reformed EU. He does well, but I wonder how many minds were still focused when we got to 'subsidiarity'.

In the car from the speech to the helicopter, I get the PM to call Tony Gallagher, the editor of the *Sun*, attempting to push how remaining in the EU works for working people.

The helicopter is circling above a pleasant military outpost, while we look up from a field below. When it lands, we wait for its blades to calm and we climb on board. The sun is out and we approach London from the south-west, providing the most stunning views of the city I've ever seen: the glistening river snaking through all the landmarks towards the horizon.

In the car at the other end I raise John Witherow, the editor of *The Times*, and then Lionel Barber from the *FT*. They listen respectfully as DC explains the latest to them.

As soon as we arrive in No. 10, the PM has a call with Barack Obama.

DC does it at his desk. The rest of us listen on a 'spiderphone' elsewhere. After a short wait, a woman from the White House says, 'Introducing Prime Minister David Cameron.' The President sounds even more laid back than usual – referring to the PM as 'brother' and engaging in a lot of verbal back-slapping. DC asks him about his recent TV programme in the wilderness with Bear Grylls. Obama says he loved working with 'the stud' – though the security services would only let him do so much.

Finally Obama asks what he can do to help the UK stay in the EU. He evidently believes it is the right thing for the country, and it would be a great loss to the US and our own standing in the world if we left. He says he will come towards the end of April, which could well be the perfect time.

When the call has ended, there are two pieces of good news. First, the Labour party won't oppose any attempt to have an early referendum. Second, DC's call to Theresa May seems to have worked. She's issued a statement saying she believes there's 'the basis for a deal here'. This is immediately interpreted as the moment she has climbed down off the fence and chosen a side. After all the concern around her, it seems to have ended not with a bang, but a whimper.

The PM and I usually see newspaper editors together. The one exception is the legendary editor of the *Daily Mail*, Paul Dacre. I make a point of going and finding him in the waiting room. He's well dressed in what could be a classic Savile Row suit and I wonder what he makes of this tiny dimly lit room, with a couple of clapped-out armchairs and a water machine with clear plastic cups. Only in Britain would the head of government welcome the great and the good this way. In the hallway outside there's a tea stain on the carpet and some gaffer tape holding together a particularly threadbare section.

I ask him what he made of the PM's speech today, full well knowing the answer, and he laughs, and gives me a friendly tap on the shoulder. We both know it'll get the *Mail* attack treatment tomorrow.

The PM arrives and I let them disappear upstairs together – taking the opportunity to slip off home. DC calls me to say it wasn't so bad: 'I asked him when the *Daily Mail* became a great advocate for Out.' He can't recall it having been such a great theme. He says he pointed out that this was the paper that supported Ken Clarke's leadership bid. Paul Dacre claimed he could have persuaded him on Europe, to which DC asked, 'Have you met Ken Clarke?'

I warn DC that tomorrow's papers will be a car crash on Europe, but on the plus side, the Out camp are in disarray, taking a major blow in not landing Theresa May.

On Wednesday 3 February, the papers are indeed brutal – having seen the draft renegotiation document and heard the speech.

The *Sun* plays on the current *Dad's Army* revival theme with DC dressed to look like Captain Mainwaring, and the headline: 'Who do EU think you are kidding, Mr Cameron?' The sub-headline is: 'He caves in over benefits; Brake on Laws is Bogus; No Control of Our Borders.'

It's not subtle and it's hardly surprising. We'd always known they were going to throw a bucket of shit over the draft deal.

However DC is feeling pretty bullish about it. Others are concerned that Brussels effectively doing their negotiating in public is a serious problem for us – making a basic error of giving away too much detail about the process. The official and final deal won't be completed for a fortnight. In news terms this is an eternity – endless opportunities to pick away at something that is complex and unpopular with much of the press, without another major event to move things along. It would be better to publish the deal cold in a fortnight, explain its significance, and then be straight into the campaign.

As the PM sits in his armchair and prepares for PMQs and his Commons statement, he leans forward and proclaims, 'Maastricht, Nice, Amsterdam, Brussels. Thatcher, Major, Blair, Brown – all of them have stood at the despatch box and declared they are handing powers over to Europe. I am bringing them back.'

He goes on, 'There have been two ways in which Europe has increased its powers: through treaty change and the European Court of Justice. I am standing here saying I have stopped that.' Anyone who has ever had anything to do with Brussels is convinced this is a significant deal.

Despite this, others are proving hard to convince. I run into ultra-loyalist Jeremy Hunt on the way to PMQs. He tells me he's happy to go on *Marr*, while confiding he, too, thinks the deal is a difficult sell.

And there are editorials saying: 'Even the most loyal Cameron supporter would admit that the draft text from the European Council is a long way from what the PM and the Tory manifesto promised.'

Jeremy Corbyn dismisses the whole thing as a Conservative drama – effectively claiming the renegotiation is a vast magic show, designed with many distractions.

An MP who is an old friend has a cup of tea with me. He says most Tory backbenchers are hating every second of this. They've traded on Euroscepticism for years and now they are standing on the edge of the precipice, they're realising they should have been careful what they wished for. He is clear this is a must-win situation for us, saying if we lose, 'They will come for us in numbers.' He means DC's enemies and those who believe they will fare better under a new leader.

He also believes that some MPs have taken the decision to go for Out, while not actually believing it – hoping it will make them popular with their local party associations, but thinking it will never actually happen. Now they are realising that they have only added momentum to a campaign that could prove unstoppable.

The next day the *Mail* has an extraordinary front page, head-lined: 'Who Will Speak for England?'

It is so over the top, it seems like a parody. 'Today the *Mail* asks a question of profound significance to our destiny as a

sovereign nation and the fate of our children and grandchildren.'
It goes on to say that its headline is inspired by the events of
2 September 1939 – the day after Hitler invaded Poland and
Neville Chamberlain gave an ambivalent statement to the
Commons. As the Labour party deputy leader was set to respond,
Tory backbencher Leo Emery bellowed, 'Speak for England!'

It's a curious comparison. Parliament debating on the eve of
the Second World War, the pivotal event of the twentieth century,
and people now deciding how they feel ahead of a debate to
leave the EU. A few paragraphs down, the paper agrees that it
would be absurd to draw a parallel between the EU and the
Nazis, which begs the obvious question.

Of course, they're hoping to tempt big figures into realising
that leading the Leave campaign could be a real career opportunity. Theresa is no longer an option, but what about Boris?
What will Gove do?

On seeing the paper and hearing that Nigel Lawson is to be
on the board of one of the Leave campaigns, a senior figure marches
me down the corridor of No. 11, takes me to the stairs leading
to the PM's flat and shows me a cartoon on the wall. It shows
John Major and Margaret Thatcher rowing in opposite directions,
with Major taking us towards European Monetary Union. On the
riverbank are people urging in or out. His point is that Lawson,
now an Outer, was part of those taking us deeper into this project.

DC seems to be taking it in his stride. Standing in his office
at 8 a.m., he says to me, 'This is a battle we were always going
to have to fight – the right-wing press trying to kill us on this
issue.' The Out campaign currently has no serious leader and is
widely believed to be in disarray.

IDS announces he is coming in to see the PM. He's a proud
and formal man and we are expecting him to revolt on principle
against the fact that Cabinet ministers who want to leave the
EU aren't allowed to campaign until the deal is formally signed
off. The thought is he wants to go on *Marr* to speak out. I say

to the PM, 'You've got to appeal to him as a military man. If no one follows the leader, it's chaos.'

DC agrees this is a good approach. I also say we should try to persuade him to do nothing, but if he has to, he mustn't breach the collective responsibility line, 'because if he does, the first question we'll be asked is: Are you going to fire him?'

I make myself scarce. Fifteen minutes later, I'm called back through to the PM's office. It turns out IDS has had a change of heart. He doesn't want to speak out now, but he does want the Cabinet after the European summit to be brought forward, either to the Friday night or the Saturday. My view is we need space to drive home our points before the cacophony surrounding the bigger story of who is In and who is Out. DC isn't sure that's sustainable.

We start talking about what we need to do to get some momentum back on our side. My thought is that with Theresa May having announced her plans, Boris and Gove are now the focus of attention. If we're sure Gove has said he'll join us, we should try and get him to find a way to come out. This morning's *Times* suggests he's wavering – it would be a great moment to confound those thoughts. DC agrees – he seems utterly confident Gove is on side after discussions he had with Sarah Vine at New Year.

Late in the day, Ed says he has spoken to Gove and he is equivocal. I've spotted a tweet from Rupert Murdoch that seems to me is aimed squarely at him; 'Cameron's deal with EU a nothing. How can sensible Cabinet colleagues accept this? Loyalty to country more important than friendships.' Gove is very close to Murdoch – he goes to his dinners when he is in London and will be at his wedding to Jerry Hall.

George comes in as I'm saying Gove going to Leave would be as big a problem as if Theresa had done. He disagrees – saying Boris is the one to worry about.

I'm not so sure and find myself thinking more and more about why Gove is perhaps the key figure in all of this.

# Chapter 6

## What It's Like to be Ed Miliband

IN NO. 10 there have always been two big assumptions about Michael Gove: he has no leadership ambitions and as a close friend of DC and George, he would never do anything to undermine them.

I have always questioned both of these claims and having dealt with him over a number of years, I'm left asking the same question: Would the real Michael Gove please stand up?

On the leadership, he had always told people that he recognised it requires special qualities to be Prime Minister, which he did not possess. This is what he told Sky News in 2012:

> I don't want to be Prime Minister . . . Having seen close up how [David Cameron] does the job, I know that I couldn't do it . . . if anyone wants to get me to sign a piece of parchment in my own blood saying that I don't want to be Prime Minister – if that's what it takes, then I'm perfectly happy to do that.

His set of friends agreed he wasn't the man for the job, saying he was not worldly enough, and claiming, 'This is the man who had to be stopped trying to unblock his loo with a hoover.'

Gove also told a lot of people he would be loyal to David Cameron to the very last, when he would switch his allegiance to George Osborne. A small moment made me doubt that. Very early on in my time at No. 10, I accompanied Gove and the PM on a visit to a free school. Michael was entertaining, gossipy and preoccupied by what would happen if Boris got into

Parliament – would he create an alternative powerbase from the backbenches? After a while it was clear that DC was bored with it and said, 'I don't know – that'll be something for George to deal with.' I could see that, as the PM went back to his work, Gove looked crushed. It struck me at the time that he hated being dismissed as a potential leader by this casual comment – even though DC did not realise what he was doing.

I also noticed that Michael was assiduous in courting back-bench MPs and assumed this was part of keeping his options open. Others said, never mind what Gove wants, think about what Mrs Gove wants.

Looking back, I now see Gove always hated the idea that some saw him as David Cameron's court jester. He was rightly valued for his jokes – regularly called upon at prep for Prime Minister's Questions to sprinkle some much-needed humour into the occasion. Some found the cumulative effect of being hit by a round of his jokes the equivalent of eating too many chocolates, but there was real talent there. When being asked about Ebola, he suggested, 'When it comes to communicable diseases, it's quite clear that the honourable gentleman doesn't know his Sars from his Ebola.'

Although Gove was praised by many for being an intellectual, I struggled to see how all the positions he had taken hung together. A man who presented himself as a modernising liberal could also appear to be a reactionary. In a paper entitled 'Northern Ireland, the Price of Peace', he claimed the Good Friday Agreement was a capitulation to the IRA; and in a newspaper column he argued in favour of the death penalty, writing that for there to be fair trials, they needed to be held 'under the shadow of the noose'.

And it was the apparent desire to still be a columnist that was part of his downfall as Secretary of State for Education. While a growing coalition accused him of failure to explain one of our flagship policies and alienating all teachers, he found time to write some curious pieces. One criticised the TV series *Blackadder* for misleading people by suggesting the First World War was futile, because, in his view, the reality was that we had been fighting anti-democratic forces bent on imperialism. I called him up to ask, 'Michael, given it is the settled view of most people that the First World War was a waste of life, and that at the time Britain occupied more than half the globe, why did you think it was a good idea to write this stuff? You seem like you're not interested in your day job.'

The more I looked at him, the more everything he did appeared to be an act or a performance. Watching him in various situations, I was reminded of the line in T.S. Eliot, 'To prepare a face to meet the faces that you meet.' In Cabinet while others sat still, he would flick through his notebook and scribble theatrically. His now legendary politeness seemed forced, particularly for someone so skilled at dinner-table character assassinations.

Polling showed he was deeply unpopular – not just with professionals, but with the wider public. Educational reform that should have been a jewel in our crown was becoming tarnished. He was moved to Chief Whip, a job the PM said Gove had told him he'd always wanted to do. In DC's mind he was protecting his friend – giving him an important role, while preparing the ground for another promotion at the next reshuffle. Gove accepted, but he appeared not to realise it meant a pay cut, and his champions in the press said he had been humiliated.

His wife, Sarah Vine, tweeted: 'A shabby day's work, which Cameron will live to regret.' Were they really people who wanted the PM to succeed and did not harbour their own ambitions?

On Friday 5 February, I wake early, but allow myself the luxury of reading the papers and listening to the *Today* programme in bed. My ears prick up at an item saying the group most likely to vote to leave the EU are those with few educational qualifications.

When I get into work, I make myself a cup of tea in the kitchenette area of the basement. Sean the driver is down there. He's a sharp, older, sensible guy and I value his opinions. He says in his group of friends, largely ex-servicemen, all want to get out. They're sick of being told what to do, and with the impact of immigration, struggling to get on the housing ladder. He says he heard Nigel Farage on the radio and was taken by him saying, 'This is all about the bankers and the posh boys.' It's a cynical ploy – he was in the City and isn't exactly from a poor background – but it's clearly effective.

The Vote Leave campaign continues to be a mess. The MP Kate Hoey has ended her affiliation with them, apparently sick of being treated like a fool by Dominic Cummings. It's obvious that coming from Labour, Hoey should be treated as a precious asset – someone they can point to who isn't UKIP or a right-wing Conservative – but now she's gone.

The one card Cummings does hold is that he may be able to deliver Gove. On that front, George texts DC having seen Gove to tell him it is definitely a serious prospect.

The next day, the papers continue to be bad on Europe. Charles Moore writes in the *Telegraph* that he's been polite about the deal so far – but enough is enough. He says there's nothing in it and now people have to decide.

In the *Guardian*'s comment pages there is a thoughtful piece from Martin Kettle pointing out we really look like achieving a lot.

We seem caught between those in the EU who don't like our supposed belly-aching, think we've been offered too much and want us to get less, and those who don't like us at home who think we've been offered too little, want us to get far more, and will keep screaming until we do.

The Sunday papers are as bad as it gets. An almost universal and systematic trashing of the renegotiation – particularly by voices in the Conservative party. We can pretend we aren't flying into the teeth of an outright campaign, but the truth is we are, and it feels uncomfortable.

I email the PM saying we need to have a fightback, but the problem is that while we're still negotiating, we can't seem too much in favour of staying in.

Late last night it emerged the *Telegraph* is running a story headlined: 'Cameron: Brexit will bring "Jungle" to Kent.' The BBC calls to ask if it is true. I can spot trouble. The *Telegraph* has clearly taken it from a briefing the PM did with their editor and political editor last week. They didn't tell us they were planning to run it. If they had, we'd have corrected parts of it. What we mean is that if the so-called 'Juxtaposed Controls' were ended with France, everyone in the camps would naturally want to come to the UK, and not that they would set up camps here. We're now in a situation where the lobby can play a game – is the story true? We then have to explain what was meant, to which they say, 'So the story is bollocks?' If we answer that, they say No. 10 'backs away'.

There's concern about where the story came from. ('Um . . . the PM . . . but they've massively over-written it.')

I have a particularly frustrating call with the *Evening Standard*, who say they are going to write the story is true or that we are backing down. When I say we can't be mocked or back away from something we didn't say, they act dumb and pretend not to be able to see the point. I tell them if I see either version of the story I will take it as misrepresenting us.

DC says this is why he hates having cosy chats that are supposedly off the record – because this is what happens. Of course, he is right that the *Telegraph* should have told us what they were planning and we'd have told them they had the wrong end of the stick, but that is not the world we live in, and we need to keep as good relations as we can.

The PM has to rush off to give his prisons speech. When he

does Kate, Ed and I reflect on where we are. The problem is all the negativity in the papers is winding up the party.

I'm made to feel a little better by some fresh polling, which I summed up in this email to the PM:

> Andrew Cooper called me with some fresh polling.
>
> A phone poll shows – Remain: 59 and Leave 41.
>
> He asked if people support or oppose the renegotiation – with 42% saying Support, and 31% Oppose, with 27% Don't Know.
>
> When people are given more detail – support for renegotiation rises to 50%, but opposition also rises to 40% with 10% Don't Know.
>
> His view is stick to the big picture – we can have the best of both worlds.
>
> Craig.

That brief moment of relief is ended by Ed suggesting we may need to walk away from the February Council without a deal. Tusk is now suggesting they could release a second draft text, which might be worse for us than the first. Obviously we couldn't accept that – and would be in an even worse position with the papers than we are now (if that is conceivable).

Meanwhile the tale of who will support Out continues to torment us. Boris writes a piece in the *Telegraph* which is an exemplar of his policy on cake: having it and eating it, too. It's basically, 'On the one hand . . . and on the other . . .' with no firm conclusion.

It makes me think how the arguments are boiling down. Out is essentially motivated by 'sovereignty' – saying it's ridiculous that a country that has been under the rule of law for centuries can't have proper control of its own borders, is regularly overruled by foreign judges, and whose parliament can't pass all its own laws. Ours is – we can have the best of both worlds, all of the economic advantages of being in the EU, without the downsides of being in the Euro or the Schengen 'no borders' agreement.

As the day goes on, the Calais story gets better. For a start, the Leave campaign claim it's no more than scaremongering, which shows they are rattled. The former head of UK Border Force comes out and says it is absolutely correct – the French would drop border controls like a hot brick. I joke with the PM at the end of the day that it's been another triumph of media strategy and he winces.

A few people are now beginning to realise that we are in a looking-glass media world, where everyone we traditionally chalk up in our column is on the other side and vice versa. There is almost nothing as formidable as the campaigning power of the right-wing press. As Ameet puts it, 'We're discovering what it's like to be Ed Miliband.'

I meet with the BBC, who dominate the media landscape in this country. In the face of a powerful newspaper campaign against us, they are going to be desperately important in reaching undecided voters.

The main purpose of the meeting is for them to get the logistics going forward, but they also bring up that they are determined to sort out the problems with online and morning bulletins the BBC has had in the past over big campaigns. I've heard this before and am sceptical. They tell me they plan to have a hotline for both campaigns that nominated people will be able to call at any time.

Having worked as the editor of the *BBC News at Six* and *Ten* and controller of the World Service, I know the organisation backwards.

The best way of understanding it is likening it to a huge vineyard, renowned throughout the world for its vintage wines – like the *Today* programme, the *News at Ten* and the World Service. As well as wines of distinction, it also mass produces more basic product in the form of short radio and TV bulletins and online copy, consumed by literally tens of millions. Understandably the management are obsessed with getting the big 'reputational' programmes right. They are less concerned by the mass-produced products. The 8 a.m. bulletin on Chris Evans' Radio Two show is the most listened-to output from BBC radio news, but I doubt any senior editorial figures ever tune in.

Too often in this job, I have struggled with these bulletins and online stories being wrong or misleading. It's not just an issue with me. When I have spoken to figures in Labour and the Liberal Democrats, they have had the same complaint. It's also not about believing them to be biased. They're not. It's about being slapdash in these areas. At core, I believe the BBC is a fundamentally good thing. Its heart is in the right place, with a public service ethos and attempting to be impartial.

What bothers us all so much is it is a leviathan – dominating journalism on radio, television and online in this country. If they get it wrong, it's a serious issue. For years no one has been in overall charge of morning output. We have frequent issues with BBC Online getting things wrong, and it seems to take a minimum of six hours to get anything changed, even when they admit a mistake.

Given their scale, how they perform in this campaign is going to be crucial.

It seems certain Donald Tusk will put round a second draft text on the renegotiation ahead of next week's council. It's thought it will weaken the original proposals. Given how bad it was for the first draft, I am seriously concerned.

I run into one of the lead negotiators coming into the back of No. 10, looking dishevelled, wearing an old beanie hat, his face gaunt and weather-beaten. He tells me he's been dealing with well over twenty other countries who want to water everything down.

He declares in the PM's office, 'There's been lots of moaning, but nothing fatal,' before going on, 'It's going to be OK.' The main concern is chipping away the language around ending the concept of 'ever closer union', the idea that we are on a fast track to a European superstate.

There's a lot of debate about the vagueness around how long we will get to extend the emergency brake on welfare to end the 'pull factors' for migrants. The PM says it's enough for him to make an argument. I worry we're too close to it. A lot of this stuff is gobbledygook to the average person – easily hijacked by the Leave campaign as not good enough.

Later on, the PM's mind turns to the drink he's having with Michael Gove. We discuss what might work in persuading him not to go to the Out campaign. George says, 'There's no argument that really persuades him. There's a little bit around "What does Vladimir Putin want?" But nothing more.' That argument is that Putin wants to destabilise the West and what it stands for. With a hawkish mindset, Gove would not want that to happen, but it's unlikely to weigh heavier than all his other doubts about the EU.

I ask, 'Has he considered what happens if he's successful?' My point is that Gove could destroy David Cameron, the man who is supposed to be his friend and close political ally, someone who has made the Conservative party electable again – and is in large part responsible for getting him into and prospering in politics. It could poison everything and result in years of internal fighting over managing Britain's exit and attempts to re-establish itself in the world.

DC comes at it from a different angle, 'Michael, we set out on this process of uniting the Conservative party. You've been a key lieutenant in that . . . I never thought you were going to vote against me.'

DC moves on to the argument he's used with Priti Patel and Liz Truss: 'You're going to be a big figure in the Conservative party. Do you really want to spend the next ten years dealing with the fallout of this?' It's a powerful argument and one that's integral to our comms strategy: who the hell knows where we'll land if we take the Brexit leap?

The next morning, DC reports back from his meeting with Gove. It sounds like he's heading towards the exit. This view is confirmed when I talk to George about it, as we are walking down the corridor. He says Gove is well and truly out, 'He's totally unpersuaded by the arguments and it's only personal loyalty to both of us [meaning himself and the PM] that's keeping him from saying so.'

If the renegotiation is successful, we need to ensure the docking of No. 10 with Stronger In goes well. I whizz over to Great North Street, which is where David Sainsbury has some offices. Inside they look stark, the light grey walls interspersed with the odd piece of modern art.

I sit the No. 10 comms team round a long table, shaped like an African warrior's shield – their comms team facing ours. I lead them through an agenda of the first seventy-two hours after the renegotiation, looking at how we handle broadcast, print and digital. I pair members of the No. 10 team with their team and task them with coming up with a plan that covers the first three days – where every theme of the campaign will be played out in miniature. These extraordinary people, who were each other's opposite number in the election, are now being asked to work together. No one is immature – there are no jokes caricaturing the flaws of our respective parties.

Our main researcher, Adam Atashzai, is paired with Labour's Joe Carberry. Both are remarkably similar, early thirties, excited by detail, fazed by very little. Caroline, who covers broadcasting in No. 10, pairs with the Labour party's Amy Richards, both young, very capable and well-liked.

What's clear from the meeting is quite how small an operation they are. The idea of even a rudimentary media monitoring team is beyond them.

I come back to Downing Street feeling sober about the battle ahead. We have the might of the Government on the one hand – they have the right-wing press, who are more than prepared for a fight to the death.

# Chapter 7

## The Domino Theory

As we face the crunch European Council, with information about the likely deal widely available, and the press totally unconvinced, a truism is being established that we aren't getting much. That feels desperately unfair, but I've been around long enough to know that if something takes root in journalism, no matter if it is wrong, it's almost impossible to dislodge.

There's a morass of confusing detail to explain. How do you begin to get across the importance of not having your currency discriminated against — when intelligent journalists aren't even aware that was a possibility or why it matters?

George says this isn't so bad, 'I had nine years of this kind of thing when we were up against New Labour.'

The conversation moves on to which Cabinet ministers are Out. George says Priti Patel, the dynamic, ambitious Minister for Employment has confirmed to him that she is for Leave. He also thinks the Business Secretary Sajid is wobbly again. Then there's Gove . . .

I take a moment to think through the absurdity of the situation:

- A Business Secretary, who may be against the overwhelming view of business.
- A Justice Secretary, who says he thinks he can't deliver our European Court of Human Rights reforms and wants to leave the EU.

- A Welfare and Pensions secretary, IDS, who claims our European welfare reform is unworkable.
- Lynton Crosby reports that Zac, our candidate for Mayor of London (the most cosmopolitan city on earth) says he'd vote to Leave. When asked why, he says, 'Zac thinks it would mess with his brand.'
- Boris – and several other Cabinet ministers – still uncertain.

It's a mess.

Someone compares Gove going to the Domino Theory: 'If Vietnam goes, then Cambodia and Laos are soon after . . .'

And yet we are having some real successes. We are taunting the Leave campaign with 'You don't know what "Leave" means.' Experts are lining up to make our case – and we're pushing them out.

Zac Goldsmith comes in late in the day with his campaign manager, Mark Fulbrook. Zac cares deeply about being elected London Mayor, but there's something about the combination of his good looks, easy-going manner and the way he sucks on an electronic cigarette that makes him seem indifferent. His campaign team has helped sharpen him up a lot and run through how they think they can close the 6.5-point gap.

The crunch moment comes when we discuss Europe. I can feel DC channelling me (something he confirms afterwards), when he says, 'You're giving Khan a massive gift – a massive "in" with business. And I can hear every interview with you – how can you argue for Out and be Mayor of London?'

I swing in behind, 'It makes you easy meat for interviewers, who won't just leave you alone. You claim you are close to the PM and can work with him, but you oppose him on something this fundamental.'

Zac isn't having any of it: he was happy to stand on the manifesto, but he doesn't think we will get enough back. 'It's about integrity – it's about people believing in me.'

When it is done, DC and Ed think he can be swung round. I really doubt it. More to the point – I feel sure he will lose and make life a hell of a lot harder for us in the referendum as a consequence.

My thoughts about Zac are confirmed in the next day's *Telegraph*, with this quote: 'I'm definitely a Eurosceptic . . . if you look at the reforms that are currently on offer, they are not very impressive.'

Someone says, 'Well, sod that. I don't think he's very impressive either.' It's an adage that has become a cliché: there are no friends in politics.

I discuss with Ameet how that doesn't stop it being hard to swallow when you experience it. It's perfectly acceptable for the people who have argued for years to be Out, but I think DC will find people seeing this as a career opportunity the hardest part of all. He asks of several people going against him, 'When have you ever argued for this?'

I'm reminded of the great claim in *The Godfather*, 'It's not personal, it's strictly business.' The statement seems utterly amoral – as if the furthering of a business proposition ends all obligations to another human being.

Politics is a rough game.

It's Monday 15 February, and we are getting close to the climax of this renegotiation.

Donald Tusk calls to run through where he's got to in terms of a suggested deal. He says his biggest worry is the French President, Francois Hollande, who is fighting hard over our plan to ensure countries that aren't in the Euro are protected from policies that might suit countries that are, but harm us.

He goes on to suggest that he amend the text in favour of Hollande and the ultra-European Belgian PM, Charles Michel. DC goes from sounding smooth, to being slightly menacing: 'I know Charles Michel doesn't like it, but this is existential for me. It isn't for him. He needs to be told.'

Tusk sounds utterly depressed, like a child being told he has a lot more homework to do. DC is on to the next thing – going into the Cabinet Room to host a roundtable with big business on mental health.

Normally this event would be the centrepiece of our day. We've arranged a £1 billion mental-health announcement and we've agreed to do an interview with the BBC. As I listen to some of the stories, including one about a man whose wife had severe mental health issues for years, but never felt able to discuss it, I wonder how much better things might have been if there'd been more that could have been done for several people I know and love.

Theirs and so many other lives might not have been blighted by something seen as shaming and ugly. If they'd had the equivalent physical illness, they would have been smothered in help. This is important – but it's barely on the news agenda.

Afterwards we are straight back into what feels like a rolling meeting on Europe. I walk into the PM's office. Every seat is taken. A number of people offer me theirs, but I prefer to lean on the desk.

I look at my Blackberry and see the following email: 'Nightmare lobby on the European Parliament and their role on welfare brake. Could be a major problem. On way back now. We should discuss whether to issue a further line.'

Nick Herbert, the thoughtful, but tough MP who is running the Conservative In campaign, comes over. He's done a survey of the party. Of the 330 MPs he believes:

- 175 are in.
- 33 saying 'Don't know' or 'Won't say' (worrying).
- Everyone else is out.

He caveats all of this by saying, 'You're dealing with the most complex electorate in the world – so you need to take this with a pinch of salt.'

He has a system of marking MPs:

1 = Def in
2 = Likely in
3 = Don't know or won't say
4 = Likely out
5 = Def out

We then spend the bulk of the meeting with him naming every backbencher and allocating the numbers. There aren't as many '1s' or '2s' as we'd hoped.

He says a couple of interesting things. 'The Outers are shocked, panicked or opportunistic,' and, 'We need to be confronted by the reality that this is a renegotiation most can't defend.'

Research has been commissioned to look at the PM's interventions on Europe. The conclusions are worrying. Arguments about uncertainty, economic instability, geo-political instability, business and jobs seem to be falling on deaf ears.

Many voters believe the reforms the PM is in the process of securing are essentially worthless, and the paucity of concessions is proof that Europe does not take us seriously. In some ways this is inevitable – the anti-EU media has been relentlessly negative, altering the debate.

Many also believe that Europe needs us more than we need them and if Britain leaves, the whole EU project will begin to fall apart. Worryingly, that is seen as a good thing. They reason, if we vote out, the EU will come running with proper concessions and a far better deal. In other words, they don't think a vote to Leave is a vote to leave.

Finally, there's a sense among many that a vote for Leave is a vote of belief in Britain. They think anybody who supports

Britain to Remain is essentially admitting that Britain is weak and can't stand on its own.

Various hopes that Michael Gove will go for In are entirely misplaced. Many arguments have been tried on him, including the fact that there will be real damage to the economy. Confronted with that, he accepted there will be 'scarring and burning', but we will emerge from that situation and end up far more like Singapore.

I am horrified. 'Did he really say that? "Scarring and burning"? If that got out he'd be torn apart – with people saying, "It's all right for him. He'll have a job. What about us?"'

We clear the room because Boris is due in. I take up a desk at the back of the private office, and watch him. He pulls off his beanie hat, leaving his hair looking like he's just stuck his fingers in an electric socket. It's the harried and windswept look to the max.

The few snappers and hacks in the street alert the rest of the village – and while he is in with the PM, I get a series of texts, expecting me to provide a running commentary.

When Boris leaves, DC declares, 'He simply hasn't thought it through. I mean, he seems to think Britain would have a seat at the European Council table when it is all done!'

Apparently he is planning to write something to clarify his thoughts and then make up his mind.

Jim Messina, the US strategist and pollster, arrives. He commands the room when he speaks. He says his understanding is that there are twenty-five per cent in the middle, who need to be fought over. They aren't going to be won over by telling them how wonderful the EU is – they want to know the cold, hard economic facts. Will it hit them in the pocket or not?

Jim goes back to the general election and how we realised there was no point trying to persuade people we'd done lots of good things on immigration. All they saw was the problem.

What did work for them was, 'Look – do you really want Ed Miliband running this country, or do you want David Cameron?' We need the equivalent question.

The conversation moves on to dealing with the press. I tell them we are in a looking-glass world, where we need to think about how we traditionally sell stories. Contrary to my reputation for being focused on broadcasters and social media, we spend a lot of time on the papers. Now we are going to be doing a lot more work exclusively with broadcasters and social media. The former Chief of the Defence staff, Lord Bramall, came out for Remain today, warning about security, but many papers buried it under a morass of anti-EU stories.

It's agreed our approach will be to talk about economic uncertainty – then make it personal: the risk of fewer jobs, less investment, fewer opportunities, the risk of greater uncertainty.

The rest of the day is spent in the minutiae of sorting out a media plan for the end of the renegotiation. It's like doing a party conference; every broadcast front needs to be covered, every newspaper needs to be given someone. There's a big social media plan.

We really have our work cut out.


Thursday 18 February and we are due to fly to Brussels for the crunch renegotiation summit. As I pull up to the back gate of No. 10, my eye is caught by a mangy fox trotting along past the back wall. It's carrying something in its mouth, which at first looks like a rolled-up, soggy magazine. Looking closer, I see that it's a dead duck. The police pause before opening the gate and we watch together before it scampers off.

This is the second time I've seen a fox up close at Downing Street. The other was during the election campaign. Perhaps I'm being told something. The rational part of my brain rejects this. The suspicious, primal part can't help wondering . . .

There's a quick strategy meeting. France is kicking up because they think we've suddenly thrown in a veto over financial regulation.

Then we get into the cars at the front of No. 10. There's a real sense that something that's been long on the horizon is finally about to arrive.

The sun is shining as we head to RAF Northolt in west London. I get a call from an MP, who is worried about a woman trying to sell a story to the papers. The way he puts it – he just kissed and cuddled her. It's obviously a massive deal in his life and he's going to be struggling to explain it to his wife, but it's a tiny issue for us. I give him some advice about minimising the impact.

There's a scene in a Guy Ritchie movie where international travel is represented in a fast-cut montage – passport handed over, take off, a drink, plane lands, passport stamped. I'm reminded of it as we arrive at Northolt – step on the plane, read documents, eat a dodgy lunch, land, be whisked towards the Justis Lipsius building in Brussels.

We are taken to the seventh floor and sit in the lounge area, with an array of differently upholstered armchairs.

DC rehearses his arguments. He thought we had a deal with France and we must pitch the need for clarity, or there will be a huge fight. He says, 'If we aren't allowed to take action to protect ourselves from financial problems, that is a real reason for us to leave the EU. If it turns into a big argument, we will be back here in September.'

We are shown into a meeting room for the bilateral meeting with Donald Tusk, who looks fresh and reasonably relaxed. Early on he asks, 'What is your priority? Because five priorities is no priority.'

DC isn't falling for that one. Instead he says everything that is being argued over is an 'existing problem' before adding, 'None are new, so all of them are important.'

The conversation doesn't seem to be getting anywhere. DC

says, 'The problem is we have now had three versions of the renegotiation document. The fourth one has to be better.'

We disappear upstairs to a couple more bilats, before DC goes in for the pre-dinner session.

While he is there, I busy myself by looking at the press conference options. I'm positive that he cannot do a press conference saying he's delivered a deal standing in front of a European flag. Liz thinks we are in danger of causing a diplomatic incident. I suggest we should simply move the EU flag to the side, making a joke of dragging it to the furthest corner of the room. My more serious suggestion is to have European flags at the corners of the stage, while putting a British flag in shot, just behind him.

I also fill my time making sure we have enough Cabinet ministers ready to go out and do media over the weekend if a deal is done. Theresa May could add a lot of force, but we are getting reports that she is unprepared to help, saying that it would be awkward for her, because immigration numbers are coming out next week and she will face difficult questions. The fact is, I am worried that if the issue is forced she will say something unhelpful.

Word comes back from the initial session DC is having with all the other European leaders. A lot of them are saying the UK is asking for too much.

When he emerges DC seems relaxed and realistic. He gives a list of all the areas they challenged him on. All of them are to be expected, but it certainly looks like there is a hell of a lot of persuading to do. He keeps repeating how often he told them he doesn't have to do a deal now. We'll be seeing Tusk in a bilateral after the dinner, DC says, 'I'll tell Tusk I wouldn't get this deal through the Cabinet, let alone a referendum.'

This sinks in among the group. In order to manage expectations, we disappear downstairs to tell the hacks. Everyone seems depressed by the idea that this really could drag on.

By midnight there is no prospect of a deal and it looks like we will be up all night. Word from inside the Council, where no aides are allowed, is that no progress is being made and people are getting tetchy. They spend two hours discussing whether inverted commas should be put round a phrase.

Finally the PM emerges. What's frustrating is that we are into a new day and no progress has been made.

DC looks fresh and neat as he sits in one of the swivel chairs. He says Tusk is too willing to let people waffle. At one stage Hollande said, 'Come on Donald, just end the meeting.' Tusk responded feebly, 'But people still want to speak.'

The PM then goes into a small meeting with Tusk. We sit in the meeting room, put our feet up on some swing chairs, and sleep. This pattern is repeated three times throughout the night, with the PM coming back to wake us up and update us on how little progress is being made.

Finally everything breaks up at 5.30 a.m.

We traipse down to the entrance, where a few hacks are waiting, before being taken in convoy to the residence. The police drive fast and put on the sirens, patently not giving a damn about the locals.

Back at the residence, the staff have been waiting for us to emerge and are standing by a drinks trolley when we arrive. No one is really in the mood for this. DC stands around for a few minutes, clearly not sure how momentum can be developed to do a deal.

I go to bed with a low-level headache, knowing that I will get less than three hours' sleep.

# Chapter 8

## Clash of the Titans

I AM WOKEN UP by calls at 9 a.m. Brussels time (8 a.m. UK) – and listen to poor Amber Rudd, a pro-EU Cabinet minister, who we've put out to defend this with virtually nothing to add. She does an admirable job.

It's a relatively leisurely start to the day. The Commission are trying to have a scrics of bilats, before talking to us again. We sit at breakfast, which is served silver-service style by men in black ties. Over the fruit salad, egg, bacon and sausage, it's obvious that everyone thinks this could go either way. We really could be in a position where we have to walk away. The PM's view is that it would mean we kissed goodbye to another summit next month – we would be revisiting this in the autumn. An alarm bell is clanging in my head. Something tells me if we walk away this is going to get worse, with other European governments entrenching and assuming we are not serious.

I suggest the PM does do a short clip on the way in, which is essentially a repeat of what he said yesterday: battling for Britain, not going to take a deal that isn't right for Britain. It helps them fill the vacuum.

By lunchtime there's a sudden sense this process is moving. The biggest symbol of this is the 'English Breakfast' that had been scheduled has turned into a lunch and then a tea on the Council schedule – they're giving time for a deal to be done.

The PM is lying down on a raised section of floor by the windows, trying to rest his sore back, when we hear Angela

Merkel wants to come and see him. The room is a mess, bags and papers strewn across the seats. There's a flurry as he stands up and I clear up.

Merkel sits down opposite me. She is wearing chunky black shoes, a pair of dark trousers made of heavy material and a blocky fuchsia jacket. It's pretty clear this is the first time she has focused properly on the detail of a deal. DC goes through what he wants, including an emergency brake on welfare payments to help curb immigration, which starts at seven years and is renewed for two bursts of three years.

DC goes on to say that he will face 'a barrage of criticism' if there's seen to be any further watering down of the deal.

Angela Merkel turns to one of her aides. 'What is barrage?' The PM offers up 'blitzkrieg' as a translation. She smiles like he is a naughty schoolboy.

She leaves to consider.

It's 4.30 p.m. and way past the point where we could be flying back to Britain for a Cabinet tonight.

The next hour or so is filled by bilats and people munching on bad food.

At 5.45 p.m. I get a call from Laura Kuenssberg, the BBC's political editor. She's heard that Michael Gove is confirmed as Out. I know she can't tell me her source, but I need to know if she's fishing or knows for a fact – after all, her opposite number at ITV, Robert Peston, has been reporting it's believed Gove's heading in that direction since Wednesday. It sounds like it's credible. The PM is with some policy people when I break the news. He says Michael has always told him he'd let him know in person before others learned.

I call Michael Gove, telling him what Laura is saying. He acts as if it's the most natural thing in the world and there's no real news here. I ask him what his team are going to say when asked and he responds, 'We're not saying anything until after the negotiation.'

I say, 'You do realise that will be seen as confirmation you are Out?'

He says he's aware of that. It's all done in his usually ultra-polite way, but there's no doubt this is the moment he makes clear he is going against the PM.

I speak to DC, telling him what's been said. He's not angry, but there's a tinge of sadness in his voice as he tries to make light of it.

'That's him off the Christmas card list.'

Later Kate Fall tells me Gove's people believe I am responsible for outing him. We agree it's absurd. Why would I want to do anything negative that cut across the renegotiation deal?

We build up to the PM going to the dinner. When he does, I disappear downstairs to talk to the hacks who've spent all day bored out of their minds, sucking their pens and desperate for information. They horde around me and I have to be tough in saying we can't give you anything. They're reduced to asking how many bags of Haribo sweets have been eaten in the delegation room.

Suddenly the log-jam breaks at 9.20 p.m. UK time – it looks like they have done a deal. I immediately email the PM – we need to get him out there for the 10 p.m. news. He responds he will try, but his draft speech is nowhere near ready.

His first-class, immaculately dressed speechwriter, Tim Kiddell, has been hanging around all of this time and suddenly has to explode into life. I watch him try to log in five times – more hurry, less haste. I start to dictate what he should say: 'A few moments ago . . . etc.,' expecting it will be collaborative, but find it's easier just to dictate.

We need to explain why this is a success and that Britain has a truly special status in Europe – already out of the Euro and the Schengen cross-borders agreement, we now have four clear successes:

1. People told us the EU was too much of a political project – we are now exempt from the idea of 'ever closer union'.
2. They worried about too much rule-making and interference – we've secured a target for reducing bureaucracy.
3. There was too much of a focus on what was right for the countries that are members of the Euro – there will be protections for the pound.
4. Finally, and crucially, people worried about the pressures of freedom of movement – we have secured massive benefit restrictions, reducing the 'pull factors' for migrants.

We send a version to DC.

I warn the broadcasters in London he will be able to do a live statement during the 10 p.m. news. Having edited both BBC and ITV programmes, I know not to come out bang on ten – not to interfere with their openings, etc. – and suggest we do it about nine minutes past. DC gives the thumbs up to the new version and we print it.

He comes downstairs just before ten. There is a bit of back-slapping, which I want to allow, but quite quickly push him towards doing the press conference. It will be a real coup if we get his statement broadcast live on both main news programmes.

We get into the lift with his printed speech and I march ahead into the press room, which is hot. No one seems that fussed about the EU flag being marginalised and the Union flag being prominent.

We are on course, but it seems to take him an eternity to come in. I bring up the ToView app on my phone. There's a thirty-second delay, after he walks in, but I can see the *BBC News at Ten* took him from the moment he started.

It is a full-on speech, where he speaks for around fifteen minutes. TV takes the first five. After a number of questions that were eminently predictable – we are gone. There's a real mood that it went well as we walk out and get into the cars. He has managed to look better than when we went in, though I suspect all of this will drift away as this becomes a binary In/ Out argument.

The mood on the plane is light, filled with relief. This could have been a disaster and it wasn't. All of us have a drink – it's a mini party, with most people standing up and mingling. The PM tells us about how the other leaders were in celebratory mood, feeling they'd achieved something . . . but there's a sober realisation among us all that things are going to get even tougher.

A car takes me to the foot of my road. It is 1.15 a.m. I take in the cool air for a moment. The next four months are going to be a giant fight.

On Saturday 20 February, I wake up exhausted, the alarm the only thing that's making me surface.

Broadcast and social media couldn't have gone better. The papers range from actively hostile to sniffy, with even the *Guardian* claiming it shows the EU is a flat-footed organisation. It's strange talking to others at No. 10, who seem rather pleased with the papers. It's all relative, I guess, after the kicking the first draft received.

Everyone is in complete overdrive: the papers packed, the broadcasters wall to wall. There are endless vox pops – my favourite is of a woman saying, 'I just want people to understand we are a maritime nation,' with no further explanation.

I get into work early, going through the media plan. This is a major operation – we need to fill the waterfront showing why we've got a good agreement. I have done a deal with the *Sun* to run a piece exclusively from DC.

I go into a small group meeting with the PM. He's trying to frame what he wants to say to Cabinet when he looks at his BlackBerry. He takes some time to read a message, elbows on his knees, glasses on the tip of his nose. With a resigned look DC says, 'Well . . . it looks like Out.' In fact, the email left no room for doubt, it's clear Boris is going for Out.

He then reads it out. It is written in very human terms, beginning by explaining how he has been a tortured soul, but he has to 'go with his heart'. There's a real concern that what he calls a 'hate machine' will try to destroy him after taking this decision, saying there are plenty out there who will want to attack, 'some of whom will earn good money'. He suggests at the end that he thinks we will end up staying in.

There's a moment when we absorb what has happened. Some look sick, others resigned. Ed and I are impressed by how well-written, thoughtful and generous the message appears.

Some wonder if we should leak it. I am clear we should not. We need Cabinet to have its moment and don't want to wind him up by starting a 'Clash of the Titans'-style war and stealing his thunder. That will detract from our message and anger MPs.

Later in the day, about four hours later than the initial message, at around 1 p.m, I get a call from DC to make sure I am stopping anyone tempted to reveal Boris sent a message saying he will support Leave. The reason is there's been another text suggesting he might change his mind and back Remain. I'm struck by how reckless Boris is being – we could just blurt all of this out at any time. His big moment could end with him badly tarnished.

I ask DC what makes him so sure Boris is wobbling. He reads out some parts of the text including the phrase 'depression is setting in' followed by a clear sense that he's reconsidering. Neither of us is left in any doubt.

I am struck by two things: Boris is genuinely in turmoil, hating having to make this decision and flip-flopping within a matter of hours; and his cavalier approach. He must understand that the stakes are even higher for DC than for him. So why is he unburdening himself in this way to the man who could be so damaged if he chooses to go for Leave? Perhaps it is out of respect and friendship, communicating with one of the few people who must understand what he is going through. Perhaps it is just insensitive.

The PM says, 'If he is in that much doubt the logical thing to do is go with the status quo.' Others are less charitable, questioning his motivation.

In the time between the two messages, Cabinet files in. I see Liz Truss and chat with her about her decision to be In. She is concerned by Michael Gove being Out, but says she is persuaded that she doesn't want to spend the next decade of her life wrestling with Europe.

There's almost a festive atmosphere as everyone gathers, all with their pre-prepared speeches.

The PM comes in and sits down, and runs through the documents that outline his deal. The only emotional moment is at the end when he refers to 'my team' and there is a crack in his voice.

George is clear – the deal is good. He warns about the problems of trying to engage with the single market outside the EU. He points out that the Governor of the Bank of England is certain there will be an economic shock, meaning serious issues for ordinary people. Finally he speaks of the good sense in being part of a multilateral organisation of Western states versus taking a leap in the dark.

That phrase 'leap in the dark', elevating risk, is to be central to the Remain campaign.

Michael Gove ladles on the praise, talking about the 'commitment, passion and patriotism' of the PM. But he's quick to say the renegotiation does not fundamentally change the direction of the EU, which is towards political union. He says there are taxes set and laws passed that we cannot amend or improve, and he cannot say to voters that he is accountable for every decision.

He ends, 'The cumulative impact is this country does not

have the freedom of manoeuvre I believe it should. I can't do anything other than to go with my deepest instincts. I do so with a heavy heart. I will vote to Leave.'

Many others speak, but for me, Patrick McLoughlin is typically wise. He is an ex-miner, with a big physical presence and a gentle voice, and I have always felt there is something right about a world where he is a significant Cabinet minister. He says, 'I'd love to live in Utopia – the only trouble is, we'll find Europe's already there. The party basically destroyed itself between '92 and '97 on this – let's not do it again.' His point is profound. Our geography dictates that we will be impacted by Europe whether we are in or out. We can't slip anchor and float off towards the United States or Singapore. Surely it is better to be at the table, influencing things, rather than standing on the sidelines complaining?

Sajid is habitually practical, warning there will be a significant downturn and the cost of leaving to the British people is too great. He says, 'With a heavy heart and very little enthusiasm – I will vote Remain.'

When it is done, we send the PM straight out into Downing Street to deliver a statement, which I have tweaked to make it work better for the evening news bulletins, adding the drama of the fact it has just happened and, 'My recommendation is clear – Britain will be stronger and safer in a reformed EU.'

The wider team watches it on Sky News in his office. He nails it. When he comes back in, he says he was genuinely fascinated by the argument he just witnessed. 'It's interesting – it boils down to a debate about sovereignty versus influence. Do we have more genuine control over things that matter through greater sovereignty at home or through having influence over an organisation that'll continue to exist and affect us even if we leave?'

The rest of the day is spent getting the PM to talk to editors, as well as fielding calls.

I'm up early again on Sunday to prep the PM for *The Andrew Marr Show*. I try to synthesise my reading of the papers into a note for DC:

- Inevitably the papers see the EU debate in extreme terms – though our piece representing our case in the *Sun* worked, with a double-page spread and a cut-out of our five reasons to stay.
- The *Sunday Times* says you are 'declaring war on the rebels' – saying they are misleading the public by claiming they can seal our borders and challenging them to define what Out looks like. You won't get much chance to do it, but you need to say in clear terms on *Marr*. Leave simply won't define what Britain would look like outside the EU, because they know there are so many serious problems with each option.
- Boris is reported to have said, 'I'm veering all over the place like a shopping trolley,' over getting a deal. Most hacks say they now expect him to Leave. You are reported to be furious at his inability as Mayor to see its impact on the City.
- Boris has been pictured at Gove's house on Thursday night. What do you make of that? Marr may also try to trap you into saying something insulting about Boris (or Michael). I'd leave it to – I'm sure Boris will make his intentions clear shortly and you don't know what they are.
- You need to be clear if asked in attacking the idea of a second referendum [Many in the Leave campaign seemed to be arguing we could vote Out and then have another renegotiation to get even more favourable terms, before putting it to the people again]. Are they campaigning to leave or not?
- You are likely to be challenged on Grayling's claim the population will rise to 80 million if we stay in and public services can't cope. This may get mixed in with the argument that the welfare brake is negated by the minimum wage.
- Gove focuses on sovereignty and the fact British politicians have laws imposed on them, without being able to amend them.

- Another line of attack comes from Dominic Raab, who says a £33 billion burden will be removed from small business – and he is fighting for 'the little guy'. Food bills will be cut, he claims.
- Finally, you may need to clear up claims the deal is not legally binding.
- There is an expectation sovereignty legislation will be addressed in the coming days – and Marr has said you will be asked about it. I've said not to expect much.
- Most important of all, you will be on the defensive – keep turning it to the positive case: Britain can have the best of both worlds, all the benefits of jobs and investment, while keeping the pound and not having open borders.

I find the PM in the windowless canteen of Broadcasting House, spreading jam on a croissant. He looks remarkably confident. He agrees with me that Boris's description of himself as 'veering around like a shopping trolley' is hardly a great look.

I'm slightly more worried about Farage, who is on before us, trying to hijack him – and demand that he debate him. We spend a moment thinking of an answer (this is about the future of the country – not personalities on TV).

We head through to make-up, where Nick Robinson is waiting to say hello. I've known Nick for many years. I was an editor both at ITV and the BBC when he was political editor. Our friendship has survived some robust exchanges of views in my former and current jobs. As he does the paper review at the opening of the programme, DC and I work up some lines we want to deliver, warning that people need to 'beware the illusion of sovereignty' outside the EU, and warning Boris not to 'link arms with Nigel Farage and George Galloway and take a leap into the unknown.'

Nigel Farage walks off one side of the set, and DC comes on the other. I sit just off camera with Nick Robinson. After a slow start, DC is on top form – landing his lines and adding a couple more: rejecting the idea that he is part of an establishment stitch-up, pointing out Jeremy Corbyn and the Greens aren't seen as being part of that network. The weakest moment is when he is pushed on phasing of the welfare brake to curb welfare (no surprise), but, as he puts it when he is talking privately with Andrew Marr and Nick at the end, 'I've been PM for six years. I know the arguments and I totally believe them.'

I spend the next couple of hours on the phone before taking my three daughters, Maya, Iona and Honor, to lunch with my brother. It's very sweet of him, but getting across London to Greenwich is a nightmare and the rumours about Boris coming out today are growing stronger. The calls keep coming.

Then, in an interview with the BBC, Iain Duncan Smith claims Britain is more at threat of a terrorist attack if it stays in the EU. That goes straight to the top of the BBC website. So much for a sensible debate. I spend most of the lunch standing outside the restaurant trying to get key figures who can rebut this to answer their phones. George and the PM are irritated nothing is happening. The Home Office doesn't want to put anyone up.

I'm on the phone all the way back across London.

The frenzy over Boris being about to announce his intentions reaches fever pitch.

He comes out just before 5 p.m. with a typically chaotic press conference on the street outside his home and announces he will be supporting Leave. All the key journalists are waiting – and must have been warned something was up a while ago to give them the time to get there.

I get endless calls about when the PM knew. The answer is more complicated than people realise. Boris's team say he informed DC on Saturday morning. That's true, but they are missing out the subsequent wobble, which we didn't disclose at the time. Speaking to one of Boris's aides – with whom I have a good relationship – I get the distinct impression he is not even aware there was a wobble that was shared with DC.

I call the PM. He received a final text from Boris just nine minutes before he told the world. This makes it tricky for us in terms of letting people know what really happened. We agree I should say, 'The final confirmation to the PM was made shortly before the announcement,' though I won't reveal the wobble. If pressed, I do reveal that final text came in the quarter of an hour before the press conference. Again, that doesn't reveal there was a wobble, though some of the smarter journalists think something strange has gone on.

The Leave campaign say it is an extraordinarily brave act of leadership. Many in No. 10 are smarting, annoyed that there has been so much dithering over something so crucial. A few believe it's little more than a straightforward political calculation to ensure Boris has the best chance of sitting in No. 10 in just a few months. Many refuse to believe that he is even an Outer, because much of his argument seems to be voting Leave need not mean leaving, but another opportunity to renegotiate better terms and have a second referendum.

Later on, DC calls me just as I flop on the sofa exhausted. Both of us reflect on this being a defining moment. He tells me that Boris's final message was clear he doesn't expect to win, believing Brexit will be 'crushed'. He says Boris is really a 'confused Inner', and their previous conversations confirmed that view to him, with discussions about tactics to get the best possible deal, and, 'He actually said he thought we could leave and still have a seat on the European Council – still making decisions.'

The bottom line is, this is the new reality and we need to get used to it. It will be a proper fight now, with the papers billing it as a 'Clash of the Titans' – the two biggest Conservatives locked in mortal combat.

# Chapter 9

## I Have No Other Agenda

THE NEXT MORNING, Nick Herbert, who is running the Conservative In campaign, sits us down and runs through his latest numbers on Tory MPs likely to be In or Out:

116 for us + 59 likely (though by no means certain) = 175
30 won't say or undecided
40 not yet publicly declared (almost certainly Leave)
85 declared Leave
Total = 125 Leave

He says we are 'perilously close' to a scenario of half the parliamentary party being Out. The fear is that Boris has simply added to the number of people feeling emboldened. Ministers like Penny Mordaunt, the Defence minister, have come out, contradicting her boss, Michael Fallon.

The conversation turns to the PM's Commons statement. A draft has been done. It's evident we need to put to bed the idea raised by Boris in his *Telegraph* column that this should be a vote for a second renegotiation and referendum. This will be seen as taking him on. DC agrees, but there is quite a bit of legalistic discussion about what to say.

I draft the following:

An idea has been forwarded that if the country votes to leave we could have a second renegotiation. I want to be clear that I believe that is wrong. Having a second renegotiation and referendum is not on the ballot paper. For a Prime Minister to ignore the express will of the British people who had voted to leave would not just be wrong. It would be undemocratic.

This is worked into the statement.

DC wants to say that he is recommending staying in – and he has no agenda in doing so, because he isn't seeking re-election. Of course, he gets that he needs to win for reputational purposes, but he isn't making a calculation about getting re-elected.

Obviously this will be interpreted as a sledgehammer to Boris's face, and the hacks will see it as a gift from the gods – fights always make for great copy.

During a three-hour session in the Commons, DC says, 'I am not standing for re-election, I have no other agenda than what is best for our country.'

He doesn't name Boris, who sits arms folded, disgruntled, unable to fire back, but he doesn't have to. When Boris does stand to ask a question, Keith Simpson, an MP who always cheers me up by acting like the naughty schoolboy at the back of the class, sits behind him and heckles, 'Tuck your shirt in!' Boris's hand moves behind him as he begins to speak, clearly a little thrown. All he is able to hit back with is a pre-scripted question about 'sovereignty', which the PM is easily able to deal with.

A major chunk of my time at the moment is trying to get the machinery in place to fight the battle that is actually emerging – and not the one we thought it would be. There's much to be pleased about.

Amid the noise over the PM's dig at Boris in the Commons yesterday, our plan to knock on the head the second renegotiation idea is working. There was a danger that if the idea got off the ground, people could be persuaded there was no risk in voting Leave, because there'd be another vote. But now

Boris's team is briefing he never meant it, despite it appearing in print.

Another big success is a letter from hundreds of businesses stating they want us to stay in the EU. It's a big strategic goal to demonstrate that the overwhelming majority of businesses are on our side – and it is working.

Boris does do a clip late this morning, claiming the business letter is 'scaremongering' and these were the companies that said we should join the Euro (not true in the vast majority of cases).

The transcript of his clip comes through as I am in the car with DC, going to an event at the O2 HQ in Slough. We talk about if this really is going to be a Clash of the Titans-style contest, where each of them feels they need to always punch back. We agree that would be a massive distraction – though it may be unavoidable.

We also discuss plans for me to resign and go to the Remain campaign as their Director of Comms. I've had a chat about what it would mean with the Cabinet Secretary and his head of ethics, Sue Gray, who are as thoughtful as ever about how it could work within the rules. The PM is keen to know if I'll be allowed to be around at No. 10. I tell him I get to keep my phone (which the campaign will have to reimburse the Government for) and come to meetings called by him. The issue is when I leave to do it.

A few points are crystallising:

- It's becoming clearer and clearer that the referendum is being seen as a career opportunity, not just for the 'Big Beasts', but for some lower-ranking MPs and backbenchers.
- The sexiest story is the 'blue-on-blue' Clash of the Titans. That's of no use to us, because it's a turn-off for the left and centre-left, who must vote for us in numbers. We have to avoid throwing the media red meat in this area.

- The Labour party is vital. We can't win it without them. But will the voters turn out for a leader who seems barely competent and seems indifferent on the EU? Perhaps even more worrying, Corbyn was put there by people who think the system is failing them. Will they vote for the status quo option, led by a Conservative?

Stephen Gilbert agrees that if this is just about the Tories, we are screwed, so we need to do everything we can to stop Tory wars, saying, 'We mustn't put temptation in their way.' What he means is the chance for a struggling Labour party to maximise our pain. He also thinks that there would be a serious possibility the Labour leadership could change its mind and suggest at best indifference, and at worst outright hostility, to the prospect of remaining.

I see what he means as I start to spend more and more time at Stronger In. Much of the team is made up mainly of Labour figures. They are smart, professional and welcoming. The trouble is, they are from the Blairite or Brownite wings of the party – and have literally no influence with the Leader's team, one of whom doesn't seem to recoil from being referred to as a neo-Stalinist. If there is any contact with the campaign, they give the impression that it has been done under sufferance and with no trust. Will Straw struggles to set up a meeting with Corbyn.

To make things worse, everyone keeps going on about how close the campaign HQ is to Westminster, but getting used to life on the District and Circle lines is a chore.

The offices are just across the road from Cannon Street station. There are about forty people packed into a long, thin room watching news channels on three monitors, mounted on the walls.

There's a tiny meeting room, with two bikes parked in it and a long table that is too wide, surrounded by giant, leather swivel chairs. Every time someone new wants to join a meeting, everyone has to move down a seat, or the person who is late has to squeeze through an alarmingly narrow gap.

On Wednesday 24 February, I get a 6 a.m. shock. Listening to the headlines, I hear Michael Gove has claimed the European Court of Justice can overturn DC's renegotiation.

He did an interview with Laura Kuenssberg last night, embargoed for the morning. We were not contacted and consequently there is no rebuttal. Sources at the BBC tell me it was deliberate not to ask our view on this claim.

I then go through a process of trying to shake a system that is literally sound asleep into action. Ed Llewellyn and I get on to the current and former Attorney Generals. We finally get to the conclusion: 'It is not true to say that this deal is not legally binding. Britain's new settlement in the EU has legal force and is an irreversible International Law Decision that requires the European Court of Justice to take it into account.' We add some supporting material from the Cambridge professor of EU law and the actual agreement.

This is a big moment. We are slapping down a Government minister. And not just any Government minister. We are correcting the Lord Chancellor/Minister of Justice on a straightforward matter of legal fact.

Frustratingly, BBC news bulletins seem more interested in the fact that it has an exclusive interview with a leading Outer than they do with the fact the Minister of Justice has screwed up on a point of law.

It feels like it's going to be a bad day when, at the end of my 8.15 media meeting, one of the people responsible for helping put together a letter from military leaders supporting Remain, which has been in this morning's papers, comes in looking ashen-faced and says, 'I'm afraid I've got a problem for you.' He tells me that one of the signatories didn't actually sign it. It's Sir

Michael Rose, who won't fudge it and thinks – on balance – he is an Outer.

I feel slightly sick. It's 'Politics 101' – get your facts straight. There's an elaborate story about how Rose looked interested, but then the contact dried up, and it was assumed he was in. It's a basic and terrible error.

I spend almost no time with the Prime Minister's PMQs prep team – week after week it's a damp squib, and this week is only notable for Corbyn having a go at the PM because his mum has admitted she's worried about cuts and DC firing back, 'I'll tell you what she would say to Jeremy Corbyn, "Put on a decent suit, straighten your tie and sing the national anthem."'

I make a point of watching the *One O'Clock News*. They are still leading off on the Gove line – even though it has been well and truly blasted. Why not lead on 'Gove criticised . . .' or at least, 'A major row has broken out after claims . . .' After the intro, I spot instantly that they are running yesterday's package as it starts with the front page of the *Times* splashing on the business letter. To my amazement the piece keeps going for a full minute. It's clear no one in the gallery is actually watching the programme go out.

The spat over the story runs all day. We now have a wall of lawyers saying in definitive terms that Gove is simply wrong on this. When I watch the 6 p.m. news, it's claimed No. 10 is 'rattled' by Gove. I roll my eyes, exhausted by it. What hope do people have if they think his claims deserve any credence?

The consolation is the Leave campaign is doing no better. Boris continues to be wobbling like a wonky shopping trolley. The main line out of an interview he does with Rachel Sylvester and Alice Thomson in *The Times* is a U-turn on the second referendum point he made last week in his *Telegraph* column. He's now saying, 'Out means out,' and he would like to negotiate a series of trade deals when we go. He also admits there would be an initial downturn, but claims it would be like the 'Nike tick', a little down before a lot of up.

We hit this hard, saying:

> This is a major admission from Boris Johnson that there would be a downturn following Britain pulling out of Europe. He is playing fast and loose with people's jobs, with no clue over what he actually wants for Britain. Last week he was Out to stay In, now he's Out to be Out, admitting this would be a major blow to our economy.

The final Sunday in February's newspapers read like one big diary column. Endless gossipy stories magnified and amplified to give the impression Tory Inners and Outers are screaming in each other's faces.

The *Mail on Sunday* splashes on Philip Hammond declaring Bill Cash is 'a shit' for releasing a document that was meant to remain secret. The *Sunday Times* has dark warnings from Outers that DC will face a leadership challenge, come what may, if he continues to attack them – never mind the sense that one of the things they object to (Gove to be sacked) is a fiction based on an anonymous briefing.

There's also some nonsense about the Out Cabinet ministers having a '999' call – based on the British Lions all piling in if one of their players was punched.

Reading it all, I am struck by the absurdity and vanity, politics reduced to a food fight, with politicians and journalists seemingly unaware how ridiculous they look to a dismissive public.

I find myself driving in for an 8 p.m. meeting with the PM, Chancellor and Ed, in the PM's flat.

The idea is to have these meetings weekly, replicating what we did in the run-up to the election. As of next week, Liz, Kate, Ameet and Stephen Gilbert will join.

Samantha Cameron comes in with a bottle of San Pellegrino, a plastic jug of tap water and some glasses.

The PM wants to start with how we think we are doing. The story of the week is undoubtedly how Boris has put himself in the position where he could be PM by the end of the year. We're also being contradicted on everything by Leave Cabinet ministers.

On the plus side, pressure from us forced Leave off the idea of a second referendum. Businesses, economists and experts of all descriptions are being wheeled out on a daily basis to support us, while they are on the back foot over what Out looks like, suggesting alternative trade deals from Australia to Vanuatu, all of which are plainly terrible.

We have crisp, clear messages, which we are repeating relentlessly.

# MARCH

# Chapter 10

## The Price of Labour Will Go Up

I T IS THE first day of March and the Out newspapers are becoming more and more personal, more and more destructive. Here are a couple of lines from the *Sun* Op-Ed, headlined 'Panicky PM':

> Britain has a headless chicken where once was a Prime Minister . . . He is disgracefully now sabotaging his own Government – and the Tory Cabinet which only a month ago was harmoniously revelling in Labour's troubles . . . The PM's Etonian confidence is shaken.

I shrug it off, but as Philip Larkin might put it, too much of this stuff 'deepens like a coastal shelf', making a lasting impression on readers and shaping the debate.

I hold the first morning call in my office, with people from Stronger In calling in. We run through the main Europe stories of the day, including the chaos as migrants try to get out of Greece and into Macedonia and, separately, the 'Jungle' camp in Calais being disrupted.

The main task is us briefing in the Government's 'Alternatives to In' document later today. It's designed to show that there's no better deal than having unfettered access to the EU single market. We face a dilemma: do we brief it to everyone, including some newspapers who will just rip it apart? I have good relations with journalists on all these papers and try to have honest discussions about where we are. Some rant that cutting them out will result in worse coverage (as if that was possible). Others are more grown up – we find ourselves on opposite sides of the fence, but if we engage, at least our quotes and points will all be in there. Maybe. We decide to brief it all round.

Then there's the obsession with process. Instead of accepting the extraordinary good fortune of having ministers allowed to campaign for Out, while still keeping their official positions, the Leave campaign is trying to create a grievance narrative that they aren't allowed to see crucial Europe documents. The explanation is obvious – they are being given special dispensation to remain in the Government. It would be extraordinary to let them have access to material they could attempt to use to undermine the official Government position.

All of it means I need to spend a lot of time talking to broadcasters, who are prone to follow up on strongly worded newspaper campaigns. It's a frustrating, time-consuming process, but it suggests Leave are struggling to come up with their own stories. We need to hold our nerve.

It's pouring with rain when I get out at Cannon Street. The Stronger In offices seem extra miserable, too many people packed in and the blinds down. I talk with Will Straw about ensuring we dock the campaign team and the No. 10 special advisers properly. It goes from making sure we have two daily calls, setting up ways to communicate quickly and effectively, to having an awayday to sort the longer-term strategy around key areas like the economy and groups that need to be targeted, specifically young people, women between eighteen and forty-five, and BME communities.

He then leaves the room and Joe Carberry, James McGrory and David Chaplin, who've been working on the press operation, come in.

Joe is prematurely grey, but young. He is unassuming, where he could have a lot to brag about – a huge and insightful brain that is capable of processing vast amounts of information at warp speed.

James McGrory is also young and bright – with what appears to be four days of blond stubble, no matter when you see him. We crossed swords when he was working for Nick Clegg in the coalition Government, but only because he cared passionately about his cause. He's a street fighter who is popular with the lobby, and I'm glad to see him. David Chaplin is the most reserved – he gives the impression of having fallen out of love with the Labour party after all its recent travails, making the occasional well-chosen, acid comment. He's shrewd, cares deeply about the campaign and what we are fighting for. I'm glad he's on board.

They are all reasonable people – undoubtedly surprised to be dealing with others who were trying to tear their throats out last year.

They're eager to spell out that Labour is utterly riven on this – with many believing it's not their job to pull DC out of this hole. It's obvious they are struggling to pull any levers with the party or the Leader's office (which is at best ambivalent about Europe). They're also desperate for more direction.

The most interesting meeting of the day is with Andrew Cooper. An analysis of the polls puts us ahead. He says all the pollsters are still failing to get to middle-class, time-poor, risk-averse people. The gold standard of polling is to have a random sample of people, but almost no one does this because it's so expensive. The ideal method involves going back to someone until they respond (so if they don't answer their door – you keep trying).

There have been two relatively recent examples of that happening:

- The British social attitudes survey said 67% of people were in favour of remaining.
- The British Election Study was 62%.

He also says that most work shows that if it comes to a straight fight between immigration and the economy, the economy wins. We already know that there has been no election in the last hundred years where people have voted against their direct financial interest.

This becomes the foundation of our thinking. We double down on routing them on the economy and pointing out we will all be worse off if we leave. More to the point, they have no answer to what life will be like outside the EU. Ryan Coetzee's formulation that we are 'strong, safer and better off' in the EU tests well. So, too, does the idea that leaving is a 'risk' and 'a leap in the dark'. All of these become central themes.

We have made our choices. The doors are being locked and sealed – our final strategy is set.

The day peters out in a meeting with Philip Hammond on his media round and speech in the morning on the 'Alternatives to In' document, pointing out the flaws in the main options if we leave: Norway, Switzerland, Canada and the World Trade Organization. We know we have an opportunity to really get Leave on the run on this – driving them mad by making clear they have no answer that works for Britain.

Finally we have our call with the In campaign. Graeme Wilson returns from briefing the lobby on the document. It appears to have met with 'middling interest'. I worry that it's in danger of misfiring and spend some time making sure the broadcasters are teed up for the morning. As I finally get home, I get a call from the BBC. Iain Duncan Smith is calling it a 'dodgy dossier' without actually having read it.

I could be shocked, but it's actually quite helpful – making it more newsworthy – and allows us to return fire: they simply won't answer what Leave looks like.

On Wednesday 2 March, the BBC news leads with Trump and Clinton each being the likely candidates for their parties after strong 'Super Tuesday' performances.

Our preview of the 'Alternatives' if we leave the EU document is the second in the running order.

As I listen to the story unfold in the morning, I feel more and more confident. Dominic Raab, a rising star in the Conservative party, supporting Leave, starts strongly in his *Today* interview, refusing to repeat IDS calling it a 'dodgy dossier'. But he stumbles by admitting tariffs would be an issue for the UK if we left the EU.

DC feels this is a direct hit. The Outers keep talking about 'a short-term hit to confidence' – it feels like they are wobbling.

There's another focus at the 8.30 slot on which MPs are with us. Nick Herbert puts it at 163 out of 330. It is creeping towards fifty per cent and the PM says he is sure it will get there, but it feels like cold comfort.

I'm due to go out for a series of meetings. I drop into the PM's private office before I go, discovering an anxious group worrying the 'Alternatives to In' document that is due to be published imminently has a number of mistakes. If they are found, it will be destroyed as untrustworthy and the 'dodgy dossier' IDS claims.

I ask one of the civil servants if she means things that are factually wrong or if it's sloppiness. I'm relieved when she tells me it's more the latter. Apparently there are sections that are titled with one thing and are full of another.

Philip Hammond is due on his feet in fifteen minutes. I call his special adviser, Hayden Allan, and tell him to ask Philip to say the document will only be available when it is laid before Parliament. That gives them enough time to fix it and reprint. It's amazing we are at this stage so late in the day and it hardly inspires confidence.

When I go outside to head to Stronger In, it is pouring with rain again.

News reaches me that Stuart Rose, the affable and avuncular chairman of Stronger In, has admitted that wages are likely to

rise if we leave Europe, adding that it wouldn't be a good thing.
I check the transcript. He does accept that if a British exit leads
to restrictions on EU migrants then 'the price of labour will,
frankly, go up'. He also accepts that one cost of staying in will
be 'one-way traffic' of EU migrants into the UK for up to a
decade. One of the select committee members appears to have
asked him if he would mind jumping into a bear trap and he
appears to have said he'd be delighted to.

It's a gift to the Leave campaign – I imagine them mass-
ordering leaflets and block-booking advertising space to ram the
message down people's throats from now until the day of the
vote. The mitigation and explanation around his remarks are
wiped away – and count for nothing. Never mind he believes
that the economy would be hit, there would be less investment,
fewer jobs and opportunities. From now on, the Stronger In
chairman will be known as the man who believes wages will
rise if we leave the EU.

As the Leave papers make hay with Lord Rose, I feel I am
fighting on all fronts. We're making progress on getting the BBC
to tone down some of its plans for a massive debate two days
before the vote. The original idea was to have it in front of up
to 12,000 people without any proper vetting of the audience.
They now want to hold it at the smaller Wembley Arena – saying
only that the audience will be half Remain and half Leave. With
no vetting, I worry that it could turn into a bun fight.

Several people in Downing Street have also picked up on the
reporting of Kamal Ahmed, the relatively new economics editor,
who keeps suggesting that business opinion is more split than
it is. Our media monitoring unit picks out this egregious example
of him reporting from a business conference:

It is very interesting that both the In campaign and Leave EU
campaign are keen about the business voice. I picked up quite
a sceptical tone today regarding the UK staying in the EU. John

Longworth revealed that he thinks Out isn't that scary. Many large businesses are pro staying in the EU, but the whole community is very split.

I complain to the BBC that it is absurd to suggest 'the whole community is very split':

- Over a third of FTSE 100 companies have come out in favour of Remain – none have come out in favour of leaving.
- The SMMT today came out by a factor of 8–2 in favour of staying.
- The CBI has been clear on the dangers of Brexit.
- Two thirds of BCC businesses want to stay in the EU.

The weight of business opinion is clearly and heavily on our side.

A view is beginning to crystallise in No. 10 and at the campaign that the BBC is in some areas doing too much 'on the one hand . . . and on the other . . .' reporting, and not enough legitimate editorial comment on the strength of our support in key areas like business. With so many newspapers campaigning against Remain, this is a problem. Yes, they have a duty to report what each of the campaigns thinks and says, but their duty to the audience to provide the proper context, even and especially in shorter bulletins, is also vital. Too often it is missing.

I manage to watch the PM's press conference at the Anglo–French summit in Calais. Hollande's first answer is a little disappointing, given how strong the French economy minister, Emmanuel Macron, was this morning about allowing migrants to cross the border into the UK if we leave the EU. But he really delivers with the second – saying there will be 'consequences' if there's Brexit. It feels like a threat, meaning it will be magnified and plant seeds of doubt and concern.

The Out campaign start complaining about it being an establishment stitch-up. We are dismissive, saying to journalists, 'That's right, the socialist President of France is part of a vast conspiracy with a Conservative PM.'

Blue-on-blue attacks are at a premium as a story. On Friday morning the BBC is strangely leading on a story the *Mail* has relegated to page 2.

Iain Duncan Smith has written a piece claiming 'spins, smears and threats' are being used by the Government machine to bully Britain into staying in the EU. It comes amid a cacophony of Outers shouting 'Project Fear' at everything we do.

They are patently doing two things: distracting from having to answer difficult questions about what Out looks like – and injecting poison into the bloodstream.

We fight back against the first. In my briefings with Sunday commentators, I point out that it is hypocritical to portray themselves as victims of dark and sinister oppressors, given what they have been saying:

- IDS himself warned of Paris-style attacks if we stay in.
- Priti Patel spoke about us being on the *Titanic*, heading for an iceberg.
- Boris described us as a frog in a slowly boiling pan of water.
- Farage claims the NHS will be privatised if we stay in.

I go on to point out the only negative thing we've really done is the PM asserting he has 'no agenda' in this, a clear dig at Boris's leadership ambitions. Our bottom line is we want this whole thing put back together again when it's done. It's increasingly apparent that many Outers don't share that desire – wanting the house to be brought down on us, whether In or Out.

Stronger In is pushing hard to send round social media interventions about IDS, essentially claiming he's a hypocrite, who was prepared to use dodgy stats in something completely unrelated last year. I call Will Straw, admitting I don't want to wind this up on the Tory side, but more importantly we can't give them examples of us slinging mud. We have to be the sensible people who rise above it, no matter what the provocation.

He accepts this and I share my thoughts with the wider No. 10 team: 'We have to avoid looking as if we are playing the man, not the ball. My deeper concern is that people are being turned off and utterly confused by it all. They just get a sense that people are rowing with each other and end up thinking: a plague on all their houses.'

I hope the weekend will provide some respite.

The main news on Saturday 5 March is George declaring he won't go ahead with a plan to remove tax relief from pension contributions – rebalancing the system away from the rich. He and the PM don't want the right-wing press to have another excuse to get on our backs about it while we are going through the referendum.

YouGov produce some analysis suggesting Remain has won the opening skirmishes. I forward the piece to the PM. All it says is that we have gone from being behind, to being (narrowly) consistently ahead. DC responds, 'Good news. And good for the blood pressure.'

The other big story of the day is the British Chambers of Commerce (BCC) suspending their chairman, John Longworth, for speaking up for Brexit during the week. It was a surprise to me when it happened last night.

Bernard Jenkin, a Brexiteer, is said to be claiming it was down to No. 10 putting pressure on the BCC.

I check in with Daniel Korski, a SpAd who has been one of No. 10's link people with business. He made his bones in the building as a fixer who gets results. I'm a fan, but others find him a little too enthusiastic. He's been spending the weekend with his young family, whom I can hear in the background. He tells me he did send quite a few shocked texts when he heard Longworth speaking up for Out, despite a survey of the organisation showing a big majority of its members want us to Remain. Later he sends me all of his contact with the BCC. I am satisfied there was no pressure to get John Longworth to resign.

It makes for awkward conversations – saying we didn't pressurise, while not denying there was contact.

The story is going to be big in the *Sunday Telegraph*. We issue a statement saying there was no pressure. Graeme has been dealing with a reporter who he thinks isn't interested in giving our side. When the copy drops, he berates the reporter for failing to include our short statement on the front page, given the gravity of the claims, and despite being prepared to run an anonymous quote from someone claiming there was pressure.

I text the editor, who replies immediately, saying our denial will be much more prominent in the second edition.

I can see this is going to run and there's a danger Daniel's fingers will get caught in the mangle.

I call Ross Hawkins at the BBC. He had sent me some manic texts just before the ten o'clock news – having just read the *Sunday Telegraph* copy. I tell him we are clear that no pressure was brought to bear, and John Longworth's suspension was as much a surprise to us as it was to everyone else. I call him again, knowing he will be writing a morning piece. I run him through what has gone on here and give him a statement as a Stronger In spokesman: 'Crying "Project Fear" is a smokescreen, so that the Leave campaign can avoid answering difficult questions about what Out looks like.'

I also point him to the front page of the *Sunday Times*, which has Gove claiming the EU has allowed fascism to rise to levels not seen since the 1930s. And Leave are suggesting we are responsible for a fear campaign . . . ?

They are deploying classic disreputable tactics – get everyone to scream blue murder and hope that no one notices there isn't a body. There's another small example, with Bernard Jenkin saying it would be a disgrace if the Queen were to be dragged into the referendum, as if we are somehow planning to.

On Sunday morning, I text the PM to ask if he wants to talk about the Longworth/British Chambers of Commerce story.

I explain the BBC is leading on Boris's claim in the *Telegraph* that we interfered in the suspension of John Longworth. He gets to the heart of it immediately: we shouldn't be shy about the director general of the organisation speaking for Brexit, when nearly two-thirds of his members want to Remain.

We issue a further statement to deal with the myriad of new questions:

> Given that sixty per cent of BCC members say they want to stay in the EU, No. 10 was surprised to see the director general of the organisation come out for Brexit. We are clear no pressure was put on the BCC to suspend him . . . This decision is entirely a matter for the BCC.

I watch Boris on *Marr*. There's a lot of build-up. He's great at the huge statements, capturing a vision of a prisoner who sees the jailer has left the door unlocked, but who is afraid to run free. Where he's not so hot is when pressed on detail – saying some jobs 'might' go if we left the EU, then getting into a mess over whether we'd be part of the single market or not.

The pack decides he was terrible – with poor Twitter reviews.

Stronger In pump out a press release criticising his cavalier attitude, '[Brexit] might or it might not' lead to job losses, and criticising him over the following exchange over the single market:

> *Andrew Marr:* One last time for clarity – just tell me are we going to be in it or not in it, and if we are not going to be in it, are we going to negotiate a similar kind of deal?

*Boris Johnson*: We are going to have our own British arrangements which will be . . . will give us access to the rest of the European Union, to the European Union.

*Andrew Marr*: Without paying any money, and without free movement?

# Chapter 11

## An Honest Man

O N MONDAY 7 March, the *Daily Mail* excels itself in its coverage of Longworth's resignation.

As I'm ploughing through it, I get a text from one of my team: 'It's completely over the top – anyone who supports Remain is a spiv and traitor; anyone who supports Leave is a saintly hero . . . the leader is awful. No evidence at all, but the *Mail* still "suspects" No. 10 forced him out.'

I want to go through it in more detail, because it's worth understanding what we are dealing with.

The front page headlines are:

> AN HONEST MAN 'KNIFED BY No. 10'
> Downing St accused of ousting anti-EU business chief.

Note those quotes around 'KNIFED BY No. 10' – it's a quote I can see nowhere in the piece.

The intro drags the PM into it, even though – again – there's no evidence: 'David Cameron was accused last night of orchestrating the removal of a business chief for speaking up for Brexit.'

The article quotes 'friends' – anonymous, of course – who say they believe No. 10 'had a hand' in his downfall. This despite his own quote saying pressure was not exerted. There is no shortage of Tory Outers prepared to go on the record, with no evidence to condemn us.

One calls Longworth 'the first Brexit martyr'. He goes on: 'If it transpires that the Government have had any role whatsoever in costing this man his career, simply because he voiced an opinion over what he believes to be in the national interest, it will be beyond scandalous.'

There's nothing I can disagree with in that statement, because No. 10 didn't cost him his job.

UKIP's Douglas Carswell says, 'A decent man has been hounded out of office simply for expressing a personal view, which is that we are better off out of the EU. Project Fear is orchestrated out of Downing Street. This is what the nasties at No. 10 are up to. Well done, Downing Street, you got your man.'

Only towards the end of the *Mail* piece does the BCC statement appear:

> No politician or interest group had any influence on the BCC Board decision to suspend Mr Longworth. His subsequent resignation was agreed mutually between Mr Longworth and the BCC Board, and there were no external factors involved.

But turn a few pages and there is a double-page spread, under the banner headline: 'CRUSHED BY PROJECT FEAR'.

Beneath it is a piece by Ruth Sunderland, headlined: 'Hero who didn't hide his contempt for those in power,' and a separate piece by Peter Oborne: 'Chilling Witch Hunt against Free Speech.'

Turn the page and you find another banner headline: 'Boris: Leaving the EU would be like breaking out of jail.'

That isn't the half of it. It is total overkill. I wonder what normal people buying the paper make of it all.

Ironically it emerges that Boris's team is being hypocritical about unfair pressure by No. 10. There were some extraordinary quotes in the *Sunday Telegraph* about people being gagged and calls for an 'open debate' and yet this is the advice being handed out to key staff at London city hall:

The advice also makes clear that GLA officers can, when not at work, express personal opinions (which can be contrary to the Mayor's views). Whilst this is the formal position for you also, I would expect, given your roles, you either to advocate the Mayor's position or otherwise not openly to contradict it.

Given the nonsense over Longworth, and the extent of the freedom to roam granted to Leave ministers, we aim to maximise discomfort on this.

I spend a couple of hours at Stronger In this morning. The reality is I am making calls and responding to emails from there, rather than at No. 10, but it's important to be visible.

I go to Will Straw's executive meeting. This is the bread and butter of running a campaign, with subjects ranging from what they do with all the hate letters they get, to whether we should raise money through a merchandise shop, to the document defining how and why Stronger In should be recognised by the Electoral Commission.

I rush back to Westminster for a meeting with Theresa May. Ameet and I are shown into her office suite in the Home Office. Her private secretaries are brought in to make a note of the meeting.

We discuss that it would be good to have an intervention from her soon. The PM is looking like he is the only one out there fighting the campaign. She nods – and agrees that later in the week she will be asked about Europe and she will be categoric in expressing her view. She wants to give a full speech 'after Easter', but we settle on next week. 'After Easter' feels like an eternity away.

On the way back, we talk about how in terms of pure politics we have to hand it to her – she is playing it well. She is on the right side, making clear she is In, but not looking overly enthusiastic. It's making life uncomfortable for us and many feel she owes DC more, but in purely selfish terms, this positions her best.

In political cabinet the next morning, Boris makes a point of catching my eye. I nod and he nods and smiles back. He's spent the morning unpicking the mess over the advice to his staff to avoid contradicting his view on Brexit. He appears to be saying, 'Fair play'. He then makes a big show of ruffling his hair and making sure he looks at me and rolls his eyes when George is discussing the economy.

I can't help feeling these meetings have become a bit pointless. The economy and party reform are two subjects that fill the space, and stop everyone discussing Europe. Fair enough – but you can almost see the 800 lb gorilla in the room.

Other meetings are involved with big decisions being taken over the budget and whether the Queen's Speech should be held before or after the referendum. It emerges the SNP is going to back away from an agreement to support our Sunday trading plans, despite the fact they mimic what's already happening in Scotland. It's no great surprise – one of the first rules of Government is the opposition will screw you over if they can.

Some want to pull the Sunday trading vote. I'm with those who think we've marched everyone up to the top of the hill on this, it's better to go down to glorious defeat than look cowardly.

That evening, I get back from a drinks reception organised by Stronger In for International Women's Day, when Will Straw texts me some copy from the *Sun*:

QUEEN BACKS BREXIT

The screaming headline is followed by: 'EXCLUSIVE: BOMBSHELL CLAIM OVER EUROPE VOTE.' And beneath that: 'EU going in wrong direction, she says.'

The story is that Nick Clegg and the Queen had a bust-up

over Europe at a lunch attended by other ministers. My assumption is that it was linked to the Privy Council, because Nick was then the head of it. The Queen is alleged to have snapped at Clegg that Europe is going in the wrong direction.

A source is quoted, 'People were left in no doubt about her views on Europe . . . It really was something. The EU is something Her Majesty feels passionately about.' There's then a load of stuff from Brexiteers like Jacob Rees-Mogg: 'I'd be delighted if this was true and Her Majesty is a Brexiter.'

Then it gets tricky. The paper claims that neither the Palace nor Clegg expressly denied a heated debate had taken place.

The Palace says: 'The Queen remains politically neutral, as she has for sixty-three years. We would never comment on spurious, anonymously sourced claims. The referendum is a matter for the British people.'

Clegg's response is a bit of a car crash: 'I have absolutely no recollection of it. I think I would have remembered something as stark or significant as you have made it out to be. No doubt you'll speak to someone else and they'll say, "I was there, I heard it." Fine. But I really can't remember it at all. Anyway, without sounding pompous, I find it rather distasteful to reveal conversations with the Queen.' I can hear him saying it – being reasonable instead of categoric and thereby leaving the door wide open.

I text the PM, but he doesn't respond. I also call Ed and Simon Case. We quickly work out that I should call the Buckingham Palace press office, Simon should call the Private Secretary and Ed should call Clegg.

My contact at the Palace is just coming in after an evening out. As we talk, I can literally hear the front door close.

The Palace has known about the story for hours. It's repeated to me that sixty-three years of neutrality cannot be breached by revealing what went on. It's the Palace's view that it will just open a can of worms.

I don't want to push it, but find myself pointing out that a pretty big can of worms has already been opened. The Queen is on the front page of a national newspaper with a headline claiming she is pro-Brexit. Some more flesh is put on the bones. I'm told the lunch was in April 2011 – and Michael Gove was there. There seems to be a particular emphasis on the last piece of information.

Ed, Simon and I have another conference call. Ed says Clegg is going to tweet the story is nonsense, he doesn't recall it, and he would have remembered something that big. I groan – that will be seen as another 'non-denial denial'. Ed says I should call him.

When I get through, the poor guy seems exasperated. He thinks it was some lunch or other where Gove 'and one of those other wankers' were there. He says the story is simply not true. I say if that is the case, he needs to ensure there is no doubt. He agrees – he will get his press person onto it now.

I go to sleep feeling the beginning of the day was a long time ago.

On Wednesday, I wake up sure that we must not add any fuel to the Queen row. I send a WhatsApp message to No. 10 and Stronger In saying we must be careful. Our response should be, 'The Palace has made its position clear, so has Nick Clegg. We have nothing to add.'

More detail emerges. The lunch when it allegedly happened was in April 2011 – and Clegg, Baron McNally, Gove and Cheryl Gillan were there. Everyone feels there's been an appalling breach of trust somewhere along the line and plenty of topspin added. In 2011, the Prime Minister would have been endlessly critical of the EU – it doesn't mean he would ever advocate leaving it.

DC's dismissal of the story is simple, 'There were no plans for Brexit then – so how could the Queen back them?'

The Palace is to complain to IPSO – the Independent Press

Standards Organisation – under the first paragraph of their code, which deals with accuracy. Their argument is that even on its own terms, the piece doesn't work. The headline is 'Queen Backs Brexit', but the piece is about a claim she berated Nick Clegg about Europe going in the wrong direction. It's not the same thing. Apparently IPSO has been very keen in the past that headlines must match the supporting copy.

I head over to Stronger In. One of my calls is with Francis Elliott, the political editor of *The Times*. His question is: how can things possibly continue at this pace? The 'burn rate' of stories is so high, it can't be sustained. A story emerges and is devoured in a fraction of a news cycle. Things that would normally have played out over days go in hours. I suspect the pace won't slacken – it's the logical conclusion of the biggest political story for a generation colliding with a digital revolution in media, shortening attention spans, and the need for more and more sensation.

The PM's afternoon meeting is in the Commons because of votes. It's followed by Andrew Cooper coming in and presenting some polling. He sits at the end of the long wooden table in the PM's office and runs through a document he hands round.

The good news is we appear to be ahead.

He goes through the segmentation of the electorate and says there is a lot of churn in the key sections: 'Hearts *vs* Heads' and 'Disengaged Middle' (the people who will decide the election). He makes a number of key points:

- ABC1s are pro remaining and vote.
- C2DEs are pro leaving and tend to be less likely to vote.

There are several alarming facts:

1. 43% think staying in is riskier than leaving (pointing to immigration as their main concern).

2. In a world where almost no facts are known and nothing sticks, a surprising number of people think it costs £350 million a week to stay in the EU and this money could be spent elsewhere if we left. It's not correct.

3. Many think the benefits bill, unemployment and NHS waiting lists will all fall if we leave because of reduced immigration.

The 'Queen Backs Brexit' story is still big on Thursday 10 March. Full credit to the *Telegraph*'s young, tenacious Peter Dominiczak, who chases down everyone at the lunch. Gillan, Clegg and McNally all deny being the source and don't recall the story. That leaves Michael Gove. 'Friends' of his (i.e. the person themselves or someone speaking with their knowledge) say he has no idea who the source is. My gut is he means he didn't directly brief the story – leaving open the possibility it was someone he told.

The *Mail* gives Gove a pass on the story. Others sniffily avoid it. I try to imagine the explosion if it had been the reverse, 'Queen Backs Remain'.

The *Sun* has a picture of an angry-looking Queen on the front page, with words to the effect that she has savaged DC. Turn inside – and it is a reference to her irritation at the breach of protocol when DC was unintentionally caught on camera saying she had 'purred with pleasure' over the Scottish referendum result.

We're about to do a regional round of interviews. The PM is understandably preoccupied with learning his brief, because he could get any number of detailed questions about local issues. I'm worried he will be asked if there is going to be an investigation into who briefed the Queen Brexit story.

For me the obvious questions are: 'The Lord Chancellor is accused of breaking one of the most precious protocols of all – why is no one going to ask him about it?' and, 'Have you asked Michael Gove if he is responsible? If not, why not?'

None of us want to look shifty, but neither do we want this story to run and run.

We go up to the Thatcher Room, where an imperious portrait of her gives the impression she sees all. The first two radio interviews done over an ISDN line don't push the issue. The third presenter is smarter, clearly getting it and pushing the PM. DC gives the 'Friends of Michael Gove have made clear he doesn't know where it has come from' answer we settled on. The presenter pushes – suggesting that if it came from a Cabinet minister it would be very serious. DC agrees.

DC is glad we didn't add much, but is also glad we underlined it's a serious issue. I wonder if Gove is getting nervous and if he'll sustain the battering of persistent questioning.

Ultimately, what might save Gove is a simple thing: there may not be the appetite to go for him.


My next meeting is at News UK. I'm seeing John Witherow and his key editorial team at *The Times* with Will Straw. Inside I find Will and we have a brief chat about how we should play it. As we chat, Francis Elliott rocks up. I ask him if I should verify it is all not for use, unless they ask us and we agree. I'm really telling him, and he says, 'It's always worth making something like that clear.'

John Witherow is waiting in his office. He is a tall man with grey, curly hair, dressed like an editor from a 1940s movie about the heyday of print: expensive, grey suit trousers held up by thick red braces, ballooning shirt with sleeves loosely rolled, and two buttons undone at the neck.

We sit round the table. The meeting begins slightly testily. One of the Stronger In board has been in to see them and told them they can have access to people like Jim Messina and Craig Elder and Tom Edmonds, who do our digital stuff. I draw a clear line – this isn't going to happen. John complains this isn't very transparent, and I suggest he allows the *Telegraph* into his editorial meetings, or business boards. He says that's ridiculous – and I say the point is the same, we're not in the business of handing out information to rivals. He stretches out his long legs, leans back and pauses, before deciding to move on.

They bring up all the criticisms of the campaign to test us. My sense in reading the paper is that John's heart says Brexit, but his head sees the economic case against. We take them patiently through every argument. Where I think we make real progress is telling them how we've had two strategic victories:

- forcing everyone (including Leave) to accept that there would be a downturn of some kind if we left.
- driving Leave with questions about what Out would look like.

At the end John asks, 'So you are quietly confident?'

Neither of us are stupid enough to say, 'Yes.'

My final meeting of the day is with the Education Secretary, Nicky Morgan, who we want to do more. Her take is, 'This is a fight that's been coming for twenty years in the Conservative party and it needs to be had.' She's right. It's a bloody civil war.

I make a quick trip to Dublin to see an old friend and watch the rugby. As I check my BlackBerry, I spot that Gove appears to be admitting he was behind 'The Queen Backs Brexit'.

PA reports:

MICHAEL GOVE DOES NOT RULE OUT BEING SOURCE OF QUEEN BACKS BREXIT STORY

Michael Gove has refused to rule out being the source of reported comments made by the Queen on the EU. During a Brexit campaign visit in Hampshire, the Justice Secretary said he did not know where the *Sun* got all of its information from.

It's a form of denial, but the use of 'all' is a weakening of his position.

Soon after, that mysterious 'friend of Michael Gove' is at it again, calling round to say, 'Michael did not brief the Queen story.' It's hopeless – unless he issues a categoric denial that he has anything to do with the story being out there, people will always suspect him.

The most interesting piece in the Sunday papers is by Peter Preston in the *Observer* on the problem with anonymously sourced journalism – which is the foundation of political reporting in this country. On the *Sun*'s 'QUEEN BACKS BREXIT', he points out, '. . . there's nothing in the *Sun*'s body-text report that justifies those three lead words in big, booming type . . . they at the most provided second-hand evidence of a couple of conversations up to five years old in the midst of the Eurozone crisis – when no referendum had been agreed and "Brexit" might as well have been some new patent loo cleaner.'

The most interesting part of the piece explains how the *Sun* rests on two anonymous sources. One, who is 'highly reliable' and 'senior', heard the Queen hold forth on Europe at a lunch after a Privy Council in 2011. A separate Parliamentary source (i.e. an MP) noted her 'venom' and 'emotion' about EU affairs at an undated Palace reception.

Preston goes on to ask what the *New York Times* would make of all of this, pointing out that its code says 'anonymity is a last resort'. Margaret Sullivan, their public editor, says 'the paper needs to show far more scepticism – a kind of prosecutorial scrutiny – at every level of the process.'

I watch *Marr*. George is on ahead of the budget this week. DC calls me after to get my take – he was unable to watch, because he was out with his children.

I run him through it, saying George did well. I wonder if we should be clearer about Turkey not joining the EU – the supposed doubt around it (when there really isn't any) – is being used by the Outers as an example of why the risks of staying in are greater, opening the back door to the most unstable part of the world, and allowing floods of immigrants to come in.

DC says it's not going to happen, but it's hard to be categoric for diplomatic reasons. Anyway, 'France needs to have a referendum before they get in – so it's not going to happen.'

I drive in to work for the 8 p.m. meeting. Several bottles of wine and a few bottles of Becks are laid out on the coffee table in the PM's office. I'm asked to open a packet of cashews, the PM delves into a big bag of Doritos roulette – where you risk eating a super-spicy one.

The agenda is long. The top issue is a report that is coming out on 24 May explaining why there is a big discrepancy between the official migration and the 'Nino' or National Insurance numbers released. It is obvious that there are far more active 'Ninos' than there are migrants being counted. The problem is if all of that comes out a month before the referendum.

The conversation segues into whether or not we will go ahead with a leaflet to every household, paid for by taxpayers' money. I want us to properly think through what we are doing. My conclusion is, 'If we win, and it's close, we're handing them an excuse for why they were cheated. That shouldn't necessarily stop it, but we should think about it.'

Stephen Gilbert says we should not underestimate the row this will cause. He would go 'fucking tonto' if someone was doing it to us on the other side.

The other big topic of conversation is Turkey – when do we affirm we would never let them join the EU? DC wants to wait until after the migration summit, but agrees this is coming, and we need to neutralise it.

We talk about Gove for a bit. It's agreed we have to hold on to the fact that he's suggesting it isn't him. DC's view is he knows it makes us look naive and credulous, but we really don't want to be seen to be shoving him.

I drive back home – back in time for the 10 p.m. news and bed. Life is one big barrel of laughs at the moment . . .

# Chapter 12

## Well, This Is a Mess

MONDAY 14 MARCH begins with a throbbing head, toothache and low-level sore throat. I've been run-down and ill for more than a couple of weeks now. I tell myself I'm going to have to do more than pop painkillers to mask it all, but I can't think how I'm going to get to a doctor, who would probably just tell me to slow down.

It's clear we're just going to have to face up to the issue of migration and 'Ninos' coming out only a month before the campaign.

Then there's the mailshot to every household – setting out why the Government believes we should Remain in the EU. We've decided to bring it forward to before the official ten-week period designated for the campaign, to stop it being criticised by the Electoral Commission. But that means it will come out in the 'purdah' period for the local elections, when the Government isn't supposed to do anything – so the Electoral Commission will probably still hate it. It's not even clear the Royal Mail can prepare itself to deliver that amount of material in such a short period of time.

Meanwhile, Bernard Jenkin is doing everything in his power to kill Daniel Korski over the John Longworth affair. One suggestion is that we allow Daniel to go before Jenkin's committee and release all his texts and emails on the subject, on the grounds he will be completely exonerated.

DC pushes back hard – saying he's not appearing and we

won't publish. He is utterly committed to protecting his staff – and this will set a dangerous precedent. It's one reason why we feel so loyal to him.

I get on the Tube to News UK again. This time to see Tony Gallagher, the editor of the *Sun*. It's fair to say we have more than our share of history, but both of us want to play nice.

When I'm shown into his office, which has an amazing view of St Paul's, he's kicking Sunday supplements into a pile. He doesn't have much success and they look like he's thrown them everywhere.

The conversation goes on for an hour. He tells me he thinks IPSO will rule against the *Sun*, but says he doesn't mind.

My main point to him is, let's not allow this to become personal about the PM. He says he won't. I offer to get the PM to write for him and do an interview – telling him that doing so is probably a risk. He assures me DC will be fairly treated.

My last meeting of the day is at Stronger In. It's chaired by Peter Mandelson, who is smooth, with hair that is well-groomed, but somehow also thick and fluffy. His schtick is to make, 'What do I know?' points, which are designed to show he knows a lot – picking up that although Will Straw thinks we won the first couple of weeks of the campaign, polling is going in the wrong direction.

He follows the opposite approach to Lynton Crosby, yearning for a room full of politicians chewing the fat and directing the campaign. He asks if more should be at this meeting. After a couple of gentle hints that I think we should be business focused, I finally say, 'It's your meeting, but I'm worried we can create situations where people just yak.'

We discuss it after – his critique of the Conservative way is that you miss good ideas ignoring people. I agree up to a point, but a lot of people don't know the facts, have a theory and just commentate.

He also worries that youth-focused campaigns won't get in

the papers or on the news. I point out that the average *Sun* reader is forty-nine – something Tony Gallagher pointed out earlier. We need to be making sure we are going where young people actually are. He argues that people need to see it as a 'good' campaign. I don't point out that no one thought Lynton Crosby's general election campaign was great – until we won . . . and then people called it a classic.

Mandelson disappears out into Cannon Street, briefcase in hand, saying he will next be available after Easter, because he's on a speaking tour of China and Singapore.

He isn't the only one doing a stock take of the campaign. Lynton points out in analysis he publishes in the *Telegraph* that we should stress how important the vote is in fairly neutral terms, in order to drive up turnout. The belief among all poll-sters is: the higher the turnout, the better it is for Remain (though some worry about a scenario where turnout is so high, it could mean traditionally disengaged voters are turning out in force to send a message). One way of doing that is underlining the real possibility that Remain may not win.

It's also clearer than ever that for undecided voters, the biggest hesitation about voting Remain is the impact of uncontrolled immigration, while their biggest hesitation about Leave is the potential to damage the economy.

Many of these voters are women, work in some capacity, tend to be aged 35–44, have a mortgage, voted Conservative in 2015, and are divided over whether the country is going in the right direction. Essentially, they are in the most exposed position in society – they have worked hard and cannot risk what they have strived for.

That means the Remain campaign should focus on the certainty staying in the EU provides and raise the personal relevance of the outcome.

In other words, we need to do more to underline personal risk, so that it is specific to the voter: your job could be at risk, your mortgage could be at risk, the funding that pays for your child's school and your local GP . . .

I am responsible for the 'Air War', the media side of the operation, and the team work to ensure our stories focus on that personal risk. Ameet has been creating a grid of stories that we roll out daily for some time now, but we also have sub-grids aimed at the nations and regions, young people, social media, the BME communities, and softer, lifestyle media.

Elsewhere, Stephen is focused on the 'Ground War' — monitoring what is going on in terms of targeting people across the country. How many campaigners are out each day? How many phone calls have been made? How we get regular nationwide reports on contact. The plan for material to be distributed, including how many leaflets and which letters go out — often written to a specific householder and focused on their specific concerns.

On Wednesday 16 March, everything stops for the budget. As we have wrestled with the campaign, the Treasury has been beavering away — regularly coming into No. 10 for small group meetings to discuss the plan.

The budget speech trundles through. The showy 'sugar tax' on fizzy drinks is met by silence in the Commons — apart from the thud of what's assumed to be a dead cat being thrown on the table to distract the media from some other unpalatable news.

The idea of a dead-cat strategy is part of the legend of Lynton Crosby. Boris popularised it by describing it: 'There is one thing that is absolutely certain about throwing a dead cat on the dining-room table — and I don't mean that people will be outraged, alarmed, disgusted . . . everyone will shout, "Jeez, mate, there's a dead cat on the table!" In other words, they will be talking about the dead cat — the thing you want them to talk about — and they will not be talking about the issue that has been causing you so much grief.' And since he described it, everyone assumes it's a Machiavellian manoeuvre employed by all good political strategists.

As with all budgets, its true impact will only become apparent in the coming days, when the experts have had a proper look.

The next day, the response is a mixed bag. The *Sun* predictably slams George for the fizzy drinks tax – the *Mail* applauds the tax measures, but is critical on debt. In the distance, I can hear the slow train coming on the Personal Independence Payment. Ameet has been flagging that this will be a disaster for weeks – inevitably billed as taking money from people with disabilities, though it is not as clear-cut as that.

Anna Soubry, a business minister and passionate Remain campaigner, alerts me to the problem – having been monstered on the issues on BBC Radio 5 Live: why are you cutting benefits at the same time as cutting taxes?

At the 8.30 meeting, I warn the PM it could be a serious problem. He is angry that the Department for Work and Pensions has done a poor job in controlling its budget, which is ballooning. There's been a recent judgment that has significantly widened the people who can get a repeating Personal Independence Payment. The aim is to reform the system to stop that. The problem is how it is being presented. Ideally, it should never have been associated with the budget, but the damage is already done.

While this is going on, I'm in another tussle with the BBC.

At 7.09 this morning, Justin Webb introduced a piece on the *Today* programme claiming 'most small businesses tend to be Out' in terms of the EU referendum. This simply isn't true and is part of the misleading picture about the weight of business opinion.

I send them several proof points, including: '71% of small and medium-sized businesses back Remain in CBI ComRes poll.' (*CBI ComRes poll*, 15 March 2016.)

One thing that lightens the mood is the fact that Sir Alan Duncan MP is coming out as a Remainer in the next few days. He drafts a statement he thinks we should use as a speaking note:

> In a major blow to the campaign to leave the EU, senior Tory MP Sir Alan Duncan has today announced we should remain a member. As one of the few undeclared MPs, he is seen as an experienced and reasonable figure of influence. Known as a longstanding but thoughtful Eurosceptic, his declaration will be seen to have a pivotal bearing on the many voters who are still undecided.
>
> To have won over such a senior and experienced political figure will be seen as a significant coup both for the Prime Minister and the campaign to remain, all the more so as Alan Duncan is seen as independent minded and someone who cannot be pushed around.

We tell him, 'Maybe it needs a little rewriting.'

On Friday 18 March, the morning's news bulletins focus on comments made by Nicky Morgan on *Question Time*, which appear to back away from the Personal Independence Payment proposals. She has the right tone – taking the heat out of the 'proposals' and buying time to come up with something more palatable. I call IDS's special adviser, who tells me she has been calling round the media suggesting that Nicky Morgan doesn't understand the proposals.

I'm concerned to hear her using the phrase, 'we are not in concession territory.' I tell her it isn't wise to look like you are in a spat with another Cabinet minister. I also make clear that IDS needs to get out there and explain what is going on, i.e., we are taking time to assess all of this. Most significantly, she says IDS is refusing to go out on broadcast, though he will consider a statement.

DC and George aren't in Westminster, but I let them know what is happening. I ask if we should just let this cool down and not throw another log on the fire.

I go up to the Thatcher Room to go through the Government document that will go out during the referendum with about a dozen people from across Government. It's a slow process – with attention to every word. My phone keeps ringing. Emails keep arriving. The view is that IDS should go out and defend the Personal Independence Payment proposals.

I step out of the leaflet meeting, go and lean on the banister at the top of the stairs lined by pictures of all the former Prime Ministers, and set up a conference call with the relevant special advisers, saying, 'We could go round in circles on this, but it's been decided Iain needs to go out and clear all of this up.' Neither argue. I tell them it's in danger of spiralling out of control – and they need to make sure they are singing from the same hymn sheet.

At 10.24, I text IDS: 'Hi, the PM wants you to do a clip on welfare today to make the position clear. I have spoken to your team and am happy to discuss.'

At 13.06, he replies: 'Just come out of a funeral. I will call.'

I respond – sorry to have disturbed him at a funeral: 'Thanks.'

I give him a fair bit of time. I ring him again at 14.46. He doesn't answer or call back.

I make clear to the PM and George that he isn't calling me. I don't want to keep poking the hornets' nest.

Everything goes quiet until around 7 p.m., when I get a call from the PM saying, 'IDS is raging about this. I think it's serious.' He tells me to stay by my phone.

This feels like it's going south very quickly.

The call comes from Ed Llewellyn just after 9 p.m., when I am at home. He tells me, 'IDS says he is going to resign.'

In the background, I can hear DC saying in a raised voice, 'You are literally resigning over SpAds briefing against each other!'

I race to put on my shoes, grab my keys and jump in the car.

I am already getting calls. First Peston, 'Well, this is a mess.' I tell him I will be in touch shortly.

I call Ed – it's out there. He's resigned. In the background, I can hear DC say, 'It's on Sky now.' Clearly we need a statement before the 10 p.m. news.

I get across IDS's letter. It's a missile aimed at George Osborne's heart, concluding we should question the Government's mantra that 'we are all in it together'. He goes on to claim that the PIP reforms may be defensible in narrow terms, but not in the context of a budget that benefits higher-rate tax payers.

I park at the back of No. 10.

As I get out of my car, a Range Rover swishes in. I jump backwards to avoid it. George gets out – wearing jeans and a jacket. His wife Frances is with him. We go in the back door together, awkwardly acknowledging the situation. They have been at a dinner.

George and I go to the PM's study, Frances up to the flat.

DC and Kate are waiting for us.

We spend some time talking through the lines I should give to the press. I call Laura Kuenssberg and Robert Peston, making clear that we are bemused that he's resigning in these circum- stances: the policy came from his department and was defended by him in a letter to MPs last night. IDS is now saying he had problems with it, but he didn't raise them when he had a chance.

The counter-briefing is that it all became indefensible for him when he heard there were welfare cuts at a time when Capital Gains Tax was also being cut. In fact this language is bogus – the PIP budget is rising, it's just some people aren't getting money they might have got. He doesn't seem to have got his story straight – he was anti the policy, but defending it in a letter to colleagues . . . then he appears to be complaining that he felt undermined when others said we should back away. What really appears to be happening here is he thinks he was being left carrying the baby for a policy that is now being seen as unfair. It's not entirely the principled resignation he claims.

The ten o'clock news comes on. DC looks at me mischievously and says, 'This isn't going to be pretty. If you don't like blood sports, look away now.'

At one point there is an obituary part of the package, going over when MPs plotted against IDS and he resigned as party leader. Our thoughts turn to who should go out to defend us. I say Fallon. When I call, I can tell he is itching to do it. We agree to have a conference call at 7 a.m. I hand the phone to DC so he can thank him. He walks towards the back of his office.

I drive Kate home. Both of us agree the real danger in this is the way so much poison is being pumped into the party's bloodstream. How will it be survivable when the referendum is done?

I try to get some sleep, but my phone keeps ringing until 1 a.m. and I need to take the calls.

# Chapter 13

## The One Word He Didn't Use

I'M UP EARLY on Saturday 20 March to make endless calls about IDS.

Everyone wants to know the details of the resignation. Yesterday's long round with the Sunday commentators has to be repeated. So, too, do conversations with political editors.

From what I can work out, IDS still doesn't seem to have got his story straight. On the one hand he agreed there was a need to reform PIP and was prepared to explain that need. On the other, he was angry he was left carrying the baby – fearing that having defended it, there would be a decision to soften it or move away from it.

I push back with our story:

- There was a problem with PIP.
- DWP accepted something needed to be done and made this proposal.
- They then defended it, including writing a 'Dear Colleague' letter to Conservative MPs on Thursday night.
- How is this a principled resignation in opposition to the policy?

At 7 a.m. I have a call with Fallon, who is going on the BBC. He is totally in control, getting this point and using a rapier rather than a sledgehammer to make it. We are lucky to have him around – it makes me smile that he relishes it so much.

Amid the endless calls and the craving for detail – 'Did DC

call IDS a "shit"?' 'How did he receive the letter?' 'Is it true he was on a call with IDS when the news broke on Sky?' (The answer to this is 'Yes.') – DC calls to discuss the reshuffle. He wants to ensure the Chief Whip and I are involved. His tone is decisive. He has decided he wants to replace IDS with Stephen Crabb, the up-and-coming Welsh Secretary. He says he thinks he'll be a calming appointment. Alun Cairns will replace him in Wales.

Philippa Stroud, IDS's former special adviser, is on the radio ramming home his 'not all in it together' message.

We regroup after the morning news cycle on a conference call and we agree that the lines I have taken are still the right ones.

This proves useful when I'm talking to the likes of Simon Walters, the political editor of the *Mail on Sunday*. Simon and I have a close relationship, but occasionally I feel that it's like the one between the boy and the Bengal tiger in the book *Life of Pi* – there's never any doubt the tiger is a natural-born killer.

He starts by claiming we are in trouble, but when I talk him through the precise chronology, he knows it isn't a good look for IDS – is he resigning because he was briefed against (a questionable assertion), or because he disagreed with the policy? Any answer to either question doesn't work for him.

Of course, the bottom line is, it isn't a great look for us either.

As I go through the calls, it is hard not to feel that this is a bitter and bloody fight that has direct links to the referendum and the soul of the Conservative party. As things keep coming at me, I realise I am suppressing a deep emotion – this is upsetting, I'd rather not be doing this, I need sleep, I need a moment to switch off from all of this.

The acronym used by Lynton Crosby's business partner, Mark Textor, rattles through my brain – TTFU. Toughen the Fuck Up. On a practical level, it's great advice. Swallow it – get on with it. But increasingly I feel days like these are corrosive, stopping anything like a balanced life.

DC calls to go through why he is so irritated by IDS's behaviour. 'He never asked to see me about policy. He called me four times and he kept saying he would come back to me. As he was on the phone to me, his announcement popped up on Sky.'

The afternoon is a write-off, as I patiently explain the story to journalists. Some have only just worked out that IDS sent a letter on Thursday night defending the proposals. It never ceases to amaze me the number of times you can make a point before it finally lands.

I read through the Sunday papers. They revel in the gory detail of knifings and claims of betrayal. We have given as good as we got – forcing more questions on IDS than he has on us.

I watch IDS on *Marr* – and yet again think he really doesn't have his story straight. The first half of the interview is a confusing mess. Finally IDS revs up and delivers his blows, questioning George, and the 'One Nation' credentials of the Government.

There's no point pretending – this will look bad for us when it is clipped on news bulletins. Why he resigned will be diminished – the attack on the Government as uncaring will dominate. He looks indignant, saying he wants the children of people on welfare to have the same opportunities as him. The challenge: 'Yes, but if you don't have sound public finances while welfare budgets like PIP are spiralling out of control to the tune of £1 billion a year, and you still have a deficit, you can't help those children,' does not come.

On a conference call after, we are all agreed that it looks like a bloodbath, but IDS didn't properly connect. It's like he has delivered a cut that creates an awful lot of blood, but which isn't fatal.

George points out, 'He explicitly supported both of us continuing.' IDS could make a statement in the Commons tomorrow, which might be a serious problem, but it seems he doesn't want to. DC's view is, 'Don't goad him.'

Nevertheless, everyone is kicking themselves. IDS was given the pretext to resign and portray himself as a martyr. We had not properly prepared people for why there was a good case to do something so controversial. Were too many people too focused on the referendum to pay attention to other things that were inevitably going to be connected?

We need to move on. I get an idea. The next call is with the *Telegraph*. I tell them DC will make the case that he is the true advocate of modern, compassionate Conservatism, setting out his achievements in this field when he goes to the Commons tomorrow.

At 7 p.m. I drive into Downing Street. I'm supposed to be talking to Greg Clark, the unassuming, but highly capable Secretary of State at the Department for Communities and Local Government, but the switchboard is down and there's no chance of it working any time soon.

The meeting takes place in the PM's study. DC and George in their usual armchairs, the rest of us on the sofa opposite and chairs dotted around. We agree not to send anyone out on the morning media round. We want to slow it down, take it easy. If the burn rate of these stories is as fast as it has been, the less energy added, the better.

At the end of the meeting DC wraps up, saying, 'It's odd they said I called him a "shit". That was the one word I didn't use.'

I drive home and watch the news – both on the BBC and ITV. I've briefed them that the PM will make the case for modern, compassionate Conservatism in his Commons statement and that Crabb will confirm the PIP reforms won't happen. DC calls straight after. He says I did really well briefing Kuenssberg and Peston, before asking what I thought.

'Bloody – but not fatal. I think we can turn this tomorrow into a fightback, but you'll have to dig deep and be magnanimous to IDS.' He agrees.

The next morning, as predicted, the papers report the bloodbath in all its gory detail. It's a mess, but my view that it's like a flesh wound, which produces a lot of blood but isn't life-threatening, is confirmed.

The CBI is out saying Brexit is a disaster and is running mid-bulletin, which is pretty much where it should be, given the circumstances. I get calls suggesting we should try to move it up the running order. I don't point out that might happen if we could stop stories about the Government tearing itself apart.

Michael Howard does a good job of reminding MPs to support the manifesto they stood on and that they're very good at opposing cuts, but not great at supporting measures designed to control budgets.

Next, DC decides we will accept both 'rebel' amendments on the budget – one on the so-called 'Tampon Tax', the other on solar panels. It's painful, but a quick way to cauterise the wound.

Finally the PM is magnanimous to IDS, but also underlines that he doesn't accept that his team are anything less than modern and compassionate Conservatives. The lines I put out to that effect are leading the BBC news and are the splash in the *Telegraph*. Encouraged by that, I have a sense of calm. This is a balloon that has been blown up to the verge of popping, but no one seems to want to prick it. All the while, we are letting more and more air out of it.

DC says, 'We've just lost a whole load of money,' meaning the welfare savings. 'We need to take our time in working out how to deal with that.' Meanwhile, George Osborne pads around Downing Street like a caged tiger. It goes against all of his instincts to lie low.

There's a small group meeting not involving the PM about Europe. We discuss the fact that the Government leaflet making the case for Remain is going out – and the level of anger it'll spark. Even with what feels like the whole of Government poring over it, I still don't think everyone has quite grasped what a big deal this will be for the Leave campaign:

- Nearly £10 million spent on it.
- Done against the advice of the Electoral Commission.

Our defence is that there was a leaflet in the 1975 referendum and in Scotland. The thing about the Scottish leaflet is that it was balanced by one released by the Scottish Government. To make matters worse, it's coming out as we are holding an awayday/night for MPs. This prompts discussion about whether we should just can the whole event.

I decide to watch the PM's statement in the Commons. He does well – the assertion about being the leader of a modern, compassionate, Conservative Government goes down well with his backbenchers and badly opposite. There's a lot of noise, but he soldiers on. I can see tweets suggesting it looked good on TV. Corbyn begins by complaining that the PM only gave him half of his statement in advance. It's a tactic that undeniably worked, because to the astonishment of everyone, he doesn't mention IDS once, though several people point out that he could have read it on the front page of the *Daily Telegraph*.

The Labour MPs look glum – how can it possibly be that the PM isn't being eviscerated? How can he have got away with it?

Later on, DC calls. I tell him I think we have taken the heat out of it. He agrees and says, 'Well done.' The story is burning itself out.

By Tuesday there's a real sense that we are turning this around. The tide is changing in our favour – as enemies fail to exploit our misery.

There's a brilliant demolition of IDS by William Hague in the *Daily Telegraph* that concludes devastatingly:

. . . presented with the idea that he resigned over a policy he defended the day before, which was being revised before he quit, and because it was combined with policies that could not possibly have come as a surprise, I can come to only one conclusion. This resignation was totally unnecessary and unequivocally wrong.

Tube passengers stare at me as I laugh out loud at another quote by Nicholas Soames, lamenting the failure of successive Tory leaders to confront the Eurosceptics:

If you have an Alsatian sitting in front of you, and it growls at you and bares its teeth, there are two ways of dealing with it. You can pat it on the head, in which case it'll bite you, or you can kick it really hard in the balls, in which case it'll run away.

The humour drains out of everything pretty quickly, as it starts to emerge there's been a terror attack in Brussels.

As I walk into DC's office, he is commenting on a line in one of the papers that Michael Gove should be made Deputy PM. He turns to me, knowing I will wholeheartedly agree with his view: 'Can you imagine him ever being left in charge of the country?'

He doesn't yet know about the attack and I warn him it is looking like a major act of terrorism.

News starts to flow in – the airport and a metro station have been hit. The images are horrific. I have an empty feeling in my stomach – shock, horror and empathy for the people there, blended with a dread that it could happen here.

There's a Cabinet, followed by a political cabinet – where Zac, Mark Fulbrook and Lynton Crosby report on the London mayoral race.

Zac stands on the fringes, refusing to sit at the table. There's more passion, but he still hasn't shaken that diffident vibe. He claims hc is 'closing in fast' on Sadiq Khan and alludes to a hustings he has just been at, where Sadiq 'blew up'.

I also sit on the fringes, on a chilly window seat, monitoring the situation in Brussels. The bodies are still being removed from the airport and metro station and some extreme Brexiteers are already trying to make political capital.

Allison Pearson, who I had thought of as sensible, writes: 'Brussels, de facto capital of the EU, is also the jihadist capital of Europe. And the Remainers dare to say we are safer in the EU! #Brexit.'

The responses are shaming and condemnatory – most ironic in pointing out how classy she is; some sickened that bodies are still being pulled out. Another UKIP supporter tweets a picture of someone lying bloodied on the ground, clearly pleading for help – saying it shows we need to leave.

After sitting around the coffin-shaped briefing table in the Cabinet Office Briefing Room, better known as COBRA, it's impossible not to shudder again at what happened. The PM does a clip on the attack for the news bulletins in the Cabinet Room and we disappear into more Europe meetings.

The main topic of discussion is how we get the Labour party to be more involved. My sense is that the likes of Mandelson and Alan Johnson need to be meeting with the PM. Not because it will get anything done, but more as a diplomatic exercise to show how willing we are. Others aren't convinced, but DC is irritated. 'There's no point sitting on the sofa rolling your eyes. We need to win this and if that means meeting with people – that's fine.'

The conversation moves on to the Conservative party. There are a lot of people telling the PM he needs to stand back, claiming he is damaging himself. DC says he doesn't know how to lead other than from the front. He's right.

After another COBRA, we go to DC's office to prepare for PMQs. It's likely Corbyn will ask him to apologise to people with disabilities. If he has his wits about him, which recent days have proven is by no means guaranteed, he'll ask about the prospect of further cuts to welfare and the budget black hole of £4.4 billion.

This should be deeply uncomfortable, but we have been handed a gift by a Sam Coates piece in *The Times*. He has been given a document from the Labour Leader's Office grouping MPs according to their relationship to Corbyn.

The categories are: Core Group – including Corbyn; Core Group Plus – neutral; Core Group Negative; and Hostile Group.

As we are discussing it, Michael Gove walks in, making a joke about being 'Core Group Negative'. I find it hard to be in the same room. He is chairing the Leave campaign, which is doing all it can to tear us apart. Fine – that's his choice, but let's not play the happy families game. I just need to swallow it, as DC seems prepared to do.

When I return for the final half hour of prep in the Commons, the breakdown of Labour MPs is returned to. DC studies it carefully – looking for opportunities to smash Corbyn. Amazingly, Corbyn's own Chief Whip Rosie Winterton is considered hostile. 'And I thought I had problems!' he quips, rehearsing his lines.

DC waits for his moment in the Commons and then is lethal, tearing into a glum-looking Labour party. He should be on the rack, tortured for the budget and the IDS resignation. Instead he is on the front foot – laying into them. Before it is over, the whole thing is summed up by a Labour MP, John Woodcock, who tweets: 'Worst week for Cameron since he came in and that stupid fucking list makes us into a laughing stock.'

He deletes it quickly, but it's too late. It's been captured – cementing a desperate day for Labour.

The key meeting of the day is in the PM's Commons office. The In members of the Cabinet crowd round the long table, the afternoon sun outside dissolving into dusk.

Andrew Cooper stands in front of a screen, presenting fresh polling, a reminder that this is by no means won yet.

- 46% of people now think it's more risky for their family to remain in the EU.
- Who is best for 'Strong Public Services', 'Jobs' and the 'Economy' are all moving slowly in the Leave direction. That is a real concern.

DC sums up, 'In some ways that is a depressing presentation. But in others it is optimistic. If we get the economy and national security in the right direction, we'll win.'

A couple of days later, with DC in Lanzarote for a short break, Andrew sends through more polling. It shows that most Labour voters aren't aware that the party wants to stay in the EU. This is serious. We need to put the party at the centre of our comms plan – with clear messages that voting to Remain is the best option for working people. That's an easy sentence to type, but delivering is going to be like bailing out a boat with a sieve.

Over the weekend, the big political news of the day is Matthew Parris slamming Boris in his column for *The Times*. It feels like a drive-by shooting – blasting his reputation in the face with a sawn-off shotgun at point-blank range.

It's all in there – every difficult thing in his private life.

The next day the *Mail on Sunday* also does a hit on Boris in the form of a long piece from his former lover, Petronella Wyatt.

DC texts to say he thought it was quite sympathetic.

'Up to a point,' I reply. 'It may be sprayed with perfume, but it's really a pile of dung.' She says he has no friends, he has depression that's so bad he can hardly climb the stairs, his hate of conflict leads him to lie on a regular basis, and he has a 'European' approach to fidelity. Part of me feels for him and his family – none of this can be pleasant.

APRIL

# Chapter 14

## It's Been a Difficult Few Days

O<small>N APRIL FOOL'S</small> Day, I try to take stock again. I believe the campaign is on course, but the ship is being buffeted all over the place. There's also the sneaking suspicion that we may make it into port, only to find the harbour is mined and snipers are waiting to pick us off.

I set out the problems:

1. The realisation that the Conservatives running Vote Leave (chaired by Gove) intend to continue fighting dirty. Today the National Living Wage came into force (complete with a Treasury press notice hailing it as 'the Chancellor's National Living Wage'). John Whittingdale and Chris Grayling were straight out of the traps, trashing it for acting as a magnet for EU migrants – despite the fact that they are Cabinet ministers who have fully signed up to the policy.

The news comes as we get a leak of a letter that Vote Leave are encouraging doctors and nurses to sign – it specifically attacks the PM and the Health Secretary, Jeremy Hunt, for their handling of the NHS and claims it could be better funded if we left. It's unacceptable and utterly inept at the same time, directly attacking the PM on the NHS, while pleading they 'desperately need' signatures.

I put the letter straight out there with a press notice high-lighting their desperation, several quotes from leading health professionals, and pointing out how leading figures including Vote Leave's Chief Executive, Matthew Elliott, have supported a range of policies that would seriously damage the NHS, including: Cuts to spending and ending the ring-fence; cuts to NHS staff pay; increasing prescription charges; allowing NHS Trusts to fail; increased NHS privatisation.

The cynicism of their approach is breathtaking – presenting themselves as champions of something they do not value.

I follow it up with a note to the PM saying there will be a lot of questions about what Gove's role is in all of this, running the Vote Leave board – and, is challenging Government policy what we meant when we said we would free ministers from collective responsibility? Needless to say it will cause bad blood.

The PM was told by some of the Cabinet ministers who joined Leave that they would 'police and call out bad behaviour'. Destroying the Government's track record on the national living wage and the NHS is hardly doing that.

Amid all of this are constant briefings that Michael Gove should be DPM, coming in as a 'unifying figure'. It seems obvious who are the people pushing that around.

2. A deeply divided Labour party, whose leadership is at best laid back at the prospect of staying in the EU. Reports are that Corbyn's office is deeply split and there's a nagging question facing them all: Why help Cameron? Those who are on our side are struggling. Alan Johnson, the well-liked former Home Secretary who is running Labour In, seems unable to get on air.

Part of my week is spent working up a plan to get more Labour voices out there. The *Today* programme isn't interested in taking Johnson, though (despite allowing John Redwood and Dominic Raab to go on and make the case for Out last week). They take Cabinet ministers, who are often caught up in wider issues – and that counts as part of our quota for In. I call Jamie Angus, the editor of the *Today* programme, and explain to him that the campaign wants Labour voices to be heard – not just Conservative cabinet ministers. He says he plans to take Corbyn on Tuesday, but not Johnson on Monday. I sigh heavily, knowing Corbyn won't be on message.

3. 'Events'. We are working hard to get a message across, but 'events' keep happening . . . the resignation of a Cabinet minister . . . the threat to Port Talbot after Tata Steel bailed on it . . .

4. Debates within Stronger In over our message. This all starts with Andrew Cooper pointing out that there has been a 3.5% swing to Leave in the latest polls. He puts this down to Labour and Lib Dem voters thinking this is a Tory war, and not getting the signal they are supposed to be on board. He suggests that we start using the idea that we can have 'the best of both worlds' by staying in the EU – i.e. all the benefits of being able to trade freely in the single market, with the jobs, opportunities and security that brings, without being a member of the Euro, or the Schengen open borders agreement. He also feels we need to play a different tune, because the strong days on the economy are not moving the polls enough.

Ryan Coetzee feels that we should be almost exclusively on the economy: the single market is the best trade arrangement Britain can have, and is better than all the alternatives.

Andrew worries we are losing the importance of the idea of 'having the best of both worlds.' He also fears that we aren't doing enough to explain to people that one of the keystones of the Leave argument, that the EU needs us more than we need them, is being destroyed.

And round it goes . . .

On Saturday 2 April, the PM arrives back from the nuclear summit and we hold a conference call that I have asked for.

We focus on Out ministers trashing Government policies, specifically the NHS and the National Living Wage.

DC says he accepts it is a big problem and thinks we need to do all we can to get the press to call out Gove. That would be fine, but he is currently doing no media, hiding, I suspect, from the question of whether he was the source of 'Queen Backs Brexit'.

George puts his finger on the issue. The problem is the Conservative party is divided. Our bottom line is we want to try and keep this show on the road, minimising disputes. Theirs is – we are prepared to walk out at any time, causing even more chaos.

Some suggest doing more to shame them: getting senior figures out to say no Conservative should be associated with attacking major Government policies. DC thinks this just creates another Tory row story.

Later in the day, there has been some contact with Gove, who says he hadn't seen the NHS letter attacking the PM and Jeremy Hunt, but agrees the attacks shouldn't be personal, or on policy. I am sceptical.

Chris Grayling claims his remarks on the National Living Wage were 'grossly oversold'. Just don't say them then.

I have the strong feeling of being taken for a fool. To be clear: Michael Gove is the chair of an organisation that is trashing our key policies. He stood on a manifesto based on them – and voted for them. He is almost certainly behind the 'Queen Backs Brexit' story. Do we need any more evidence?

Late in the afternoon, Leave tweets an attack story on the NHS with a picture of Jeremy Hunt. Gove, who has claimed this should stop, now says the tweets are automated – so this one couldn't have been stopped. Pull the other one. But even if that is the case, why were they happening in the first place?

Gove may be avoiding interviews, but he makes some impact by writing a book review on Yanis Varoufakis, the Greek finance minister at the height of the Euro crisis. He uses it as a way to forward the Leave case.

It's over-written, declaring anyone who claims to be interested in the poor should cry 'hot tears of rage' over what is happening in the EU, suggesting it is a 'gateway to despotism'.

I talk this through with friends at No. 10 – several of whom are shocked by his behaviour. One who has known Gove for years describes him as 'out of control' and willing to sacrifice relationships to get what he wants. They see the constant briefing about how he should be Deputy Prime Minister and fear he is trying to engineer a post-referendum world where he is allowed to rule the roost.

Things feel like they are stepping up a gear in the week beginning 4 April.

Stronger In tell me on our 8.10 a.m. call that the leader of the Labour In campaign, Alan Johnson, pulled out of doing morning media, because he wasn't being taken by Radio 4's *Today*. ITV's *Good Morning Britain* were prepared to send a satellite truck to his house, but he pulled out around 8 p.m. last night.

I'm told he said, 'There's no point in doing media for the sake of it.'

I have a quiet word with some of the Labour people at Stronger In. They totally understand that persuading the *Good Morning Britain* audience is vital – and so is getting big Labour figures out there to make the case.

Will Straw says he knows it is a problem and is just as concerned as me. My gut is there's a grain of vanity in this. Politicians want to know their peer group sees or hears them, and none of them watch the ITV breakfast show.

The key meeting of the morning involves bringing together

the key stakeholders around the leaflet setting out the Government position on the advantages of staying in the EU. I am handed a final version of a document that I and dozens of others have crawled over.

I set out a plan to brief the broadcast political editors on Wednesday, in order to get it on the evening and late news bulletins. The hope is to give it a good run before it is monstered by a number of papers. Any idea that this won't drive the Leave campaign wild is dispelled by one page that says 'EU membership brings economic security, peace and stability.'

I propose sending it to the papers at 5.45 p.m. on the same day.

I also want every penny of the spend on it out there and transparent from the off – I don't want any suggestion that we are hiding anything.

I head over to Stronger In to meet Will Straw. I'm standing on the eastbound Tube station platform, when James Slack, the political editor of the *Daily Mail*, calls across the tracks to me. We chat about how he's heading to HQ to do a shift writing the editorials. I'm struck by how we have such a good relationship, despite the vitriol of so much in the paper.

At Stronger In, Will Straw and I head into a booth off the main campaign room. I see others wondering if they are going to be invited, but we both avoid their gaze.

I show him the leaflet and warn him of the storm it'll provoke. He seems pleased and impressed. We talk a bit more and he lets me see quite how tough it is dealing with the Labour party at the moment – they are lost in their own internal world and battles.

The BBC has joined forces with the International Consortium of Investigative Journalists to do an exposé of a Panamanian law firm, Mossack Fonseca, accused of aiding tax avoidance on an industrial scale. Millions of documents have been leaked, and lumped in with characters like Putin, and African and Middle

Eastern despots, is the PM's dad. Every time I look up at my TV screens, I see a still of him, or file footage of the PM going over to kiss him and his mother at a campaign event sometime before 2010.

The PM has been comforting his mother and says he knows little about his father's business, as he is now dead and most of it happened decades ago. It's clear we need to get more of a sense of what went on with the PM's tax affairs. At lobby the Prime Minister's official spokeswoman quotes a line that seemed to settle this the last time the issue was raised, saying the Cameron family's tax affairs are a 'private matter'. This time that phrase is seen as a red rag to a bull.

As the papers drop, I can see there is a real danger of this going out of control, with the *Mail* saying the PM has 'questions to answer' about his father's business. It's happening as we are trying to land perhaps the most controversial thing in the campaign, a £10 million taxpayer-funded leaflet explaining the Government position. We are stretched, to put it mildly.

The next morning it's obvious to all of us the use of the phrase 'private matter' regarding the PM's finances was a mistake.

DC is heading off for a campaign visit on Europe. As the morning meeting is drawing to a close, it is agreed that he should make a statement making his financial position clear then. It is all done in a hurry, but he will answer that he does not have any shares.

I watch him at the Cameron Direct event. Faisal Islam asks him a question about Blairmore, his father's company, and he delivers a spiel about not owning shares. My heart sinks a little, as I see we are opening the door to more questions. We are leaving threads dangling, almost begging a bored media pack to pull on them. The hacks want to know – you say that about yourself, but what about Sam and the kids?

I should be focused on the leaflet, but instead I am running around trying to work out the situation regarding the PM's family and shares. I start with Laurence Mann, the PM's political secretary, and we spend an unhappy couple of hours in calls with DC, Sam and their accountant. I release the following statement:

> A No. 10 spokesperson said: 'To be clear, the Prime Minister, his wife and their children do not benefit from any offshore funds. The Prime Minister owns no shares. As has been previously reported, Mrs Cameron owns a small number of shares connected to her father's land, which she declares on her tax return.'

Of course, the problem with all of this is we look like we are on the run. It's also distracting us from the serious work of winning this referendum.

On Wednesday morning, there's no doubt about it – we *are* on the run on the PM's father's offshore company Blairmore – and his connection to it. When we think we have sealed off the exits, another one opens.

I call DC to go through it all. He tells me that as part of a portfolio of shares his father operated for him, he did own Blairmore shares.

We go through the difficult questions about the past and if he thinks what his father did was wrong. We are back to the fact that the PM's father set up this company thirty-four years ago. We don't know enough about it to be categoric and we don't want to appear to be misleading.

This is a pain, because it's also the day when I'm supposed to be briefing the fact that the Government is spending £9.4 million on a leaflet explaining why it believes we should remain in the EU. It's by no means nailed down. There's now endless buggering around about the wording of the associated website. I'm literally chased down the corridor to another meeting by people who have a series of finicky, late questions, which they should have had the answers to days ago.

Meanwhile, I've asked Graeme to spell out the key questions on Blairmore:

1. Have you benefited from your father's offshore activities in the past? Were your school fees/home, etc. paid for from the funds?
2. You've talked in the past about people who don't pay the taxes they should as being immoral. Were your father's actions immoral?
3. Do you think your father was wrong to have gone to such great lengths to avoid paying UK tax?
4. Does your mother still benefit from offshore trusts or funds?
5. Do you or your family have any connection to the Blairmore fund?
6. You inherited a significant amount of cash from your father in his will. Did that money come from his offshore activities?
7. You are hosting a corruption summit next month – aren't these revelations a huge humiliation for you?

Next up is a meeting to brief Michael Fallon and Liz Truss about the leaflet. Both of them look genuinely surprised that we are doing it – though they conclude it's a good leaflet and we need to be on the front foot about the Government not being neutral in this.

I have carved out half an hour to read the very detailed Q&A on the leaflet. I'd love to delay the whole thing, but with millions of these documents already printed, the story is certain to leak soon without us being able to shape it, if we don't go ahead. I know a lot of it, but I need to be totally on it. The draft isn't finished. There are seventeen minutes before I am due to brief the broadcast political editors.

The briefing goes well. But what should be the biggest thing we do this week is looking like an aside in my day. Graeme and I return to worrying about the PM's shares.

We hold a conference call, hoping to get to the bottom of it all. DC sprays a lot of jargon at us. He's been on the phone to accountants and he's had it all explained. It's all to do with a time when exchange controls were lifted and stockbrokers were allowed to buy 'dollar denominated shares'.

In a machine-gun delivery he explains that Blairmore was registered with the Inland Revenue and above board. He decided to sell his shares in Blairmore in 2010, along with others . . . all totalling £155k. He says we should meet with his brother Alex and someone called Nick Peppiatt, who understand everything about this.

The concern is how it will look that the PM sold his shares in Blairmore in January 2010. Will it look like he was getting rid of something that could be conceived to be dodgy?

Half an hour later, Nick Peppiatt and Alex Cameron arrive in the PM's office. Alex looks like an older, heavier version of his brother. Peppiatt a classic City man, wide-eyed and looking younger than his years, his thick curls cut short, and wearing a Hermès tie.

Alex takes the lead in explaining what has gone on:

- When exchange controls were lifted over thirty years ago, people were suddenly able to buy dollar denominated shares without paying a premium.
- There was a rush to take advantage of this new market – creating funds to buy, fund and sell global equities.
- You could buy an off-the-shelf company in Panama to do this. You needed a lawyer to do this and the best one turned out to be the now infamous Mossack Fonseca.
- The company was renamed Blairmore and the Bahamas was chosen to be its base. (I ask why not somewhere more reputable? And he says that these were the only kind of places where it could be done.)
- Administrators were put in to run the company, including Bahamian directors.

- HMRC was informed that the fund was set up. It was listed in the *Financial Times*.
- Crucially when an investor sold a unit in the fund, they should and would comply with their own country's tax laws. The Camerons did this.
- The fund moved to Dublin in 2012 to comply with EU regulations. An alarm bell rings in my head at this point – the *Telegraph* today was all about the 'mystery' around the fund moving to Dublin in 2012, when it was renamed Blairmore Equities Fund.

We ask a series of questions and it is made clear that if it was in the UK, it wouldn't pay any more tax.

I go from feeling sick about this – and having a small worry that this could all unravel to the point where the PM ends up having to resign – to thinking this is OK.

A plan starts to come together in my head: if we are to get the PM to defend his story, it needs to be clear that Blairmore isn't dodgy. I call Robert Peston, ITV's new political editor, *The Times*, the *FT* and the BBC.

When that is all done, the PM arrives looking as cool and in control as ever.

I'm keeping it together, but I notice that each time I finish a task related to this or the leaflet, I sigh heavily.

We quickly boil all of this down to one question: was there any tax advantage to the fund being held offshore? The answer is no. The reason is important, because it allows us to be clear that the fund was not about tax avoidance.

I take a break with the comms team to watch the BBC 6 p.m. and ITV 6.30 news on the release of the Government leaflet.

The BBC piece is a dream – taking people through all our key points and why we are doing it. Robert Oxley, the Leave person put up to respond, hasn't thought his attack through properly. He says it's all about distracting from the PM's tax affairs. Seriously? But it does reveal a strategy to make DC appear dodgy wherever possible.

I literally punch the air when I see ITV is leading on this. They have Peter Bone MP wearing his fluorescent green 'Grass Roots Out' tie saying it is an abuse and the PM will have to explain himself. The package repeats the BBC in being a brilliant exposition of our case.

When that is done I sit at my terminal and begin to write what the PM is going to say on his tax affairs tomorrow. Nick Peppiatt stands next to me as we go through the finer details. It's not too painful a process and this is what I start the statement with:

> It's been a difficult few days, where I've seen my late father, who I loved very much, being criticised for his business dealings. The hardest thing of all is a lot of it has been based on a misunderstanding – that Blairmore was created to avoid tax.
> It wasn't.

Then we go into the facts of what actually happened. Some think the opening is a little cheesy, but DC is happy with it.

The next hour is spent going through the Q&A. It's real in-the-weeds stuff that will mean little to most people, but could trip us up if we don't get it right.

At 8.30 p.m., I say, 'I haven't stepped outside the office since I got here at 7.30 a.m. this morning.'

As I get up to leave, I have to chat on the phone to a tax lawyer, who can look at the fund and say it isn't dodgy. I get into a cab, so I can talk to him all the way home. When I arrive and hang up, I have six missed calls I need to deal with.

Graeme and I chat later on about our current hellish situation. He describes the sensation as like driving at 100 mph towards a series of brick walls and then swerving at the last second to avoid a smash.

The truth is – we haven't handled this well. The whole building is laser-focused on Europe – and it's another thing that slipped. We have looked on the run and not been in full possession of the facts.

# Chapter 15

## We've Just Got to Win This Thing

On THURSDAY MORNING, I'm cheered up by the leaflet still being the lead on BBC News. The Leave campaign continues to do our work for us – screaming either that it's not fair or that we're doing it to cover up the PM's tax affairs.

Instead of going into No. 10, I'm driven to Northolt, where I am to be taken by helicopter to pick up the PM in his constituency.

I'm in email hell with several chains adding to and clarifying lines to take on tax.

We land in the field next to the PM's home. A minibus and a police Range Rover are waiting nearby. DC and his protection officer join me and Will MacFarlane, the private secretary on this trip. Between me and the PM are a basket of fruit and two flasks of coffee. It's a strange mix of luxury and cheap – the coffee served in too-thin paper cups, which mean gripping the rim with fingertips to avoid being scalded.

We start by looking at the papers. The leaflet was a late drop for them, but just enough time to ensure it ends up on a lot of front pages. The Leave camp still haven't settled on a line.

It's job done in comms terms, but I ask DC how much bad blood the tax issue will have caused. He turns and looks out the window at the rolling fields and Cotswold stone houses and says, 'A lot . . . it's bad . . .' He pauses for a moment before saying, 'But look, we've just got to win this thing . . .'

We spend the rest of the twenty-minute journey with me

putting him through his paces for the interview I have arranged with Robert Peston. I know there will be next to nothing on the leaflet and a lot on Blairmore.

We arrive at the business school, which looks like a very agreeable campus. There are a couple of protestors as we get out of the car, who can barely muster the energy to shout, 'When are you going to do the right thing by junior doctors?'

After a few preliminaries, we're into the main event – telling young people why they need to vote to remain in the EU. The line we've agreed is, 'Young people have the most to gain by remaining in the EU – jobs, education, travel – and the most to lose by leaving.'

He's surrounded by around 250 students, some on a spiral staircase and balcony. He takes off his jacket and Hugo Swire, the local MP, who is sitting in the audience, grabs it.

It's quite a feisty encounter, but nothing he can't handle. I stand in the audience, with a good view. To my left are a few hacks. To my right, a number of young Conservatives. One can't be more than twenty-two, but is wearing the fustiest of tweed jackets and a red tie. Every time the PM says anything vaguely good about the EU, he mutters, 'Rubbish!' under his breath, but it doesn't get more raucous than that.

It's going well – apart from a slightly weird moment where he says he likes to watch Glastonbury at home with a fire, despite it being in June. Apparently he does watch it with a fire.

We are taken to another part of the building to do the interview. Peston has no knowledge that he's about to get a big story. I take him into a side room and say, 'He's going to talk to you about his tax affairs.' I'm not sure he registers what I've said.

We go through to a low-lit room, where the interview is to be done. There's a handshake shot and then we are into it.

We start on tax. The PM gets what he has to say out, but he isn't quite as fluent as usual. We've been discussing if he will say he will publish his tax return, and agreed to leave some wiggle room, but in the interview he is clear he will do it. This is a major story.

I let the interview run – it's important he makes clear as often as possible that Blairmore wasn't a tax avoidance scheme. He keeps saying, 'I have nothing to hide,' which seems to have unfortunate echoes of 'I am not a crook!'

At the end, I conclude it was fine.

DC disappears into a political reception and I call back to base to let people know what's been going on. I decide that we should get a transcript of which parts need to be sent to the lobby, but will only confirm when I've read it properly.

The helicopter journey back to his home at Dean is a case of four seasons in one day, blustery wind, then sunshine, then flying into hail, which is like suddenly flicking on a radio that is tuned to static at full volume.

We land back in the field next to his house. Then I take off without the PM – back in Northolt at 4 p.m. My phone doesn't stop ringing for the next few hours. I agree on which extracts can be put to the lobby, brief Anna Soubry, catch up with most of the home team . . . then watch the Peston interview before talking it through with the PM.

The next few hours are blotted out with calls again. At one point, I walk back from Waitrose in the pouring rain, answering questions about when the PM put the Blairmore shares in his and Sam's name, because by splitting it in two, it meant they both avoided capital gains tax.

I find myself in the hell of painstakingly going through the detail with journalists who are clearly bamboozled, but have to write a story. The crucial calls are with the BBC's James Landale and Peston again. At 10 p.m. Peston is particularly good, saying that we need to remember that politics is also about real human beings and that the human response to people attacking a man you loved was to tell them to 'Bugger off!'

It's clear that's why we got in trouble this week – and people will get that.

When I have watched both programmes, DC calls. 'I don't know if it's just that I've had a couple of glasses of wine, but that seemed a hell of a lot better.'

Tomorrow we will have to look at releasing his tax returns, but I feel I can sleep easy tonight.

The joy is short-lived and ends when Friday's papers come through.

It's starting to feel like we are in a perfect storm. Much of the Conservative party is going nuts about the leaflet and many MPs are threatening not to cooperate with any form of parliamentary business.

A friend who is a backbench MP calls to say, 'It's now certain that there will be a leadership challenge after the referendum.'

A few of us gather round the table in my office and begin the process of working out the release of the PM's tax returns.

The fact is we're utter novices in this world. We discover the PM invested in something called the Vietnamese Enterprise Fund. We're told it's perfectly legitimate, but will the lobby see it that way? Who knows what it invested in? We think it's fine, but what if it's not?

Another bit of paper points to £3,089 in royalties on the book *Cameron on Cameron* by Dylan Jones. We work out he gave the money to charity.

There's money from the rent of his house and it's also clear that the PM's mother gave him two gifts of £100k in 2011, following the £300k he received from his father's will. The question is – was this a deliberate attempt to ensure he did not pay inheritance tax? The £300k in the will is below the inheritance tax limit. Had his father given him £500k, it would have been significantly above. Was this planned?

We move on to the speech he is due to give at tomorrow's

Conservative Party Spring Forum. I'm told to come up with an intro that will work – acknowledging it's not been great this week, but we haven't been misleading people.

I spend the rest of the day running people through our side of the story. The most effective line is that this was about a son protecting his parents and his wider family. I use it fairly shamelessly, to the extent that I feel the need to call him up and tell him what I'm up to.

Endless meetings, endless calls . . . all firming up getting the tax returns out there.

Yesterday I called a halt to them going out today. Boy are we glad about that now. There are endless finicky details . . . experts to be called . . . payslips to be checked.

I leave late, knowing I will be back in early. I thank the press team. We are all feeling shattered – not knowing where this is heading. The whole thing really could blow up . . .

On Saturday 9 April, I come in exhausted – at my desk by 7.45 a.m. I go downstairs, but of course what passes for a canteen is empty. I go to where the 'House' staff make tea and find Laurence Mann hoping to get some, too.

He tells me he hasn't been home since Wednesday night.

A financial expert called Graham Aaronson and his assistant are already waiting in the political office – super smartly dressed, and straight out of central casting. DC comes in, dressed for his speech. He wants to run a rule over what we are announcing, and to know the accountants are happy. Of course, what they think is normal might not live up to the lobby's world view.

The big sticking point is over whether we should reveal that DC's mother gave him two £100k gifts.

The reason she did was that his brother inherited the family home and his sisters got the mews house in London. He was supposed to get the pension. But of course, it was completely gone. His mother wanted to balance things out.

After going round the houses a bit, I say, 'The lesson of this week is supposedly, "Get it all out there." If it's true people will be able to work out from this that there is some missing cash, we do need to put it out there.'

There's a bit of black humour about how all the advisers in No. 10 are being written off as complete morons and DC says, 'I'm really sorry you guys are getting all the blame.'

We feel like we are in uncharted territory. I tell him I think we're doing the right thing. It's not comfortable, but we have to have faith that he hasn't done anything wrong. He nods. He has clearly been wrestling with this.

The thing I'm more worried about is the sense that the Government is really wobbling at the moment. We need to change that.

A few of us head through to my office and plough through the document we will release later and the Q&A. It's heavy going – we don't want to make a mistake. Numbers fly around; so does financial management jargon. All of us work hard to keep up. I'm glad to have the excuse of going to the Connaught Rooms, where the PM is giving his speech.

We stop outside, ready to jog up the stairs, past a phalanx of hacks. As we do, someone shouts, 'Are you going to resign, Prime Minister?' The rest is a blur of words, where I can only pick out 'tax' and 'offshore'.

We are taken into a small room off the main hall where one of Theresa May's SpAds is waiting. I watch DC from backstage. The opening of his speech is a masterclass. He tells them it hasn't been the best of weeks and pauses for laughter. He tells them not to blame 'nameless' advisers in No. 10 . . . it has been his fault – he wanted to protect his family. Whatever you think of it, it works.

He then goes on to give eight reasons why this Government is really on the ball.

When he is done, Zac Goldsmith and Boris follow us back to the small room. Boris is saying, 'Brilliant, brilliant speech!'

to no one in particular. I find myself next to him as we jog upstairs to a room full of activists. He huffs and puffs about all the 'financial nonsense' that's been going on.

A picture is taken with volunteers from the London campaign – and we are off. DC gets into the car back to Dean. I get in a cab back to No. 10. The driver says he's never been asked for that address before. He asks me whether we should Leave or Remain in Europe. I give him the chat and at the end, he tells me I have persuaded him.

There's a crowd of about a hundred protestors outside No. 10. Some are wearing pig snouts. One has a giant rod with what appears to be a pig hanging from it with DC's face on it. They seem remarkably placid. Back in the PM's office, we watch the pictures on Sky.

The last details go into the press release and the Q&A. Everyone is jumpy and exhausted.

It's approaching 3 p.m. when I send the email to the lobby.

We all agree to go home and take the calls from there. I have got two of the trickiest customers – Tim Shipman, from the *Sunday Times*, and Simon Walters from the *Mail on Sunday*, as well as all the broadcasters.

The key thing is telling them about the two £100k cash gifts. They seem OK about this. But a couple of hours later, the *Mail on Sunday* is on saying they think it is a tax dodge. Their point is that if the PM's dad had given him £500k in the will, he'd have been liable for tax, but doing it this way means that if his mum doesn't die within seven years, he won't pay any.

I start by being dismissive. I call Geordie Greig and say I'd be surprised if the paper suggests this was wrong, given that the PM has given a full explanation that it wasn't about avoiding tax and was about evening out the will, which others accept. He seems reassuring.

But at 9 p.m. Simon Walters calls me and says, 'It's the splash, I'm afraid.'

'Seriously? The *Mail on Sunday* is critical of the PM about his mother giving him the kind of gift that happens on a smaller scale in millions of families?'

When I see the front page, it is worse than I feared: 'CAMERON TAX BILL DODGE ON MOTHER'S £200K GIFT'. The copy is shocking.

I call the PM, but can't get him. I see if the No. 10 switchboard can track him down.

They call the protection cops, who are reluctant to get him out of a function. I tell them they have to. More minutes crawl by.

He comes on and I explain the situation. I tell him, 'We are considering a statement,' and he sighs heavily.

It's past midnight when he calls again. He is worried that the *Mail on Sunday* is being so difficult. 'Labour will leap on this now. Just as we were getting out of it . . .'

'Let's see what the morning brings – it may not be that bad.' He takes a little comfort from this. We agree to talk early. I collapse into bed, wondering just how much trouble we are in.

I struggle to sleep past 5 a.m. and get up and go through the papers. This is the torturous side of this job – unable to rest properly at the crucial moments.

There's something genuinely shocking about seeing the *Mail on Sunday* splash on a claim that the PM's mother's gift was a tax dodge.

I've also started getting supportive, 'Are you OK?' texts, which is the surest of signs things are falling apart.

I find myself hoping Corbyn will blow it on *Marr* as I go for a run round the park – hoping to burn off some nervous energy.

DC calls to say the papers are better than he thought. I tell him to watch Corbyn and let's have a conference call after.

*Marr* starts well, with a press review by Iain Dale and Polly Toynbee. Polly is reduced to saying, 'He hasn't done anything wrong, but he is rich.' Iain is excellent, robust in his defence of family tax planning.

Corbyn is weak – he doesn't seem to have much of a message and as usual, there's almost no energy. At one point, Marr suggests Mary Cameron has £200 million. I text the programme editor, telling him it needs to be corrected, and it is done in the next answer.

Amber Rudd is on at the end. I briefed her earlier and she is firm but sober, pointing out there's nothing to see here.

I text DC: 'Feels a lot better than midnight. Getting out there painful, but it's done. Talk at 10.10. Craig.'

His reply is short and sweet: 'Indeed.'

On the conference call with the core team, George says, 'My political antennae have just pricked up.' The reason is that Bill Cash is planning an amendment to the finance bill, which insists the Government fund a Brexit leaflet, too.

Much of the rest of the day is spent at my kitchen table making calls and sending emails. I talk to various newspaper editors to ensure they understand why we did what we did and how publishing a summary of his tax returns is significant.

That night a few of us gather in No. 10 and run through our mistakes. The classic analysis, that we should have got everything about Blairmore out of the door immediately, doesn't work. We were struggling to make sense of a company that was set up three decades ago, by a man who died in 2010.

On Monday 11 April, we may not be out of the woods yet, but we are heading in that direction.

I wake up, wired and worn out, with the front of my brain tense as a flexed muscle.

Interestingly the *Mail* is critical of other parts of the media, particularly on inheritance tax, with an 'enough of this madness' approach. They defend the very human urge of parents wanting to pass on their wealth to children. In a strange way, the extreme coverage on Sunday provoked the turning point, with the right-wing press now understanding that some have been engaged in sawing off the branch they've been sitting on.

Some feel the decision to publish a summary of the PM's tax returns is a mistake, describing it as 'just feeding a crocodile', with more and more demands coming.

We move on to the referendum. Focus groups are showing Remain voters are weighing up the risks of leaving and the risks of remaining. Having been pushed off the economy, Leave are starting to be effective in leveraging the idea that staying is a risk – being overrun by immigrants. There are signs that this is a real motivator for those minded to leave to definitely turn out.

Finally the conversation ends up on Gove and how it is that he has made himself the darling of the Tory party. I am nervous that people will take him seriously. Others believe he can't take the pressure, saying we have seen him up close, having 'infarctions' when the heat is on. Others are more critical of 'Mrs Gove', whom they believe is 'definitely measuring the curtains'.

# Chapter 16

## Who's Up For a Threesome?

I T'S RAINING AS I make my way to the Treasury, where George and I are meeting Peter Mandelson, Nick Herbert, Will Straw and Stephen Gilbert, as part of our first attempt at getting the politicians together.

A backbench Labour MP, who wouldn't want it to be known he's at the meeting, is also there, looking nervy. What would his colleagues think if they knew he was in Osborne's office? There hasn't been a moment where we've been introduced – and he eyes me diagonally across the Chancellor's long wooden table, not sure if we can all trust each other.

George speaks first, making clear that he and the PM are available to work with the campaign.

Perfectly groomed, Mandelson makes a speech, his tone soft and insistent. His view is, 'If I were Leave, I would know the weakness of my argument – and think that the only way I can win is by making this a referendum on the Government.' He makes a point of saying, 'And things aren't going that well for the Government. So make it as much of a maelstrom as possible, so that their message is buried.' He then argues, 'The message of our campaign is not igniting. We are in a bit of a phoney war at the moment, until the local elections are at an end, so let's take advantage of that time and review everything.'

As he speaks, I notice that his tone doesn't change at all. There is no special emphasis – calm, quiet, almost monotonous. 'They will play the man, not the ball. Try to run us ragged.'

The backbench Labour MP's analysis is plain and simple. This referendum is turning into a battle between economics and immigration. He is also clear that – right or wrong – the Labour party feels the lesson of the Better Together campaign on Scottish independence was, 'Don't share a platform with the Tories, because they will toxify you.'

We could spend all day arguing about that, and whether the truth was that Labour had taken its own supporters in Scotland for granted for too long, but it wouldn't help. The fact is that it is a strong view, so we had better deal with it.

My view is that we need to lean into the fact that we have broad support – Green, Labour, Lib Dem, Conservative – and do more to show people that we are prepared to set aside our differences in the same cause.

I walk back to No. 10 with Will Straw in the rain. I half expect us to be snapped together.

When we sit down in my office, I want to talk about how we are getting across that we are a coalition. We think Vote Leave will have lots of rallies, but what they won't have is cross-party support. I suggest getting the PM at a call centre with a prominent and recognisable figure from each of the other parties. This is a clear visual that says, 'Look – you didn't expect to see us on the same side.'

The fast burn rate of stories works in our favour. By Tuesday 12 April the tax story has died down almost completely.

DC is seen as having performed effectively in the Commons yesterday, though he thinks he has been fortunate in facing a weak Labour leader, with a party in disarray.

'Yes, I meant to say that you mustn't remark, "We're so lucky!" quite so loudly when we are in the House of Commons!'

I get a call from Francis Elliott asking our plans on the referendum. I have to walk past John Whittingdale, who is wandering around early for the Cabinet meeting. I can't be overheard by a Leave minister, so I dip into Ed Llewellyn's office, only to find Michael Gove ensconced in there.

I have to go and stand in the disabled toilet to continue the conversation in private.

The key event of the day is the International Monetary Fund giving its report on the UK's finances – warning of the serious consequences of Brexit. I have gone out of my way to say it will be big. The IMF more than delivers.

The No. 10 media team sit in my office to watch the news. We find ourselves having another proof point that we are living through the looking glass – with everything the wrong way round. The person used to oppose the IMF is the former Conservative Chancellor, Norman Lamont; the one to support it is the left-wing firebrand John McDonnell.

I'm almost home that evening when I get a call from John Whittingdale's special adviser, Carrie Symonds. *Newsnight* is planning on running a story about him having had a relationship with a prostitute.

Carrie has already drafted a statement, which includes the following:

> Between August 2013 and February 2014, I had a relationship with someone who I first met through Match.com. She was a similar age and lived close to me. At no time did she give me any indication of her real occupation and I only discovered this when I was made aware that someone was trying to sell a story about me to tabloid newspapers. As soon as I discovered, I ended the relationship.
>
> This is an old story, which was a bit embarrassing at the time. The events occurred long before I took up my present position and it has never had any influence on the decisions I have made as Culture Secretary.

I talk to the *Newsnight* editor, Ian Katz, who sees it heavily from the Hacked Off point of view – the papers didn't run it because

Boris in a beanie: leaving Number 10 after discussions about which side he'd take in the referendum failed to reach a conclusion.

Days later David Cameron tells the nation he's negotiated a 'special status' for the UK in the EU. The next day Boris declared for 'Leave'.

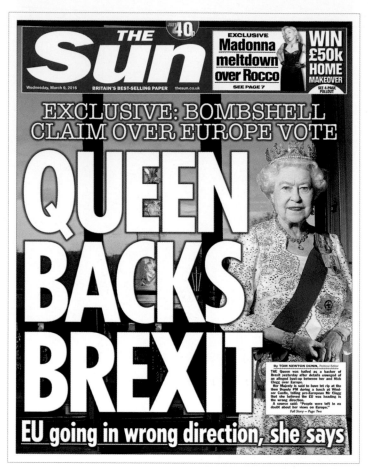

Many newspapers campaigned fiercely for 'Leave'. This *Sun* front page was the most controversial of the campaign.

The *Daily Mail*'s coverage of John Longworth standing down as Chairman of the BCC caused irritation in Number 10.

Strange bedfellows. 'Remain' made a great deal of political figures, who normally disagreed violently, working together in the national interest.

The images made an impact – but most could see the current Labour leadership was at best lukewarm, and many thought they were actively hostile.
Cartoon by Peter Brookes.

The infamous 'Vote Leave' bus with its false claims about payments to the EU and the NHS. Amber Rudd said a rainbow with a pot of gold would have been more accurate.

Getting strong images to accompany news stories was a major part of the campaign, here hundreds of people came together in Hyde Park to spell out 'IN'.

David Cameron and I arriving for one of several BBC interviews during the campaign. The 'Remain' campaign felt the BBC was struggling with issues of balance and impartiality.

No need for a body language expert. Jeremy Corbyn looks uncomfortable supporting 'Remain'. Angela Eagle looks even more uncomfortable supporting him.

Nigel Farage's notorious anti-immigration poster was released and roundly condemned just hours before the murder of Jo Cox MP.

David Cameron and Jeremy Corbyn side-by-side as they pay tribute to Jo Cox MP.

24th June: Slipping away. 'Remain' campaigners begin to realise all predictions are wrong – the UK has voted to leave the EU.

Nigel Farage celebrates. Just a few hours earlier he told Sky News he believed 'Leave' had lost.

Samantha Cameron by her husband's side as he announces he is resigning. Minutes earlier he had called Michael Gove to congratulate him – but not tell him his plans.

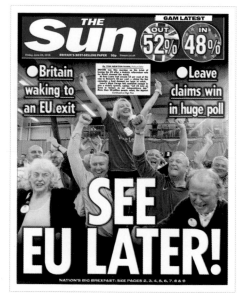

The *Sun* captures the joy of the 'Leave' campaigners

Michael Gove and Boris Johnson appear to be in a state of shock
in the hours after David Cameron resigned.

BREAKING NEWS | MICHAEL GOVE HAS BEEN ELIMINATED

16:24 CONSERVATIVE LEADERSHIP: SECOND ROUND RESULTS - THERESA MAY 199 VOTES, ANDREA LEADSOM 84 VOTES, MICHAEL

David Cameron's team watched the bloody leadership
battle from the sidelines of Number 10. This was one of Sky News'
stark captions as Amber Rudd commented on events.

David Cameron after making clear he would leave Number 10 within a couple of days. With Andrea Leadsom dropping out of the leadership race – the path was clear for Theresa May to become Prime Minister.

And then there was one. Theresa May makes her first speech outside Number 10 Downing Street.

they wanted to be able to hold a gun to his head, in case he threatened to push through the final bits of the Leveson inquiry on press regulation. This sounds like pure conspiracy theory to me.

I finally get through to DC and I propose saying, 'He is a single man who is entitled to a private life.' I have also been round this block often enough to know that we will be asked if we have full confidence in him, to which the answer is always 'Yes', until you are actually prepared to sack someone.

DC suggests Ed and I call John Whittingdale. When I get hold of Carrie, she says the call will need to be quick, because he has to go into a dinner. I ask what dinner could be more important than his career? She's embarrassed to say it's something for Vote Leave. I tell her his career may be a little more important than that and laugh at the bitter irony of spending my evening doing my best to help.

He is clear that he didn't realise he was going out with a prostitute who specialises in sado-masochism.

I tell him that the *Mail on Sunday* was on to me at the weekend about his string of Russian girlfriends. He snaps, 'My current girlfriend isn't Russian – she's Lithuanian.' He goes tortuously through the story. I tell him to release the statement and find myself in a series of calls until *Newsnight*. I watch it on my iPhone in bed, including a debate between Brian Cathcart and Roy Greenslade. Cathcart seems to have lost the plot – appearing as the champion of people's right to privacy, while demanding someone else's is invaded.

My last call on the subject is at midnight.

Wednesday is largely spent defending John Whittingdale, who is top of the news.

By Thursday we are back on Europe – with the BBC's 6 a.m. headline: 'Corbyn to outline case for staying in the EU.'

It's yet another reminder of the fact we live in strange days. The man we think would ruin this country is now an ally.

At 10.30 this morning DC and I jump in a car to the Stronger In call centre. I have pushed for a photo opportunity designed to show we have support from the Conservative party, all the way through to the Greens.

It's a classic political call centre – desks strewn with leaflets, newspapers and used paper cups, that won't be cleared up between now and the vote. The walls are badly in need of a lick of paint, and dotted with posters. In one place, the words 'Stronger In' are spelt out in photographs of the team. The young staff, wearing campaign T-shirts over their normal clothes, look like they could do with a good night's sleep and some healthy food.

A line of desks has been set up with phones and a script for participants. DC sits in the middle and puts on a blue rosette that says 'Stronger In'. Paddy Ashdown, Tessa Jowell, Neil and Glenys Kinnock, and a guy from the Green campaign called Darren Johnson surround him wearing rosettes in their own party colours. Ashdown really hams it up, swapping phones with the PM and roaring with laughter as they explain who they are to people who answer. The pool reporter, snapper and cameraman lap it up. I can see we have a hit – the clear message: a very broad coalition of people say, 'Vote Remain'.

Meanwhile, Corbyn is out doing his speech – supposedly signalling to his core supporters that we need to stay in. All his media handling around this is bad. He sounds lukewarm. I had to send a message from No. 10, through Stronger In, to Labour In, to the Labour Leader's office, to stop them doing odd things like a series of clips after the speech (what would the point of that have been?). But perhaps this will start getting Labour voters to realise . . .

The news gets better, as Lloyds Bank, the NATO Secretary General, and a union come out for us. I watch with satisfaction as Laura Kuenssberg declares that, 'All in all it's been a good day at the office for the Remain campaign.'

I get in the car with DC to an awayday at a hotel in the constituency. I need this like a hole in the head, but the PM wants the media team to do a presentation to keep them occupied.

We arrive at the hotel, where most of the MPs have already gathered. Most look relaxed and part of a modern party, but there are some 'smart casual' horror stories, including a tweed jacket with giant pink checks.

I give my presentation, which is aimed more at entertainment than to inform. There are endless clips and tweets of politicians making fools of themselves, which go down well.

I disappear to my room to work, before coming back down for Andrew Neil's presentation on the US elections – it's entertaining and informative, with the apocalyptic conclusion that mainstream politics is in serious trouble.

Dinner is interesting. I sit next to the MPs Helen Whately and Andrew Bridgen. Bridgen is the Outer's outer and a self-made man. I have fun having a robust chat with him, during which he gives me chapter and verse on his low opinion of No. 10 and the EU campaign. He's convinced Leave will win, and volunteers that even if they don't and it is close, they will demand George's head on a plate.

Over the weekend, I feel as tired and as fed up as I have done at any time since I started this job.

To top it all, I'm still dealing with calls about John Whittingdale's love life.

It starts with Simon Walters calling with the *Mail on Sunday*'s latest allegations about someone called Stephanie Hudson, whom they describe as 'a former Page 3 girl and soft porn actress.' They claim: she stayed at his constituency home and he permitted her to see confidential ministerial documents from his red box; he texted her a photograph taken at Chequers showing many Cabinet ministers and Downing Street advisers and did so without their permission; he was asked to leave the American Bar at the Savoy in December 2013 after engaging in what she describes as 'mutual drunken heavy petting, kissing and groping'.

I call John Whittingdale to go through it. He begins to bluster at the very first sentence, saying she was a Page 3 model, but not a porn actress. I ask him to let me get through it before he responds. He insists he wasn't thrown out of the Savoy, though accepts a waiter did approach when she was kissing him, after a customer had complained.

He says the idea she saw things in his red box is ridiculous. He is very dismissive of her: 'We weren't compatible, which is why we broke up.'

I discuss it with the PM and we agree to stick to, 'He's a single man, who is entitled to a private life.'

I have no doubt they will go big on it, but no one will follow it. It's too saucy for broadcast, and the other newspapers aren't about to go for him, having made a point of not going for him.

All of this takes up several hours, as does tackling a wide variety of issues about the wiring of the Remain campaign comms operation.

On the plus side, cross-party pictures at the phone bank were a real hit – they have been seen everywhere and are now being used in cartoons. My favourite is in *The Times*, the PM with Ashdown and Kinnock, asking, 'Who's up for a threesome?'

I exchange thoughts with Peter Mandelson, who also thinks we have had a good week. He hopes Labour and trade union people (e.g. Unison re the NHS) will grow in confidence now that Corbyn is out of the trap. He believes the main hit of the week was the phone-bank pictures, because if Kinnock can do work with the PM, others can.

It's still a bright sunny day when I drive in for our Sunday night meeting.

It kicks off with another round of the debate about to what

extent we should be engaging in blue-on-blue spats. This weekend Boris has had a go at the PM and Chancellor for being the Gerald Ratners of politics, dealing in crap. He's also accused them and Theresa May of talking 'bollocks' on immigration.

My view is that we can't just keep taking this without coming back. We should consider an intervention from the likes of John Major that aims to call him out on all of this. George is up for this – I think other issues are at play for him here. DC isn't so sure. He doesn't feel it is in our interests to engage at all. His point is – I keep pushing the fact we have a broad coalition of people on our side and massive third party support, and how does engaging in Tory Wars help that?

I see his point, but fear we look like we are being run ragged as a Government and there is zero incentive for them to stop punching. We are also being penned in by the reality of their position – Vote Leave only have Tories, so they can only put them up. If we don't engage most of the time, we are ruling ourselves out of a lot of battles. We're also hobbling ourselves in the social media/digital battle because, frankly, we can't take the piss. DC is adamant: 'We must not let them be able to play the victim.'

We move on to discussing what image we are portraying. There's a bit of a debate about the PM, Kinnock and Ashdown picture making Tories feel uncomfortable. Some think it was a mistake. DC says he wants to see more of it.

He believes, 'If we lose this – it will be very serious for this country for the next ten years, so we need to do what we can.'

The meeting concludes with the PM saying he wants more aggression in our responses to Leave. That will certainly come tomorrow, when George releases a Treasury document warning that the average household will be £4,300 a year worse off if we leave the EU.

On Monday, Leave predictably go bananas about the claim that everyone will be so much worse off – specifically the Chancellor standing in front of a huge sign with £4,300 emblazoned on it.

DC jokes that he is like Sean Connery in *The Untouchables*, riddled with bullets and crawling along the floor: 'They keep shooting me.'

'That's not a great analogy,' I laugh. 'He dies!'

I show him a fairly mild digital attack that's a play on *The X Files*, a picture of Boris and John Redwood beneath the title, 'The Brexit Files'. It's inspired by Boris saying the CIA set up the EU and Redwood saying, 'It's a conspiracy!' DC agrees to it, before suggesting we add a little Roswell alien to the gap in the poster.

DC isn't the only one prepared to start taking off the gloves. George gives a very punchy interview on the *Today* programme defending the Treasury document and warnings. He sounds to me like a man who isn't going to go down for the lack of shooting back – describing the Leave campaign as 'dishonest' and 'economically illiterate'.

The outrage from the Outers is palpable.

Meanwhile, the Government continues to be attacked by its own people. Priti Patel seems to be prepared to say anything the Leave campaign tell her to. She is at the centre of a story on school places today, saying it's 'deeply regrettable' that families in England would be hit by a shortage of primary school places because of immigration. There's anger at how prepared she is to hand Labour a series of quotes to put on campaign leaflets when this is done.

Andrew Cooper feeds in his latest polling analysis. It's encouraging, confirming something I sense as I sniff the air – things are moving in our direction:

- Three online polls over the last four days: two have the referendum 50/50, the other with a 51/49 lead for Remain – the consistent and familiar picture from online polls.

- The first phone poll for three weeks (conducted by ComRes) was published today in the *Sun*: Remain 45%, Leave 38%, Don't Know 17%.

One fly in the ointment is an online Reality Check from the BBC. It says that the poster behind the Chancellor et al, claiming that each household would lose £4,300 a year, 'is not true'. They put this down to household GDP and household income not being like for like. Our point is that people will be considerably worse off – and we simply changed it into something more understandable. The 'Reality Check' line is softened.

We get to hear that Gove is giving a speech tomorrow. George wants a stunt to show they are on the back foot. I set the Stronger In team to work on it and we come up with a document with 'Vote Leave's plan for the EU', and when you open it, the pages are blank. I order them to print 150 copies and to get volunteers handing them out.

Tom Edmonds, the creative brain there, comes up with a poster idea to put on a digital site tomorrow: a picture of Boris Johnson crossing his fingers, and hoping for the best. I know the PM will reject this, but I send it to him anyway, along with an image of a giant forearm and hand, with the fingers crossed. He responds that it's a big call to start attacking individuals and we should go with the other one.

# Chapter 17

## To the Back of the Queue

TUESDAY BEGINS WITH a Gove 'essay' on the *Today* programme. It's supposed to be Leave's opportunity to make their case.

It's classic Gove, elaborate and elegant packaging, which he hopes will mask the fact he doesn't have an answer to the question – what does Out look like?

It's the same at his speech later, where he attacks us for how negative we are, before suggesting that if we stay, we will be the hostage held in the boot of a car being driven to a federal Europe. I get reports back, saying our people handed out the empty document outside the venue and it was lapped up by the media. Apparently an angry Leave press officer came out and started complaining that it was illegal because we used their logo – and this was an act of war, because we would now face them hitting back with similar stunts. Good.

It feels like we are winning – winding them up, steamrollering them with our argument, forcing them to say things they haven't thought through. Gove tries to answer the 'You can't answer what Out looks like' point by saying there is a free trade area stretching from Iceland to the borders of Russia, which we could be part of. Our wonks scratch their heads over this, before saying he appears to be suggesting our relationship with the EU could be like Albania's. Great – the magical mystery tour of the world has a new destination.

I begin to wonder what it must be like for them. They like

to portray themselves as the plucky little David facing Goliath, but they must struggle knowing that we will keep putting up groups of experts and institutions to support us – with them left trying to find ways to dismiss them.

Political cabinet feels like one giant exercise in evasion. Everyone is terribly English in their small talk – pretending the blood all over the walls isn't really there. I make a point of talking to Chris Grayling as we go in. He is friendly and grown up. Determined to keep lines open. I appreciate it. People from Conservative Central Office are wheeled in to talk about the local elections – no one is really listening too much.

The *BBC News at One* is a joy to watch. Gove's speech is framed by our empty document being handed out. Norman Smith even holds it up in his live report and starts waving it around, saying it is becoming a real problem for Leave that they can't define what Out looks like.

The key meeting of the afternoon is in the PM's office in the Commons. He's pulled in George, Philip Hammond and Theresa May for a discussion.

Theresa arrives and sits next to me. Philip sits opposite, next to the PM, who starts the meeting by saying, 'Look, I feel both depressed and confident about this. Confident because I feel the campaign is going well – and we are really making the argument. Depressed because it's having such an impact on the party.'

Everyone agrees that it is toxic out there. Philip Hammond says he thinks we are winning the EU argument, but we look like we are being blown off course by events. He feels a few days out of date to me – still living the tax and IDS stories, which with the burn rate of the modern media are so last week.

George says we need an extra special focus on ensuring the morale of Remain MPs is kept high. Theresa says she feels she is starting to hear people who were strident Outers start to have doubts.

★   ★   ★

By Wednesday it feels like our campaign is out in front, but the Conservative party feels close to breakdown. I've been struggling for ways to articulate the particular psychodrama we are living, only to find that Philip Johnston has put his finger on it in his column in the *Telegraph*: 'It sometimes feels as if we are trapped inside the tortured mind of a party that has been wrestling with its demons for many years and now has succumbed to madness.'

Unleashing demons, indeed.

Johnston goes on to express concerns about the Chancellor accusing other Cabinet ministers of 'economic illiteracy' and others who voted for various budgets now denouncing forecasts on which they were based.

We've been talking to the White House about writing an Op-Ed piece ahead of Obama arriving for a couple of weeks now. It arrives in my inbox – and it's fair to say it delivers. After the usual, slightly pompous, opening, he takes on the Brexit argument that he should not interfere, 'The tens of thousands of America's sons who rest in Europe's cemeteries are a silent testament to just how intertwined our prosperity and security are.' He then argues why our power is enhanced, not diminished by being in the EU, before outlining the economic and security benefits. It will work for us.

Late in the day, on the way to a Stronger In event, I talk to the PM about how well he and Obama get on. Before I arrived it struck me that he was a little suspicious, but over time a close bond has been formed between them. DC agrees, saying, 'He once joked that before he was President his main impression of Britain was formed when he lost his luggage on a British Airways flight.'

We arrive at the Berkeley Hotel to find Roland Rudd, the campaign fundraiser, waiting for us. DC immediately snaps into 'Great to see you' mode. He's eager to get in, talk and get away, but once inside, he relaxes, happy to chew the fat for a bit. I grab a glass of champagne, then watch him as he stands on the stage, in front of a room with about fifteen to twenty tables, decked out in red, white and blue. It looks like a Fourth of July event. DC does a great ten minutes, trying out the patriotic case on the audience before leaving. Peter Mandelson texts me, 'If the PM says that to the country, which he will – we will win.'

I take my place at Stuart Rose's table and talk to his partner, who is charming and thoughtful. A lot of wine flows and Roland makes for a funny auctioneer, teasing up the prices. The evening is punctuated by speeches by Chuka Umunna and Michael Heseltine, who I am told is eighty-three. He gives an impressive speech, starting with how the desire to stop war was the genesis of what is now the EU. Everyone starts texting me, suggesting we use him more.

At the end of the evening, Stuart Rose sits at our table eating a plate of cheese and grapes and we chat. He is tens of thousands of pounds poorer, having bought things in the raffle. He's still attached to the campaign, but less front-line after his select committee performance. I feel for him – an impressive man who still cares, despite his experience in the grinder.

I'm slightly hungover the next morning as the No. 10 media team meet early in my office.

There's a feeling we haven't done enough to explain the craziness of Leave suggesting that we have a relationship to the EU like Albania and we should be part of the single market. When Caroline Preston, the head of broadcasting, hears us talking about the 'Albanian Model' she jokes, 'Oh no! Not another story about John Whittingdale.' I laugh about it all day.

There's also a brilliant sketch by John Crace on Cummings' appearance before the select committee. By the end of it you are left in no doubt he thinks he's crazy – though the best line is made up, claiming he said, 'Accuracy is for snake-oil pussies,' when asked why most of the info on his website is misleading or inaccurate.

There's been a big push to get Theresa May out there. Ameet has been to see her and she's agreed to do an Op-Ed this Sunday, *Marr*, and a speech on security. Graeme and I call her SpAd to find out more. She immediately says, 'I'm so sorry. Theresa just doesn't feel able to do the Op-Ed – she doesn't feel she's had time to think through the arguments.'

I don't even bother to argue back, it's so predictable. I write an ironic email, entitled 'Shock News', to the team to let them know she's pulling back.

I walk over to North House with Ameet for a committee meeting of Stronger In. This involves representatives of all the political stakeholders and key figures.

The blinds are being drawn so that people can see a screen with the latest polling on it. Peter Mandelson struggles with one of them for a bit and Damian Green says, 'What happened to your reputation as the Prince of Darkness?'

Peter laughs, then says, 'They tried to turn me into a nice guy.'

The polling is positive. We are creeping up. Ideas like being 'Stronger in Europe' are, understandably, associated with us. There's also an understanding of the 'personal risk' of leaving.

I feed this back to the team at No. 10.

I've asked Tom Edmonds to come in to demonstrate Stronger In's social media operation. I prompt him to show some of the negative stuff against us – it includes videos suggesting DC can't be trusted on the NHS. The most striking attack is a picture of DC and George with the caption to the effect: 'Jobs will go on 24th June – theirs'. I say, 'Actually it's quite effective.'

DC is a little shocked by it. George says he's aware of the truth behind it.

It's a sobering reminder they aren't pulling their punches and that they are attempting to steer this onto a wider referendum on the Government. It makes sense when they are being taken apart on the economic argument, and is clearly a threat to us.

It's tempting to fight back with our own negative material, but a more mature thought takes over – creating more blue-on-blue helps them more than it helps us.

It's 6 a.m. on Friday 22 April and I'm sitting on my sofa, reading the papers on my iPad, part of my brain still asleep.

I wince.

I've started a piece by Boris on why Obama is wrong to intervene in the EU referendum. It begins on the old chestnut that Obama got rid of the bust of Churchill from the Oval Office. Listing some of the potential reasons, it says, 'Some said it was a snub to Britain. Some said it was a symbol of the part-Kenyan President's ancestral dislike of the British Empire, of which Churchill had been such a fervent defender.'

It's at best a stupid thing to say and opens him up to accusations of racism. If I'd been advising him, I'd have told him to whip it out – particularly as he's been accused of racism in the past, talking about black people as 'piccaninnies' with 'watermelon smiles'.

As the day develops, anger grows – the strongest voice being Nick Cohen: '[Boris] is a braying charlatan, who lacks the courage even to be an honest bastard . . . but instead uses the tactics of the coward and the tricks of the fraudster, to advance his worthless career.'

He goes on, 'And with that cowardly sentence, filled with "some saids" so he could sneak away from its implications if needed – Johnson abandoned what few rights he possessed to be treated as a decent politician, journalist or man.' Ouch . . .

At least for him the 'some said' stuff masks the questionable claim that what the President is saying is 'incoherent, inconsistent and downright hypocritical'.

I warn the White House team to let them know they may get the question at the press conference.

They say the Churchill story never goes away – he replaced

it with a Martin Luther King bust, not out of any malice, and had a different Churchill bust placed elsewhere. On the part-Kenyan remark, they say that after seven years in the White House, they're used to this kind of crass remark.

The day builds slowly to the President's arrival. I take the chance to get in some Sunday commentators to see the PM and for Matt D'Ancona to do an interview for the June edition of *GQ*. I want a lot of long-lead stuff to land in the couple of weeks before the vote.

A little before Obama arrives, I find the PM in his office shining his shoes. He sits on the edge of his seat with one of those long tubes with a sponge on the end, saying, 'I'm sure the President shines his own shoes.'

The President arrives at 3 p.m. in a rainy Downing Street.

A few of us chat to his staff in the Pillared Room. George takes me to one side and chats about Europe – he thinks the campaign is going well and we should keep 'punching the bruise'. We talk about Gove and if he is setting himself up to take over. He isn't sure Gove thinks he's up to it, 'but it is being thrust in his direction, so it may be hard to resist.'

After half an hour, we are invited down to the Cabinet Room. I make a point of talking to Theresa, who is going on *Marr* this weekend.

A few minutes later, Obama saunters in with the PM. He swings round my side of the table, and shakes my hand and smiles as I say, 'Mister President.' DC introduces me. It's strange he doesn't do that to anyone else and I wonder if it's because he walked the wrong way round and realised too late.

The meeting is pretty run of the mill. The President rests his chin on his right thumb, his long index finger stretching up beyond his temple.

The PM explains that years ago the IRA mortared Downing Street, but the security is better now. 'Well, I feel quite safe,' Obama grins.

The conversation focuses on defeating Islamism – it's all very headline and general.

There's a moment where his interest is piqued by Philip Hammond discussing his recent trip to Libya.

George makes sure he turns the conversation to Europe, saying that a key flaw of the Leave campaign is their belief they can get a trade deal with the States as soon as we leave the EU – when, of course, it wouldn't be that straightforward.

Obama nods. He's been sending the odd signal that he wants to pile in on the economic message – asking for our lines on it – but we aren't sure how far he's going to go as we walk over to the Locarno Rooms in the Foreign Office. Later that day, it's claimed that George fed him the lines he used in his press conference, but that's not correct.

I accompany Obama's counter-terrorism expert across to the Foreign Office and we talk about the deep concerns over the rise of ISIL/Daesh.

I sit in a row at the front of the very full Locarno Room. The lobby is just behind me.

DC and Obama come in. Both make powerful EU statements, but it's the Q&A where things really deliver. The first question is from Chris Ship from ITV News – and inevitably EU based. Obama unpacks an answer that feels like it is twenty minutes long. He is languid, professorial and devastating.

Dealing with the point that it is inappropriate for the President to intervene, he points out that 'they' (Leave) have been speaking on behalf of the United States, by claiming it would want to do a trade deal immediately. Obama says he thought, given that, people might like to hear what the President of the United States has to say. He says Britain would have go 'to the back of the queue', because America would be far more interested in doing a deal with a big bloc.

I sit up immediately and whisper to Graeme, who is next to me, 'That's the story.' Obama meanders on for several minutes, but his point is made. Twitter is alive – they had expected him to throw in a grenade, not drop the bomb.

The next British question is from Laura Kuenssberg and includes a reference to Boris. The answer is a masterclass in how a true statesman can crush someone. Without mentioning Boris, he explains that there is a bust of Churchill outside what is called the Treaty Room where he goes to work – he sees it every day, and he says, 'I love the guy.' He then goes on to say he hopes people can understand why the first African–American President would like to have a bust of Dr Martin Luther King in his office. It's very subtle – hinting at a lot, without actually saying it. Someone tweets: 'The Boris takedown was as brutal as it was graceful.'

I sit back and relax. It feels like job done. When the news conference is over I rush back to No. 10 to catch it on the *Six*. 'Back of the queue' is the headline.

I get several texts saying things like, 'Oh my god, you have had a good day!! Hope you're smiling – nothing else can top that!'

It's true. The news is a dream. We couldn't have hoped for more. There's some weird whingeing from the Leavers that the fact he said 'queue' instead of 'line' proves it was written by No. 10. I slap it down. 'Nonsense. The President can speak for himself.'

A few of us go to the Red Lion on Whitehall for a drink. All of us have nothing to say for ourselves anymore that isn't EU related. We have all become utter bores – living it, breathing it. There are over sixty days to go. Will this be the best one? Will its impact be felt on 23 June? Who knows? But I'd rather be in our shoes tonight than theirs.

Early on Saturday morning, I get a call from DC. 'Well, I think that's job done.'

Obama's intervention feels as big as it can get – and rather than ignoring it or changing the subject, Leave are raging against it.

My gut is that all it does is accentuate the fact that our eminently reasonable friend is being straight with us.

DC is to play golf with the President. All week some at No. 10 have been warning it will come over as an elitist disaster. All week I've been saying, 'It's fine.' This morning DC is obviously regretting the prospect, as Obama plays a lot and he plays just a few times a year. 'I kind of wish I was spending the afternoon doing anything but this.'

In the afternoon, news comes through of the golf match. When it's done, DC texts me so we can give some colour to the Sundays: 'I got my par on the first hole. Obama and I played with an expert staffer of his each. Very even match, but he is much better than me! I only lost one ball, which for me playing eighteen holes is a record. Great game. DC.'

Everyone is asking – will the President's visit come to be seen as the moment that turned it all?

# Chapter 18

## We'll Get Back to You

THERESA MAY APPEARS on *Marr* this morning. I have a call to run her through her potential questions with Adam Atashzai at 8 a.m.

The interview is a simple exercise in defence – with Marr attempting to batter her on immigration and Theresa frustrating him. The Remain cause is not forwarded.

We have agreed with her team that they will be briefing out part of her speech. It's standard to run these things through No. 10 so that there are no surprises. Come 4.15 p.m. we have seen nothing.

I make some calls to ensure they send it. They say they are sorry, but it has been hectic post-*Marr*. When I read it, alarm bells begin to ring.

It starts well:

- She will put forward a positive case for shaping and leading the EU from within, citing security, trade and the economy as reasons to remain.

But there are phrases in there that will be catnip to a lobby suspecting she isn't fully signed up.

- The Home Secretary will call for a more mature debate, which acknowledges the complex challenges that lie ahead.
- Acknowledging it is a balanced judgement, the Home Secretary will say that she does not want to: 'Insult people's

intelligence by claiming that everything about the EU is perfect, that membership of the EU is wholly good, or that the sky will fall in if we vote to leave.'

My concern is that there are well-chosen phrases in there, which will make the story that the Home Secretary is chiding the Remain campaign for its approach and it's a fine decision between staying and leaving. In other words, in a world where the media is already speculating about her position, this drags everyone towards a discord story, rather than a positive statement in favour of remaining. That isn't helpful.

I call the PM, who is mowing the lawn at his constituency home. He sees the point.

After a lot of negotiation and very late for Sunday deadlines, it's agreed a version calling for 'a more mature debate', but without the 'sky falling in' line, goes out.

The next morning we discover the whole of her speech has been briefed to *The Times*, so that it can't be changed. The headlines are uncomfortable for the campaign – and feel like they've halted the momentum we built up with Obama.

Will Straw texts me: 'Are we sure May's not an agent for the other side!? Bump back to earth after last week.'

All of us are clear that we need to get back onto the economy. The OECD will be coming out to say there will be a five per cent drop in GDP if we leave; they will also point out that as an inevitable consequence of that shrinkage, immigration will go down. This will be leapt on by the Leave campaign. We also have the IMF to come, saying there will be a recession when we leave.

There's more than enough happening elsewhere. The build-up to the doctors' strike is the central concern. There's also the prospect of a rebellion over the policy of ensuring that every school becomes an academy.

The most difficult meeting is when we talk through the day we get the National Insurance Numbers (Ninos) for migrants –

revealing there are far more EU migrants in this country than previously realised. I keep waiting to hear a good answer, something I can use to explain it, but there doesn't seem to be one: there really do seem to be three times as many people here (albeit most on short visits) than we thought. Technically they are not migrants, but trying to explain that in this environment is going to be like shouting into a hurricane.

By Tuesday 26 April, there's no doubt Leave is going to put the pressure on public services, caused by immigration, at the centre of their campaign.

It's a smart play – softening the accusation that there is something straightforwardly unpleasant about their anti-immigration stance and linking lower immigration to a better economy.

Our response is to point out that experts believe public services will be hit hard if we crash the economy by leaving, and you are far more likely to be treated by an immigrant in the NHS than find yourself in the queue behind one.

On a practical level, we need the unions to throw their weight behind the referendum, marshalling their call centres and army of volunteers in the name of the cause. To help this process, there's a plan to get the former head of the TUC, Brendan Barber, to do a joint Op-Ed and visit with us, signalling we are all in the same boat.

I walk over to Stronger In for the board meeting. The long, modern white table at North House fills up. Stuart Rose is in the chair. He asks Will Straw to take us through an analysis of where we have got to.

This meeting is scheduled for two hours – and I have a feeling I'm not going to hear anything I haven't before.

When Will is finished, Roland Rudd chips in. He asks if it was sensible to let Theresa May do her speech on Monday. Stuart Rose looks to me to respond: 'This is a complex, multi-dimensional campaign. Would I say she was completely on message? No. But then I would also point to the fact that we are trying to win over the "Hearts versus Heads" group and a cold dispassionate analysis is something we know works for them.'

I go on to point out the positive editorials in the *Telegraph* on this. I am almost managing to persuade myself.

Ryan wades in behind me. He says there is a case for appearing cold and rational about the reality of immigration. No one really accepts our points.

Late in the day, I go to a meeting in George's House of Commons office with Peter Mandelson, Stephen Gilbert, Will Straw, Liz and Ameet.

Peter Mandelson comes in clutching a bottle of water in one hand and his smartphone, with white headphones dragging along the floor, in the other.

George sits on a green sofa, Peter in a green armchair. The rest of the group are on chairs dragged over from the office table.

Peter takes the lead in the meeting, firing questions. His approach is to put each area under scrutiny, sometimes with unfair assertions, and make us fight back.

Towards the end he asks, 'Why do you all insist on bringing a spoon to a knife fight?'

'In what way?'

'It's clear that Boris and Gove need to be taken out by big Tory hitters.'

We begin by taking him through it gently. George points out that we all agreed that we didn't want to turn this into a Tory psychodrama. Peter persists. I decide to be a bit tougher; what does he want us to do? Surely he can see that Boris has had a torrid time of it, literally accused of being a racist. What would we say to Gove that wouldn't simply elevate the soap opera? No – the best thing we can do is to keep reminding people this is cross-party and minimise all that crap. He seems to accept this.

I show Will Straw out and walk to the Tube with him. I ask

him how he's getting on with his new baby. It sounds like it's as busy a time at home as it is at work with a toddler and a new baby. I tell him I think he is doing remarkably well – diplomatically picking his way through all of this, while trying to be a decent father.

I arrive home to receive a call from Tom Newton Dunn at the *Sun*. He says they are going to splash on the fact that a core group of aides and ministers are using a WhatsApp group, with the express aim of getting round the Freedom of Information act.

I had earlier taken a call from Harry Cole and ended up saying, 'I'm not going to comment on this. It's nonsense.'

I awake to it being the splash and a curious one at that. Social media is going crazy, because yesterday the Hillsborough verdicts came through, prompting blanket media coverage – except on the front page of the *Sun*, which is seen as insensitive, given their history on the story.

I'm bemused. The headline is: 'CAM'S GROUP TEXT SCANDAL', next to a picture of him on his BlackBerry, which we don't think can use WhatsApp. It goes on, 'Aides use WhatsApp to keep EU plot secret', before going on to quote Matthew Elliott, from the Leave campaign, 'Not only are David Cameron's taxpayer-funded spin doctors running the In campaign, they have now been caught trying to hide their secrets from the public.'

All of this is justified by some guff about none of this appearing in official records or Freedom of Information requests. A leading Leave campaigner is quoted, 'Attempts to avoid the Freedom of Information Act in what is supposed to be a legitimate activity will lead to scandal and embarrassment. This will reinforce the public's view that Remain is prepared to cheat to win the referendum.'

Those of us in the group, which is actually used to make sure we are all up to speed on fast-moving stories when we are out of the office, and late at night to take the piss out of each other, are contemptuous. Does anyone involved in the story really understand what it is or why it is used? Laura Trott, who is the special adviser running the grid of stories coming up, puts her finger on it by saying, 'Basically, they are accusing us of texting each other.'

My point is that we also have conference calls — is the telephone also a nefarious attempt to get round Freedom of Information and the twenty-year rule? What about conversations when we run into each other in the corridor?

The next day, the BBC is leading in on the fact that Leave have put out eight economists in favour of Brexit. It seems to me to be the worst example so far of them mistaking balance for being impartial. Kamal Ahmad does not point out that they are wildly out of synch with mainstream opinion among economists, giving people another misleading impression of the weight of debate.

Leave have put up Priti Patel to do interviews on the morning programmes. On the *Today* programme she asserts that we'll be able to strip back regulations and take away huge burdens if we vote out. It's pointed out to her that the main ways of saving money would be getting rid of regulations that people actually appreciate (e.g. the working time directive, which says you must have a break after six hours). She struggles, unable to name any regulation she would get rid of, other than on packaging. In the end she is reduced to saying we'd have an audit when we leave and then decide. She claims Remain is all about big business and big Government abusing their power and ignoring small business and the little people.

I arrive at my desk fired up. We need to combat this message and get some people saying with moral authority, 'How dare they claim to speak for working people?'

I've invited John Witherow, the editor of *The Times*, to see the PM. We say that in a newspaper environment where so many are campaigning against, *The Times* – a business paper with a rational economic view – feels almost indifferent. He says his readers want to see both sides of the debate. Fine, but it feels to us that they are cutting Leave a lot of slack, in an environment where others are cutting us none.

DC underlines the point by saying that, losing the economic argument, Leave has gone all UKIP, 'Pull up the drawbridge and pretend it'll be the land of milk and honey.'

'Shrewd though,' says Witherow.

I jump in the car with DC to go to King's Cross. I want to lodge some ideas in his head before he spends time with Sir Brendan Barber. As the police motorbikes help us thread our way through traffic, I point out Barber is quite softly spoken and we need to make sure he has his say – making clear he is a passionate advocate for working people.

Brendan is waiting with Stronger In's Amy Richards. We walk to the train together and DC and he sit opposite each other. They discuss the importance of getting the unions fired up. He says, 'When they get their boots on, the unions are very effective campaigners.'

Brendan is completely open and we appreciate that he is taking a risk with his own reputation, working with a Conservative prime minister. They chat away for the rest of the journey and share the PM's car to a Costa Coffee in Peterborough, where we sit outside. Several people come up to DC and ask for selfies, including a guy who says he's called Nigel Lawson.

When the time is right, we move on to Caterpillar. It feels like this idea has been long in the preparation. I see two giant posters in the car park, each covered with a black sheet. Liz has shown me a video of them struggling to get the sheet off, but promises me it will be okay. DC and Brendan walk up and watch as they are unveiled, one filled with 'Experts who believe we would be stronger in Europe' and the other headed 'Experts who believe Britain should leave Europe', which is empty save for a magnifying glass revealing the words, 'We'll get back to you.'

When the picture is revealed DC and Brendan walk to the journalists and deliver their words. Brendan is great – saying this is about what is best for workers.

The new best friends go to the board room for discussions with Caterpillar's board, before a walk around the factory, where they will 'bump into' Laura Kuenssberg and do an interview.

She starts with Barber, who really delivers, before getting a bee in her bonnet about, 'You said you would be prepared to leave the EU – now you say there'll be doom if we do? Can you see why people don't trust you?' It's a legitimate challenge, but the PM is able to pivot to the fact that our economy would be under threat.

We then move to an enormous Cameron Direct – a format where the PM takes questions from people, usually at a business. This time there are 1,500 staff members in the audience. I have persuaded them that it should be the PM on his own. The line that we are setting aside party differences in the national interest is a good one, but a slip under sustained questioning will be blown out of proportion.

The head of Caterpillar UK introduces the event – he could not be clearer to his staff; the company believes it would be better if we remained in the EU.

DC runs through his now familiar arguments. The key moment for me is when a reasonable man talks about pressure in his child's classroom – with teachers having to give a lot of attention to pupils who do not speak English as a first language. It's a real issue in his life and not one that is easy to bat away.

When I get back to London, the Labour party is caught up in an anti-semitism row, partly initiated by the PM in the Commons yesterday, and now catalysed by some crazy comments by Ken Livingstone about Hitler and Zionism.

George's instinct is to keep hitting Labour hard. My view is they are already doing more than enough to cause themselves trouble on this and we need to understand that looking like we are adding to their woes is hardly going to encourage the leadership to work with us in the referendum.

Others, who are closer to the MPs, warn that they are already suspicious of the cross-party campaign and we need to demonstrate we understand who the real enemy is.

We stop to watch the 6 p.m. news, which would normally be a dream for us: ten minutes of an utter shambles for Labour. It starts with footage of an irate John Mann chasing Ken Livingstone up the Millbank stairs shouting that he is a disgraceful apologist for Hitler, before Corbyn is cornered in a 'crisis – what crisis?' moment. It is obvious to me he is still in denial about the scale of his problems. I wonder if this could be the moment when Labour goes for him, destabilising him to the point where his position is untenable. That would blot out the sun on the referendum for us for a long time. In the latest lesson about strange bedfellows, it is clear more than ever how much we need a strong Labour party getting their people out to vote, not a civil war.

The good news is the Kuenssberg piece on the PM and Brendan is great. Our pictures and the strength of our message punch through. The Leave event is a mess, a group of tired-looking economists in a hot, half-empty room.

The next morning, George feels the Radio 4 bulletin has been too negative and asks me to call to make some points.

I ring the BBC Hotline, set up so that the campaigns can supposedly complain and get a quick response.

It rings for some time before someone finally answers, sounding utterly bemused. He says, 'I should have forwarded this number to someone else. I don't know what to do. I'm putting the bulletins out. So there's not much I can do.'

So much for the 'Hotline'. I call someone else to talk them through it . . .

John Major is on the 8.10 slot. We have asked him to do the essay making the case for Remain. It's powerful stuff, though the interview off the back is a bit scruffy. There's a section when he says, 'If people want complete sovereignty, they can go to North Korea.' I know what he means – the consequence of having complete power over your affairs, while not cooperating with others, is dreadful, but it sounds like another extreme statement in a binary battle.

The PM has a call with Tony Hall, the Director General of the BBC, to discuss how its new unitary board will work. DC manages to get across my point that the BBC Business and Economics unit is giving a misleading impression on the balance of the debate. He says he will look at it.

I call DC to talk about it afterwards. He tells me he watched *Question Time* last night and it confirmed what we have all been thinking: this is now a binary argument, a straight fight between the economy and immigration. We have closed down the economic argument – pinning them back onto immigration.

It feels like a strategic victory, but in another way it's concerning. As DC puts it, 'It's an argument to which we don't have a strong enough answer – other than: wrecking our economy is no way to deal with it.' He wants us to think through our response. What are the consequences of being more forward leaning? Should we be harder line?

I tell him I'll set up a discussion and begin an email chain that lasts the whole day – and which I end up wishing I hadn't started.

The first response is that we have good lines on immigration – we just need to deploy them more. Those lines are essentially:

- accepting people have concerns.
- pointing out the significance of the reforms the PM achieved on curbing welfare payments to migrants (which test well).

- setting out the potentially devastating consequences to our economy of ending free movement and urging people not to throw the baby out with the bath water.

Will believes our challenge is getting politicians to use the script, because it jars with the more defensive position that Labour and Conservative politicians take on the issue. He suggests a big speech from the PM on the importance of the single market.

Others point out that freedom of movement is a simple fact that we struggle to get round – we cannot win an argument about control, but we can win an argument about a strong economy.

I don't disagree with a lot of this, but there's a problem. We have had a lot of success with the assertion that Leave believe a recession is a 'price worth paying'. It seems to me that the weakness in our argument on immigration is the same in reverse. These levels of immigration are a price worth paying to ensure a strong economy.

So, a question we will almost certainly be hammered with in this now binary debate is: 'Let me be clear: you are saying European immigration – whereby anyone who wants to work in our country and is not a criminal, should be allowed to come here, and use our public services – is a price worth paying?' We can keep pointing to the hard-won curbs on welfare payments from the renegotiation, but it means we will struggle with the person saying, you don't understand what it is like at my child's school, or going into my local A&E.

We are in danger of sounding like an out-of-touch elite. In a general election, immigration is only part of the argument – in this referendum, it will be at least half of it.

Ryan agrees with me that our position reads as: we think free movement is a price worth paying for membership of the single market and the economic benefits that brings. The difference between our position and theirs is that, when tested, there is net support for what we say, but not for what they say.

And this is the nub of everything.

We believe we have the winning argument.

The PM's next call is with Gordon Brown, who sounds gruff, but engaged.

DC underlines the importance of getting Labour involved and not turning this into a Tory psychodrama.

Gordon Brown believes, 'There's been some success getting the Tory vote back in the fold,' but his primary concern is that the Labour vote is not secure. He says we have to focus on different messages for different people and we have to remember that the economic message doesn't always work for people who are not already economically secure. He believes our message for them must not be one of fear, but of optimism for the future. 'Most of all,' he says, 'it's horses for courses. Including a positive voice for a better future for Labour voters.'

All of this sounds encouraging, but he then makes a rather apocalyptic point, 'You are facing a perfect storm. Immigration, terrorism and a fragile EU economy . . . No one believes leaving would make things any better,' but he seems to be pointing to a kind of anarchic 'to hell with it all' attitude.

I'm reminded of one of my favourite films from the 1970s, the seminal *Network*, where a suicidal newsreader persuades half of America to scream, 'I'm as mad as hell and I'm not going to take this any more!' and someone points out, 'The American people want somebody to articulate their rage for them.'

By Saturday 30 April, it's plain Michael Gove is prepared to embrace immigration as Leave's main argument. He writes a piece for the *Mail* that causes widespread revulsion in the Remain camp. He warns of the threat from the East, with a potential 77 million Turks and Albanians coming here with their criminal gangs. I feel increasingly angry at the tactics, though my rational side thinks they have finally abandoned all hope of winning the economic argument and are simply hammering the one point that works for them. Gove now appears to have bought, and to be selling, the UKIP argument wholesale.

DC emails – we need to be clear that we will not allow enlargement of the EU.

# MAY

# Chapter 19

## World War Three

THE STRONGER IN board meeting at the start of May begins with some polling. Andrew presents it in an unvarnished manner, which seems to spook several people. He says:

- There's an 8.8% lead for Remain in phone polls.
- A 0.6% lead in online polls.
- The phone lead is down from 20% at the start of the campaign.
- There's good evidence underlying indicators have recently started going our way.

He ends up telling a startled group that the polls are in even more of a mess than during the election, with the pollsters not really certain what the hell is going on. He predicts the polls will tighten more.

All of this leads to the inevitable question – if the polls are wrong, how can we be sure of our assertions? Particularly how, in a straight Economics *vs* Immigration fight, we will win?

There are several attempts to reassure people. Will says, 'We have a good strategy, which we can either stick to or panic.'

The group moves on for drinks at the Mandarin Oriental, where George Osborne is speaking at a fundraiser.

From there we move on to a dinner being held by Stuart Rose for us in the Lotus Rooms. It's an expensive hotel, and we eat in a grand, dimly lit room. When we enter, some are shocked to see Hugo Dixon has been invited to speak. He is clearly a very bright man, capable of creating the InFacts myth-busting website about Leave nonsense. He looks like a scruffy academic – more interested in argument than his appearance.

When the first course of avocado is gone, he sits slouched in his chair and pontificates about the campaign. He is clear that Leave are being utterly misleading, but he has what feels like a very big dig at No. 10, 'You seem to be avoiding the obvious thing, which is taking down Michael Gove and Boris Johnson. I know you feel you have a party to put back together at the end of this, but you have to get over your obsession with avoiding blue-on-blue.'

As he says it, his eyes flick towards me several times. I begin to prepare my response, which I know I will be asked for, because Stuart Rose keeps catching my eye.

When Hugo is done, Stuart asks me what way I think the papers will go. I tell him it's obvious the *Mail*, *Sun*, *Telegraph* and *Express* will all be Out. There's a question mark over *The Times* and the *Sunday Times*, though I suspect the former will be In. The *Mirror* and the *Guardian* will be Remain, as will the *Observer* and the *Mail on Sunday*.

I decide to answer Hugo. 'You did us the courtesy of being very frank in your talk earlier. So I hope you don't mind if I am frank in response: you are the siren voice that is calling us to the rocks.'

He shifts in his seat. Across the table I see Ryan Coetzee and Stephen Gilbert smiling.

'The easiest thing in the world would be for us to turn this into a Tory psychodrama. The media would love it and it would blot out almost every other story. Instead of listening to what you say – I think we need to double down on what is truly remarkable in this campaign. People from the Greens, to the Lib Dems, to Labour and the Conservatives are setting aside their differences in the national interest to say we should stay in the EU. It means we have moments like the PM standing with Brendan Barber – thank you for taking a risk and showing leadership, by the way, Brendan –,' I nod to him sitting at the top of the table, 'and show that we are the reasonable, sensible moderates, and not engaged in internecine fights.'

Ryan and Stephen wade in behind me.

As the conversation develops, I am asked to speak again, 'One of the things I have learned in this job is that there are about 3,500 people who live in the political/media village. Their values, what they think and believe, are often dramatically different to the 35 million voters we have to win over. What I have learned is that people who focus on the 3,500 and not the 35 million are almost always the ones who fail.'

On Wednesday 4 May, there's grumpiness all around at the morning meeting about the planned U-turn on child refugees.

Going through it, DC looks at the two or three MPs present who are glum and tells them, 'It's no good looking miserable about us having to make concessions, when a large part of the Parliamentary party isn't holding the line.'

I get some grim texts from Fraser Nelson, who – after rowing out for the PM in the *Telegraph* last week, saying the grown-up thing to do was to limit the number coming into the UK, because not doing so simply acts as a magnet and puts more children in danger – now smells a U-turn and is irritated. His view is if we bend on this, we are just signalling to people we will bend on anything.

I have a go at defending the PM to him. But I think we should go down fighting in the Commons. The PM and George explain to me why that's hopelessly naive, saying if you're a Conservative MP, you don't expect to lose votes. 'Well, don't bloody vote against the Government,' I say petulantly.

Most of this week is spent preparing for the local election results, but on Thursday I walk over to North House for a meeting with what has become the core team linking No. 10 and the campaign, Will, Stephen, Ryan, Ameet and Liz. We start by looking at some interesting work from Jim Messina. It breaks down the areas of the country we should be targeting. Our strongholds are Scotland, London and big university cities like Manchester. It also lists areas where there are rich pickings in terms of 'in play' households that are open to persuasion. The east of England is very well represented, so are Leeds, Bradford, Doncaster and Barnsley, which we can hit hard.

Back at No. 10, I take some decisions on which television programmes the PM will do in the run-up to the referendum. The default position has been to keep our options open, but we're just a few weeks out and I'm getting pressure, not just from the broadcasters, but from other parts of the campaign. If we don't fill the vacuum, there's a real chance we could see some people representing us that could spell disaster. The usual view is expressed that we should avoid them. I take a deep breath. 'OK – maybe I have drunk the Kool-Aid, but I don't think it's good enough. Do you really want to spend the whole period being called a chicken?'

'Not really . . . ,' says DC.

'Well – it's the fight of our lives. You're the best thing we have. I don't want to be sitting here on 24th June wishing we hadn't saved some of our ammunition.'

I appear to be shifting them. I make the case for doing a programme with Farage in it. He's the unacceptable face of Leave to millions – let's put him in the centre of the frame.

The results of the local elections pour in on Friday 6 May, and it looks like no one won and no one lost.

There's something for everyone if you're prepared to look.

We did not go backwards. Ruth Davidson's energetic Scottish campaign took her to the previously unthinkable position of being leader of the opposition. Labour's disastrous performance there is evened out by victory in London.

I spend parts of the day ensuring we are fighting our corner on all of this, but as ever, my eye is really on Europe.

At 6 p.m. I get a cab to Lynton Crosby's investiture party at the Australian High Commissioner's house tucked in a lovely street by the Albert Hall.

As I approach, I see Boris on his bike. Traffic is slow and he is literally outside my window for a couple of minutes until we get ahead. His hair is as tousled as ever – people on the pavement stare and try to engage. When I arrive, he is a minute behind. He says, 'Great to see you, Craig, great,' before walking straight by. I smile, as I get the distinct impression I'm really not the person he wants to talk to.

A big theme of his and Sir Lynton's speech is how far he has come from rural Australia. He really has achieved a lot.

On Saturday morning, I plant myself on my sofa and don't move for several hours. There's an endless merry-go-round of calls on Europe – making sure loose ends are tied, hares are set running or stopped.

The debates are definitely a worry for Leave. We are doing our usual trick of not giving anything away. They brief James Forsyth that it would be a scandal if we don't end up debating Gove or Boris, but we know any such programme would be a Tory psychodrama and won't do it.

That leads me into a negotiation with ITV, who have offered to move their programme by a week (earlier) and a *Question Time* format with Farage answering questions in the first half and the PM doing the same in the second.

I tell the PM it's as good a deal as I'm going to get.

On Sunday, he says he is moving to that view, almost winking at me. I laugh and ask, 'Any chance you're going to reach that view soon?'

'I'm moving at my own pace . . . I'm sure we will get there.'

Gove is on *Marr*. He will undoubtedly be asked about an intervention from John Sawers and Jonathan Evans (the recently retired heads of MI6 and MI5), who have been the splash in *The Times*.

I watch Gove intently. In one sense he is very polished. But, for me, he fails the blink test. There's something too fluent, too certain about him.

The opening exchanges with Marr feel like sparring. But it really heats up when he is asked about the economy. When asked if, 'yes or no', should we be in the single market, Gove goes for it: 'No. We should be outside the single market.' He then goes on about how we should get access to the market on terms we dictate. It is pure fantasy land.

I call James Chapman, who is with the Chancellor about to do the new *Peston on Sunday* on ITV. I tell him, 'Gove just made a big mistake on the single market. George needs to be clear it would be a catastrophic mistake to leave – they are being irresponsible.' They are on in minutes. James says, 'Got it!' and hangs up.

Minutes later, George goes in pounding. This is when he is at his best – spot an opportunity, grab the ball and run. I feel proud of how he delivers a great soundbite on this being about real people's jobs. This evening he jokes with me about me ringing up, getting him to say something, and it coming out on air.

I call Stronger In. We need to leap on this and get a press notice out really hammering them. The team go to town, getting every business person and economist we can to ram home the point. By lunchtime we have a very impressive press notice, ranging from Carolyn Fairbairn of easyJet to Juergen Maier of Siemens, saying Gove is playing fast and loose with jobs and the economy.

I call the PM to update him. He didn't watch, but had heard

Gove was good. I tell him the interview was fine, but the clip won't work for him and that is how most people will encounter the interview.

On Monday there's a hilarious editorial in the *Mail* in response to our briefing of the PM's 'Patriotic case for staying in the EU' speech.

It says: 'With 45 days to go, is it too much to hope Mr Cameron will tone down the rhetoric, stop pretending he's secured a game-changing deal for Britain – and start treating the electorate like adults?'

I text a *Daily Mail* journalist, 'Pot?! Kettle?!' He claims to be trying to make our case and use as many of our quotes as he can – and pleads to have early access to our briefs.

DC gives his speech early at the British Museum. I don't go, with too much to do here, but have it on in the background as I go through the meetings. It looks impressive, but it's a little long. It's designed to make the security case for staying in the EU – how the institution has helped bring peace and has been a beacon for Western values. I've been a little cynical about this, but having read through it all, I really can see the Niall Ferguson point, that it's ultimately treaties and meetings, or trenches.

I get Philip Johnston, the leader writer for the *Telegraph*, in to talk to DC. I like him very much – he's an older bloke, with a London accent, who sees the world in sensible, simple terms. I can't imagine anything ruffling him too much.

DC begins by discussing the tendency of Leave to play the man. If anyone says anything, they write them up as 'washed up' and having made errors in the past. DC laments them not engaging in the argument. Phil says, 'Well, their problem is – how do you prove a negative,' before underlining his concerns about how the party will be put back together at the end of all of this.

DC says, 'If we win, it'll be fine. I'll be magnanimous. But if we lose it will be a disaster – we'll spend years dealing with the mess.' He goes on, 'What's interesting is Gove told me he didn't actually want a referendum . . . and Boris doesn't actually want to leave.'

My day has been punctuated by prepping for a presentation to the Conservative In group of MPs. I said I would do it, but only if it was clear what I was being asked to do and we didn't all trip over each other.

This led to endless chopping and changing. To the extent I said several times I was very happy to step down . . . anyway, it ended with Stephen Gilbert, Andrew Cooper, the PM, Nick Herbert and me all giving talks. By the time we get to the end of our presentations, it is forty-five minutes in.

It seems to go OK and they like the fact that I'm able to show them plenty of shiny videos, including a very moving one of veterans of the Second World War saying they fought so that there could be a lasting peace in Europe, and the EU is part of that. The presentation goes well, though there's no shortage of people pointing out that the Union flag in one of my slides was upside down.

Graeme walks back to No. 10 a couple of steps ahead of me. He's taking a call. When he's done, he tells me IDS has done an interview with the *Sun*. He's told them Angela Merkel vetoed a proposal for the emergency brake on migrants the night before the PM gave a key speech – and at the last minute we changed policy.

I traipse through to the private office with Graeme. We agree it's an interesting approach from IDS. He's looking for ways to destabilise the Government.

In the end, our answer is rather wet. A non-denial denial, which won't help.

I get back to my office to find James Harding, the BBC's director of news, keen to talk to me. He says he saw the PM and George at Alan Parker's sixtieth birthday party and both told him we wouldn't be doing any programmes with them.

He criticises me, saying, 'I think we need to have a relationship where you tell me that kind of thing. I was genuinely in the dark about this.'

I'm surprised. I got him in to see the PM. We said we wouldn't do blue-on-blue programmes. He said they weren't in a position to tell Leave who they put up – so we were at an impasse.

He then makes an offer I thought he wasn't prepared to make. He's suggesting Gove do a *Question Time* with a studio audience on 15 June – and that we do one with Nigel Farage on the same programme, but facing the audience separately, on 19 June. I agree to discuss it with DC tomorrow – though I doubt either of us will think giving Farage such a golden opportunity four nights before the vote will make sense.

The next morning I'm in the trenches with the BBC from early on.

They arc leading on an IDS speech. They mention our letter from senior figures in US administrations going back forty years – all saying we should remain in the EU. But there is no mention of another letter from five previous NATO Secretary Generals. If I had to choose which they would report, it would be the Sec Gens letter, because it destroys the Leave case that we don't need the EU because of NATO.

I call the famous Hotline – which simply rings out.

I call the Millbank editor. No answer.

I finally get hold of the radio bulletins editor, who was, understandably, in the shower.

I point out that Leave make the case of NATO as the only guarantor of peace in Europe. This is a demolition of their case – why isn't it up there?

He seems to agree – and says it will be on the 8 a.m.

When I get in, DC is feeling a little uneasy about the response to the speech yesterday. He clearly feels stung by the hyperbolic headlines – claiming he was suggesting we could face World War Three if we left. Of course, he said nothing of the kind and it is a gross misrepresentation of a thoughtful speech. We've been around the block enough to know that often it's not what you have actually said that damns you, but what others claim you said.

In another reminder of the topsy-turvy world we are inhabiting, he says, 'I had to read the bloody *Guardian* to get balanced coverage of what I actually said!'

He also feels we signalled he was doing the speech too early, allowing Boris to cobble something together and be given equal coverage for it in another 'Clash of the Titans' TV treatment.

George points out, 'This is now a daily battle. It's like the general election.'

DC is irritated by his/our self-imposed decision to fight by Marquess of Queensberry rules, 'On IDS they [Leave] would say he was a washed-up politician. I mean look at what IDS said about John Major – saying he had a failed economic policy.'

We are all clear that we have to get back to the single market.

Having been won round to the security speech, I now see that no one really wants to hear or buy our security story. Detail on data sharing and the European Arrest Warrant is too abstract.

I email James Harding to let him know we're saying 'No' to his Sunday night before the referendum proposal. DC and I talked about it – and rejected it.

He calls almost immediately and asks why we won't do it. I explain it's not appealing to hand such a high-profile opportunity to Farage so close to the vote. He isn't happy. I suspect he thinks I'm playing games. I'm not. There's just nothing in it for us.

Later in the day I talk to DC and suggest we go with ITV and Sky and reject the BBC. He agrees, saying he may well be open to a BBC programme in the final days, but let's see how it goes.

I head to Stronger In, where we run through the final month of the campaign. We squeeze around the table that is too big for the room.

While I'm there, I get a call asking me to come to the private office.

I'm obviously unable to attend. When I get back, it is over. But the PM seeks me out. He has been caught on camera at Buckingham Palace talking to the Queen, the Archbishop of Canterbury, Chris Grayling and John Bercow saying we are building up the corruption summit, 'Actually, we've got some fantastically corrupt countries like Afghanistan and Nigeria coming.' The Archbishop looks uncomfortable.

DC says, 'I am sorry. I look terrible. I have a glass of champagne in my hand. I was trying to fill the silence. No one speaks at these things . . . no one warned me. I didn't realise this stuff was going to be released.'

The way I see it – he may have been a little undiplomatic, but does anyone think Nigeria isn't corrupt?

I suggest we point out to journalists that the leaders of both countries referred to have written in a book accompanying the summit about how corruption is endemic.

We disappear into a meeting to discuss the campaign. Andrew is here to run through more polling.

He tells us, 'Lots of people say leaving the EU is bad for me, but I'll vote Brexit.' That seems to be irrational to all of us. Surely, as in the Scottish referendum, these people will see that it could be an act of self-harm leaving and come back?

The one worry is that the statement, 'The EU needs us more than we need them' is still working for them.

Tonight the PM watches the six o'clock news and texts me his amazement that the story was fine. James Robbins did a lead story on his gaffe – basically saying the PM didn't say anything that anyone didn't think was true and No. 10 is nothing other than relaxed.

As I leave, I get a call from Simon Case. The Queen is about to knock us off the news. It's emerged that she, too, was caught on camera – talking to the Gold Commander on the Chinese state visit, saying the Chinese had been 'very rude' to our ambassador.

Apparently the cameraman, who the Palace have been employing for years, forgot to turn off his microphone. There is hours of footage of the garden party that has been put out there, in which anyone could have said God knows what.

# Chapter 20

## Welcome to the Labour Party

O N WEDNESDAY 11 May, the 'gaffes' story is still leading the news. In terms of the referendum, our decision to put Gordon Brown front and centre appears to be misfiring.

He is supposed to be working with us, but is running an idiosyncratic media strategy, which involves him briefing the *Guardian* and the *Mirror* a story about how being a member of the EU helps crack down on tax avoidance. Quite how this will persuade Labour supporters to vote Remain, or get a huge amount of attention, is beyond me.

I am assured by Labour figures at Stronger In that this works pretty well with Labour voters. Really?

I'm also concerned by the extent to which it's being claimed in the Leave media that the PM said there would be World War Three if we left the EU. He didn't – or anything close to it. It's a fiction that's now being reported as fact. What was a long and thoughtful speech about how our security is enhanced by being members of the EU is now a gross caricature.

Boris is launching his bus tour today. Labour's Gisela Stuart is next to him in most shots, looking like a hostage, being used to pretend they have widespread Labour support. As the day goes on, we see him in various locations – waving asparagus, licking an ice-cream and doing other photo-friendly things.

In comparison, Brown looks dour. There's concern in No. 10 that we are being forced to rely on Labour figures who are falling flat – while Boris looks energised.

I've been invited to a dinner at Roland Rudd's house. I find it by spotting the 'Stronger In' posters in his windows.

He is a kind and generous host, with a range of guests from Chuka Umunna to the film director and screenwriter, Christopher McQuarrie. I'm relieved to be sitting next to Christopher, because I can chat to him about movies, instead of having to talk about the referendum. The conversation ranges from his screenplay for *The Usual Suspects* to the fact that the Coen Brothers' *Miller's Crossing* is one of our favourite films.

Halfway through the evening, Roland taps his wine glass and suggests that we all talk about the campaign. 'Oh God!' I think. I'm sitting in a room including opposition politicians and George Parker from the *FT*. But for the most part, I worry about the Americans sitting round the table, who mustn't have a clue.

Roland begins the conversation by talking about how tough it is responding to people who are willing to use obscure and questionable claims. Chuka Umunna chips in, saying he wants to see more passion – and challenges me to have Conservatives attack Conservatives.

I'm asked to speak next. I reply that it may be hard for people who are 'ardent internationalists' to understand, but we are fighting for the 'Heads *vs* Hearts' group, who just don't believe the EU is all wonderful. What works for them is hard facts and we just have to be practical about that. Several people around the table join me in support of this course of action.

When I get back home, I catch up with how the news that we are doing a programme with Farage on ITV is going down. Leave are spitting tacks.

The *Sun*'s political editor has tweeted: 'Got to give it to Craig Oliver tonight. Has managed to get PM out of a blue-on-blue, and royally shaft Vote Leave and the BBC at the same time.'

I look at a bunch of raging tweets from Leave and go to sleep.

★   ★   ★

On Thursday morning I wake up to the Leave campaign appearing to have lost the plot.

In a moment of late-night intemperance, their press team sent round an extraordinary response threatening ITV and No. 10:

> The Establishment has tried everything from spending taxpayers' money on pro-EU propaganda to funding the IN campaign via Goldman Sachs. The polls have stayed fifty–fifty. They're now fixing the debates to shut out the official campaign. ITV is led by people like Robert Peston, who campaigned for Britain to join the Euro. ITV has lied to us in private, while secretly stitching up a deal with Cameron to stop Boris Johnson or Michael Gove debating the issues properly. ITV has effectively joined the official IN campaign and there will be consequences for its future – the people in No. 10 won't be there for long.

It's clear the ITV hacks are shocked that they are being threatened with 'consequences' by a group of people who could find themselves running the country. Robert Peston says he thinks someone has hacked the Leave account – he has never campaigned to join the Euro. Another tells me Dominic Cummings was 'unbelievably pissed off last night'.

I talk to Michael Grade, a Conservative peer, who is a highly respected voice in the broadcast world, having had positions at the top of the BBC, ITV and Channel 4. He's outraged that Leave are threatening ITV and says he will put out a statement.

It's also cheering to see Mark Carney, the Governor of the Bank of England, knocking the ball out of the park at a press conference. He says there could be a string of terrible occurrences, ranging from a technical recession to higher prices. It's now at the top of the BBC's running order.

Graeme Wilson and I walk through St James's Park to Lancaster House to brief the PM ahead of his press conference at the corruption summit. The sun is shining, people are in deckchairs, and it feels as if no one is worrying about the prospect of Brexit.

As we approach, we pass a large demonstration. Several of them are with megaphones shouting something I can't quite understand. They are watched by a group of bemused policemen in shirt sleeves.

Lancaster House is the most ornate of Government buildings. We jog up its grand staircase and find our way to the bilateral room, where the PM is waiting. We could be in the Élysée Palace or Versailles. He is standing – looking like he's had enough of being in a stuffy room on a hot day. There are three subjects we need to brief him on:

- Carney.
- A report pointing out the number of National Insurance numbers handed out to migrants is higher than previously thought.
- Leave attacking us and ITV over the *Question Time* programme.

Carney is a simple opportunity to put the ball in the back of the net. The Ninos story is going far better than we could have hoped, and I can only think there is too much news around for it to be covered properly. On debates, DC makes a joke about when he heard an aide to a Justice Secretary had been threatening a national TV station, he thought he was hearing about one of the countries in the corruption summit, not the UK.

Meanwhile Christine Lagarde, the head of the International Monetary Fund, comes out and says there are no good arguments for Brexit – and the forecast ranges from 'bad to very, very bad'.

I can't imagine how the last few days must feel to the Leave campaign – a constant pummelling, leading to more and more errors (forced and unforced).

Surely they feel on the ropes?

By Sunday, it feels like Leave are making even more unforced errors.

Boris has written a piece saying that for 2,000 years people have been trying to unite Europe, including Napoleon and Hitler. The EU is doing the same.

This seems curious after his Obama 'part-Kenyan' quote. There's no shortage of people queueing up to have a go. Lord Bramall, who is in his nineties and stormed the beaches on D-Day before eventually becoming Chief of the Defence Staff, is particularly critical.

Mark Carney is on *Marr*. A smooth performance – with calm authority telling the interviewer when he is simply wrong. His best quotes are that the Brexiteers are in a state of denial, and saying there will be a material impact on growth and inflation.

I celebrate the evening of my birthday by driving in to work for the Sunday meeting. Kate gives me sympathy, saying it's hardly a great way to celebrate.

Before we go in, I get a call from James Harding. He tells me the BBC is now prepared to offer the PM a *Question Time*-style programme on his own, with Gove doing a separate one on *his* own. DC agrees. It has taken months, but we have finally reached an agreement.

The Sunday meeting has an odd feel, because it's been a hot day and everyone is dressed in summer clothes. George reads a section from a speech he is planning, which includes detailing everyone who is supporting the case for Remain.

He concludes, 'This is not a conspiracy. This is a consensus.'


On Monday 16 May, the Leave campaign get a letter published in the *Telegraph* saying 300 businesses support them.

The Remain campaign response has been to mock it as underwhelming – nowhere near the legions of businesses supporting us. The PM and George question this approach, suggesting we should have woken up to an entirely discredited letter, with people up all night to achieve our goal.

I'm not convinced. The morning bulletins' lead EU story is

what the PM has, unusually, written in the *Daily Mirror*. The letter isn't much covered, though we all understand we must not let Leave argue us to a draw on business, when we have such a clear lead on the issue.

There are worrying signs that the Electoral Commission guidance, warning businesses, institutions and charities about campaigning too explicitly, is having a real chilling effect. Leading figures have contacted us to say their lawyers are spooking them. They also say there's an unpleasantness to the debate that was putting people off, with some finding there's a cost to speaking up, because Leave is so angry with whoever does. In the City, it's believed the damage to the financial services sector would be vast – with no reason to see why the EU would allow UK-based companies to have passporting rights allowing them to operate freely in the event of Brexit.

I head to North House for a board meeting. There is an endless, though very competent presentation on the 'get out the vote' strategy.

I'm asked to run through our media strategy – and then we are into a debates meeting.

We sit in a smaller room, where sandwiches and crisps are provided courtesy of David Sainsbury. We run through the debates. I tell Will the PM is signed up on the BBC now. I detect there's a bit of a question about whether we should have engaged with them on that.

The main sticking point is whether it is wise to allow Angela Eagle to be the Labour voice in the final Wembley debate. Lucy Thomas, a former BBC presenter and the campaign's sharp deputy, wants Ruth Davidson to represent Conservatives – and Sadiq Khan to represent Labour. Her point is both of them have a touch of political stardust about them at the moment, following the recent elections. As Ruth puts it more bluntly, she is too similar to Angela Eagle, and it will look like we are making a heavy-handed point.

We go round the houses . . . but don't really get anywhere.

I come out of the meeting to find a copy of a letter from the company Serco has been briefed to the *Mail*. It is dated 8 February – just before the end of the renegotiation. It offers ways of helping get big business to support staying in. The bulk of the letter is about prisons and in the top right it indicates it was shared with the Ministry of Justice. The suspicions about who leaked it are clear. It will be portrayed as part of the conspiracy – big business working with Government before a deal was done.

We leave Tuesday open for Labour again.

There's been endless messing around about getting the shadow chancellor, John McDonnell, out there. The first part of our day has been entirely built around him. We've heard he's planning a full morning media round. Then that he isn't.

I point out that we can't keep clearing space for Labour for them not to deliver . . . though I know they have no influence on the people who are supposed to be their colleagues.

Then we hear he's going to say both the Leave and Remain sides have failed to make a positive case. Of course, it will be read as an attack – rather than making a case for remaining.

This morning it's confirmed he isn't doing any interviews.

In our cross-campaign call at 7.30 a.m., Ryan Coetzee tries to say to the Labour representative that McDonnell needs to avoid slagging us off. The response is, 'I have been trying to do that for the last six months. Welcome to the Labour Party.'

The truth is the Labour leadership has contorted itself into a position where it feels it can only support us on its own, very specific terms. This leads to excruciating and baffling soundbites, such as the one Corbyn gave on Saturday, along the lines of, 'Yes, I want there to be a Leave vote. The Conservatives to leave in 2020.'

I wondered: how the hell does that persuade people to vote Remain?

Lynton's column in the *Telegraph* is a fairly devastating condemnation of Leave – he says they need to decide what their core message is.

It's too early to count our chickens, but the mood in Westminster is increasingly that we are winning. Our campaign is a steamroller, theirs a spluttering steam engine. There's a healthy degree of nervousness among us, though.

The word from European capitals is that they are 'in quite a tizzy' about if we will lose. Some wonder if they should speak out. DC and I say, 'No!' in stereo. Our fear is that they will say something that just makes people resent them more. But by the end of the day, Donald Tusk is very emotional about the fact Hitler has been brought into it by Boris.

I sit round the fringes of political cabinet and watch Boris's body language. He looks exhausted, his wide, pallid right hand spread-eagled across his face. I nudge Graeme and wonder if he is asleep. I don't blame him – the political cabinet is dull, poring over the local election results and avoiding Europe.

A few hours later, I am watching Boris out on the road campaigning. He gives a speech that sounds like pure bluster for the first few minutes, characterised by his trademark faux inarticulacy. Someone says it is all an act and he's really the most scripted politician they know.

Then someone in the crowd shouts 'Bananas!' and it somehow sparks something in Boris's brain – he claims that European regulations are ridiculous, including one that insists that bananas cannot be bought in bunches of more than two or three. This triggers an extraordinary series of events.

Several of us begin to email and text that we need to leap on this – he has said something that isn't true, consistent with all the nonsense he used to churn out when he was a Brussels correspondent for the *Daily Telegraph* about regulations on balloons and plans to blow up asbestos-filled buildings.

Someone at Stronger In goes out and buys a couple of bunches of four bananas and photographs them next to a campaign sign. We make plans to buy loads of bananas and hand them out at Boris rallies.

I report this to the PM at the start of the 4 p.m. meeting. He has been irritated by Boris attempting to make hay with the leaked Serco letter, coming close to accusing the PM of being corrupt.

When the meeting is over, I call Michael Heseltine, who is supposed to be doing more media for us. We discuss the Serco letter, the banana claims, and the suggestion that the EU has plans to dominate Europe like Hitler.

He gets in a cab to Millbank to do an interview with the BBC.

The former Deputy Prime Minister does not spare Boris in his beating. It is a relentless takedown. A spokesman for Boris issues a statement saying, 'People want to hear the arguments, not personal attacks.' This seems ironic given the abuse the PM has taken. I imagine they are feeling very bruised indeed. Laura Kuenssberg declares it a significant slapdown for Boris.

After huge amounts of provocation it is a shot across their bows.

As I leave No. 10 that night, Theresa May is just ahead of me. She gets into a black BMW. I have a feeling that with all this warring and ultra-violence, she could come out of all of this very well.

Heseltine made a big impact on broadcast last night. He's the splash in *The Times*, but there's only a tiny mention of him in papers like the *Telegraph* in an article headlined: 'Boris cries "stitch-up" over the PM's letter to business chief.' The final para says, 'Lord Heseltine meanwhile told the BBC that the "strain" of the referendum campaign was "beginning to tell" on Mr Johnson and he had begun to make "preposterous, obscene political remarks".'

The paper's leader is, however, a sustained attack on the PM.

Whoever wrote it is fulminating that when asked in an interview, DC said Abu Bakr al-Baghdadi (the leader of ISIS/Daesh) would be pleased if we left the EU: 'That is not just offensive, but politically ill-advised. Roughly half of the electorate, and most of the Conservative party membership, back Brexit. They do so honourably . . . yet Mr Cameron has suggested they are giving succour to a death cult, guilty of mass murder, rape and enslavement. If the PM faces bitter recriminations from voters and Tory colleagues after the referendum vote, he will only have himself to blame.'

I talk to the editor, who has constantly reassured the PM that he will attempt to keep the paper a fair representation of the debate. He seems to accept that it was an over-reaction to the PM saying al-Baghdadi would be pleased. DC meant no slight to their readers.

Having said all that, I'm convinced a mistake was made in making a big deal of al-Baghdadi. The problem is that it allows them to paint us as being every bit as extreme as they are. More to the point, we should discuss these things before we throw them out there.

I find myself reflecting on how bruising the campaign has become. None of us had really expected to go to war again – at least not to this extent. Ameet and I slump at the round table and talk about this. I tell him I keep being reminded of the line in 'Brothers in Arms' by Dire Straits, which feels so appropriate:

> Some day you'll return to your valleys and your farms,
> And you'll no longer burn to be brothers in arms.

Later on we have a meeting of Conservative 'In' Cabinet ministers. Sajid Javid appears to have the newfound zeal of a convert, having previously been so reticent about the case for Remain. He does a presentation about why the single market is so important, pointing out that they amount to a huge part of our economy

– and if we leave the EU, they will be massively discriminated against, having a huge knock-on effect for ordinary people.

Stephen Gilbert gives a presentation explaining how we are targeting voters – saying that there will be twelve different versions of the electoral address, including one aimed at ultra-Outers, for whom the only argument that works is: Britain's place in the world will be damaged.

On Thursday, it's hard to believe, but the lead EU story on the BBC is a Leave campaigner, Steve Baker MP, calling for a truce in the negative campaigning. The only trouble is that it's based on a ConHome blog by him suggesting all the negativity has come from Remain. I listen to him on the radio as I drive in, and his main point literally begins, 'They started it . . .'

I manage to stop myself from getting irritated by it all, listing all the crap they have thrown, including suggesting the PM is corrupt and telling ITV there will be 'consequences', before remembering, 'If you're whingeing, you're losing.' And boy are they whingeing.

Steve Hilton does us the courtesy of emailing to say he's writing a blog criticising the campaigns for treating the public 'like simpletons'. It's classic Steve, claiming (erroneously, many tell me) he was behind successful negative campaigning techniques like 'Labour's Tax Bombshell' – before saying he now regrets that everyone is copying him.

Geordie Greig comes in from the *Mail on Sunday*. It's fair to say we haven't been getting on brilliantly recently. The PM is irritated about their campaign to stop so much money going on international aid. They also showed pictures of his wife Sam in a bikini and did a story about Elwen applying for a private school, when it wasn't clear if he was in yet and the PM worried it would unsettle his son.

After a robust discussion, we are clear we are on the same side in this campaign and agree to say it's all water under the bridge. At the end, 'We have a good story this weekend. Big names from retail saying prices will rise if we leave.' He looks interested. We agree they can have it exclusively.

All day there have been concerns about an amendment to the Queen's Speech, which has been widely briefed by Leave as a deliberate attempt to destabilise the Government programme. It says the House regrets that the Queen's Speech does not state that the NHS should not be affected by TTIP (a major new deal being negotiated between the EU and America). It is a straightforward attempt to cause maximum disruption. When the wording of the motion is clear, it is decided we can accept it, because we don't actually think TTIP should affect the NHS. It's unusual and embarrassing, but a smart play, shooting Leave's fox.

It's great that we have done it, but there is a creeping dread inside me: these people will stop at nothing in order to bring us down. And that won't end if we win.

# Chapter 21

## We Can't Be Complacent

THAT WEEKEND THE *Mail on Sunday* rows in behind us, splashing on our story: 'HIGH ST BOSSES: PRICES TO SOAR IF WE QUIT EU.'

There is page after page that is pro-Remain.

The *Sun on Sunday* also gives us a good show, warning of price rises. The only real fly in the ointment is the *Sunday Times*, which buries a powerful Op-Ed from two former NHS Chief Execs warning about Brexit and writes an editorial declaring itself bored by all the scare stories.

I jump in the car to Asda at Hayes, getting there at 7.45 on Sunday morning. The bright sunshine makes the area look its best. A security guard ushers me in and I find a flagship store where everything is pristine. It looks as if no one has ever bought anything from the shop and every surface is gleaming.

The managers are clearly proud the PM is coming.

I find Harriet Harman, who has agreed to do this visit with us. She is very likeable, but does little to undermine her North London Labour caricature, pointing out all the products that are packed full of sugar.

DC arrives and introduces himself to Harriet. They are straight into the photo op.

After a few shots in the aisles, we disappear upstairs for a roundtable with staff. There's lots to be encouraged about in their chat – they get the importance of the economy. But they also raise worries about the NHS and the £350 million a week being spent on the EU. It's pointed out it is not correct, but it's clear the claim is effective. I imagine legions of people across the country, unable to have a personal chat with the PM explaining why they are being misled.

I get in a car with DC and we are rushed into Central London. As we go through Knightsbridge, there is a pack of tourists, who form into a paparazzi scrum when they spot the convoy.

St James's Park looks amazing in the lemon sun. I wonder if anyone sensible is going to be watching the PM on *Peston* on a day like today.

I take the PM through all the difficult questions – he sounds remarkably confident, and I'm soon into getting him to check the Op-Ed for tomorrow's *Telegraph*, which uses the Treasury language to warn of 'a DIY recession'. I keep trying to draw him to the positive side of things, 'There's nothing more positive than ensuring our economy is thriving in the biggest market in the world, with all the opportunities that come from that.' I also want him to nail Turkey – there's no prospect of them joining, but what we do know is there would be an economic downturn if we left.

We arrive at the South Bank. The team is grateful that we are doing this. While the PM is in make-up, I go into the studio to see Robert Peston preparing, and then DC and I watch *Marr* in the green room.

Penny Mordaunt, the Minister of State for the Armed Forces, comes on. She looks nervous. There's a key moment when she is asked about Turkey joining the EU. Marr reminds her the Government has a veto. She says that isn't the case. I am on it in a flash – she is simply wrong. I use the WhatsApp group to make sure we are winding up social media.

The PM says the programme should hammer her on it. I text the editor, Rob Burley – she is plain wrong. Ninety seconds later, Marr returns to it and again she insists we don't have a veto and tries to say we would just let it all happen. This is very uncomfortable. You rarely catch someone saying something so definitely wrong. We begin to plot what DC will say. If their judgement is so faulty on something like this, it calls into question the whole basis of their arguments.

Peston walks in and starts to chat. He seems most interested in the fact the PM won't be wearing a tie. The PM tells him his navy suit and navy shirt combo make him look like he's heading out for a dinner party.

We inform him of what Mordaunt has just said and he can scarcely believe it. Wags on social media are writing things like, 'That sound you can hear is Penny M clearing her desk after a disastrous performance.'

Next up on *Marr* is Simon Stevens, the Chief Executive of the NHS. He is a bit hesitant, but he delivers the key point: if the Governor of the Bank of England is worried the economy will go into a 'tailspin', the NHS needs to worry. He says when the economy sneezes, the NHS catches a cold.

Finally he warns Penny Mordaunt she is wrong on the NHS, too – if we leave the EU, the big worry is the impact on lots of foreign-born staff, who may just up sticks and leave, and that will have an impact on her local hospital. Penny's bad morning is about to get worse.

DC does not spare her as he relaxes in his seat. He delivers the slap down perfectly. No mercy. He also sounds good on the NHS and prices.

He comes out knowing he has done well.

He jumps in his car back to Dean – and I walk across the river and hold a Stronger In call, making sure we can capitalise on prices, the NHS and Turkey.

There are howls of protest on Twitter about the soft ride DC was given. They wanted him asked why he supported their accession in 2010 – and would he use the veto.

It's not yet 11 a.m. when I hang up the call in my Uber car home. I think how exhausted I am in my bones, in my brain.

There's no rest to be had, though. Endless people want endless conversations.

The BBC is classically reporting the Turkey spat as 'on the one hand, on the other'. I have to call numerous times to say, why won't you just state that Mordaunt is wrong on a straight-forward matter of fact? Look at Article 49, which states we have a veto. It's there in black and white.

After hours of pushing, I get them in a position where by the evening news they are saying it. So are ITV. The problem for us is they have a clip from DC in 2010 talking about wanting a road 'paved from Brussels to Ankara'. Fortunately there is a Boris quote from 2006 calling for it to happen . . . but then there's also a quote from the EU saying accession talks have been 're-energised'.

I stand and watch this with George in the private office outside the PM's study. He looks at both BBC packages and says, 'This is so confusing – what hope do viewers have?' We are caught in the grey world of compromise that marks out so much diplomacy. Our diplomatic service wants to dangle the carrot of Turkey joining the EU to encourage them to adopt more Western ways. The reality is, it cannot and will not happen. We do have a veto. We'd almost certainly use it – and many other countries, like France, would definitely use theirs. But the nuance of the diplomatic position allows Leave to create mischief.

The PM comes in around 8.10 p.m.

The first topic of conversation is that Steve Hilton has added a chapter to his book for the paperback edition. He claims that the UK is 'literally ungovernable', because of the weight of regulation from Brussels – and he saw this first hand in No. 10.

We discuss if we should hit back hard, before realising it will simply add fuel to the fire.

The bulk of the meeting is taken up with what we are going

to say on Turkey. The options are to stay as we are and face pain – or move and look like we're slipping around under pressure, though there's a hope we can shut it down.

Occasionally the pressure in politics rises to absurd levels – and what would normally be ludicrous or extreme statements become run-of-the-mill.

IDS does a media round this morning and is pressed about Boris continuing to bang on about the regulation of bananas. His response is, 'I don't know, because I don't eat bananas.'

In a separate story about the potential of Ed Miliband joining the shadow cabinet, an anonymous Labour MP is quoted as saying, 'Ed Miliband shouldn't be in the shadow cabinet, he should be in jail for what he did to the Labour party.' The Westminster village is febrile.

The Turkey argument continues. DC is tempted to say there should be a referendum if there were any prospect of them joining (which there isn't). I ask Andrew Cooper what he thinks, concluding, 'My view, for what it's worth, is that it is a very, very bad idea.'

He makes the points:

1. People are likely to be very cynical about the sudden offer of a referendum.
2. It will serve only to raise the salience of Turkey – opening a renewed debate.
3. We'd be expected to spell out the precedent we'd be setting and its consequences.

I share this with DC. He sees the points.

We dive into the debate prep deciding to focus on immigration. It's instructive – all our arguments sound reasonable, but glib. It's a classic case of dealing with what's partly an emotional issue by using only reason – it doesn't work.

We talk about showing more emotional intelligence on it.

We need people to know they have been heard. I also think we need to call Farage into question: 'He's not levelling with you.'

As we talk, I get a call from Peter Dominiczak at the *Telegraph*. He's heard there's a possible resignation of a junior minister over another Treasury document. I haven't heard anything – it sounds wrong. The PM and Chancellor hit the prospect of a recession very hard at an event this morning – the response has been rage from Leave, but it's hard for them when people like the unimpeachable Paul Johnson at the Institute for Fiscal Studies say the assumptions behind our document are fair.

Peter also points out that they are working through the latest Lynton Crosby research for tomorrow's paper. It shows a thirteen per cent lead for Remain among decided voters. His commentary is apparently a precision strike on the Leave campaign for failing to stick to a coherent message.

Whenever anything like this happens, you can guarantee someone will say, 'We can't be complacent.' Several people do.

Some of us are reminded of a scene in *Game of Thrones* where there's a duel. One of the fighters is winning by a mile – prancing around, showboating. He could kill off his opponent at any point, but he doesn't. When he finally moves in for the kill, he is pulled down, and his head is crushed.

Come Tuesday, Lynton's research lands with a thud in the village.

And yet . . . we are also swimming against a tide of excoriating reviews of yesterday's Treasury document. The broadcast news was a dream – with the Institute for Fiscal Studies calling it credible – but the papers attempt to tear it apart. The *Sun* has a picture of George mocked up as Sid Vicious, with a '*Never Mind the Bollocks*' theme.

DC wants to do more to derail the Leave campaign. He says he went to bed thinking of an attack ad on the US presidential candidate Michael Dukakis, where he was going round and round in a tank, looking like a fool. There was a cool, calm voiceover pointing out the need for someone who can take control. He slams the Leave campaign 'going on about bananas and Hitler' – before pointing out extraordinary pictures of Boris in a sports car doing donuts on last night's news. Amid the burning rubber, Boris came out looking sick. The metaphor is obvious.

There's a danger we win the campaign argument, but lose the war. We are definitely seen as the slick, sensible people, while they can be a rabble. But what if they do tap into the common rage? I think again of, 'I'm as mad as hell and I'm not going to take this any more!'

Today's *Mail* front page declares that fifty MPs are ready to demand a leadership contest when all this is done.

I have a meeting at Stronger In and I march to the Tube with my phone glued to my ear. As I do, there's a strong gust of wind which blows the wreaths placed carefully on the Cenotaph into the middle of the road. A woman and I end up stopping traffic to pick them up and place them back as respectfully as we can. Some have broken apart and I feel a real sense of sadness.

As I get to the other side of the road, I find Charles Moore, the *Telegraph* columnist, hurrying along. I always find him extremely pleasant. He asks me if we plan to continue using 'Project Fear'.

'Can I start by saying, it feels a bit rich for the campaign that claims five countries are going to join the EU by 2020, sending millions of immigrants here, to claim we are using "Project Fear". But if you are asking if we intend to keep talking about the negative impact on the economy of leaving – we will.' It's all very good-natured.

Later on, we have another debate prep session. George comes in, hoping to talk about the PMQs where he is standing in for DC tomorrow. He points out that he has the order paper from hell and wants to know what we suggest in terms of dealing with it. First on the order paper is Richard Drax, who accuses him and DC of effectively betraying the country on a regular basis, then Philip Davies, who often takes pride in being offensive.

Basically, George wants to know what we think about hitting back. DC is clear, 'In my experience being snippy is a disaster.'

He says it's far better to smother them with kindness and to keep your answers short. George evidently feels he's been given a hospital pass.

I often think our one big advantage is the Leave campaign refusing to learn from its mistakes. On Wednesday 25 May, the Institute for Fiscal Studies says Brexit poses a serious danger to the economy. Despite the fact they are commonly held to be the exemplar of independent analysis – as the BBC's Norman Smith says, 'Like Moses delivering a tablet of stone' – Leave releases a statement calling them 'A paid-up propaganda arm of the EU.' I raise a smile as Norman's report concludes that this is like 'thrashing the ball into the back of their own net.' The systematic trashing of experts seems risible – surely it can't work?

Paul Johnson of the IFS is brilliant at explaining the issues – ridiculing Leave for the claim that we send £350 million a week to the EU as plain wrong and pointing out that even if it wasn't, just a 0.5 per cent drop in GDP would wipe out any hope of saving the money. In other words, there won't be more money if we leave the EU, there'll be less, because the economy will shrink, or at least grow at a slower rate. The middle course of projections is that we will lose six per cent of GDP.

The case really should be closed. But there's a spectre of doubt that looms over us: immigration. It feels clear and present in people's lives – just as our numbers and acronyms feel distant and abstract.

When the day's polling and focus group data comes through, that point is indisputable – people are moving towards Leave and the numbers thinking the economy is central are coming off. It's causing a real wobble in our core group.

Even though the polls are questionable, they inevitably dominate our thinking. A minor uptick within the margin of error makes us feel relief, whereas a downtick makes us sag. Intellectually, we know it's voodoo, but on such things morale is built. I wonder if we will discover that all the polling was built on sand and one side will win far more decisively than expected.

I'm in a meeting on campaign posters in the tiny room in Stronger In, when DC calls from Japan. I slip out into the corridor to give him an update. He seems fairly relaxed, but he lets slip that beneath the placid surface, the undercurrents are churning. 'Every time I see a bad poll, I feel knocked back,' he tells me.

I squeeze back into the room with Will, Peter Mandelson, Stephen, Ryan and Tom. An agency has come in with a set of posters. Each of them has what could be an advert in *Saga* magazine for an over-sixties holiday or a country club. Comfortable, old people enjoying retirement. Each has a headline such as, 'We don't care if we leave the EU' and then a sub-heading like, 'We expense our travel anyway.' I have been set up by Tom Edmonds to come in as the bad cop and point out it is a terrible idea. Fortunately I have no problem, its core thought – that young people must vote because a self-satisfied, selfish group of old people do not have their interests at heart – is poorly executed.

They look like nice people. I aspire to be like them: comfortable in retirement.

I find Peter Mandelson an interesting figure – so much of his reputation as a cold Machiavelli goes before him. For the most part he's charming. He spots that I am drinking coffee and acts horrified. 'What are you doing to your skin? You will be horribly dehydrated!'

'I've got lovely skin,' I joke.

'Don't take it for granted,' he chides, 'you may lose it!'

At the end of the meeting, there's a view that we should hit Boris hard with the toughest of all posters. It is the direct descendant of the Ed Miliband peering out of the SNP leader Alex Salmond's top pocket poster that was so effective in the general election. It shows Farage sneering as he looks down at a surprised-looking Boris, peeking out of his pocket and clinging on to the fabric of a pinstripe suit. The Leave campaign will howl with rage and cry foul. I suggest we give it to the *Guardian* – with a briefing that it backs up our polling that Boris has been seen as moving ever closer to the Farage agenda.

James McGrory does the briefing. Then mid-afternoon I get cold feet. I do not think DC and George are ready for this. I say we should not give the poster over until I have had a meeting with George back in Downing Street.

Part of George sees the point, but he also realises that it would be unleashing the dogs of war. We would never hear the end of it and it would legitimise even more personal attacks on us. We decide to pull back. Will is understandably irritated, but forgiving. I apologise, thank him – and say everyone is having moments where they are failing to show grace and consistency.

I break out early to take my children to the semi-final of *Britain's Got Talent* – the one treat I have allowed myself and them as we approach the final month of the campaign. I'm just crossing the road to the studios in Wembley with them, when I get a call from Ed Llewellyn, 'I want to tell you something concerning. Jim Messina has come back with his latest polling. There's been a drop of six per cent in the Remain vote since his last big sweep. It's now neck-and-neck. And that is the case across the country. Apparently there's a bunch of Obama advisers working for Leave. They've come up with nearly the same thing, with Remain just one point ahead.'

I'm not really sure what I'm supposed to do with this. There's very little context. Should we completely review? Should we hold our nerve?

I text Stephen Gilbert, who responds: 'It says it's very narrow. Regressed a bit since his last calling in September. But it is unweighted and not in line with other polls. I am speaking to him tomorrow to properly understand it.'

I also text Will Straw to get his take. He comes back: 'Worrying. I think it stands up Ryan's analysis from earlier. Outside SW1, Leave are (1) derisking Brexit by saying it's all a conspiracy & (2) making status quo risky. I suspect that we have devalued our risk message somewhat too & need more on "stronger, safer, better off". We should think hard tmrw about how to correct.'

I try to relax into the evening. It's fun – and my children love being charmed by David Walliams. During a commercial break, we're waved onto the stage and introduced to Simon Cowell. Inevitably the referendum comes up and I tell him it's tight.

He says, 'It'll be fine,' but nagging at the back of my mind is the prospect that we really could lose this.

# Chapter 22

## A Sticking Plaster on a Gaping Wound

I T'S NOT ON the news, but Thursday 26 May is significant. It's the last day the civil service machine can be working to support the Government's position to Remain.

At midnight, we go into a period of 'Purdah', where we aren't allowed to use any resources paid for by the taxpayer. I will effectively resign and go to Stronger In. A ratio has been worked out – eighty per cent of my salary will be paid by the campaign, a fifth by the Government, because I will have to deal with issues other than the referendum.

I wake at five, knowing I'm not getting back to sleep.

I plough through the diet of pro-Brexit, anti-us stories – then send the PM a media digest. He picks up on my highlighting of the *Times* editorial saying we should be worried by how little people trust us over Europe, that we are hyperbolic and suggest we got a better renegotiation deal than we did.

We discuss whether we need to do something to correct this.

We do, but not until we've got to the bottom of Jim Messina's analysis of the worrying polling he sent through last night. He's sent through a further email, which says what we really need to care about is moving our message, encouraging voter registration, and getting out our vote.

He points out that the most important date right now is the voter registration deadline of 7 June. He also says we urgently need volunteers to make phone calls to supportive postal voters to send in their ballot. He stresses that those volunteers need to be high-quality self-starters, capable of writing a letter to their local newspaper supporting Remain and talking to/emailing/Facebooking five friends or family about voting.

The gold standard of voter contact is door-knocking, both for increasing support amongst persuadable voters and boosting turnout among supporters. Currently, volunteers are doing no real door-knocking for the In campaign.

The next best is a massive 'digital push' with a 'deadline is imminent' message for voter registration and postal voting. He details plans for Facebook, Instagram and Snapchat.

I arrive in Downing Street, ready for the 8.30 meeting to be chaired by George, but five minutes in, Ed Llewellyn and I are told the PM wants to talk to us from Japan. We make our way to Ed's office. The switchboard put the call through to Ed's BlackBerry. He places it on a chair where Larry the Downing Street cat often sits. It is thick with white fur.

DC comes on the line. He sounds remarkably cheerful, telling us he's surveying the oyster beds from his summit bedroom window.

He asks me to bring him up to speed. I tell him it's immigration day – with deeply uncomfortable Office for National Statistics numbers about the possibility of another four million people coming to England in the next few years being published shortly and closely followed by the official net migration figures, which are now 330,000 (well over three times our target). We had no control over when the numbers emerged. Our response will be that we accept immigration is a problem, but trashing our economy is no way to deal with that. David Blunkett is going out to make our case.

There's no point in hiding it, the immigration numbers will be an unmitigated disaster for the Remain campaign – and our response is no more than a sticking plaster on a gaping (possibly fatal) wound.

Almost as concerning is that a commentariat view is growing

that we are overdoing it on the economy. I sum this up in an email to him afterwards:

> PM:
>
> I wanted to send you a note ahead of your press conference tomorrow.
>
> A view is crystallising in the commentariat that we are hyperbolic in terms of our focus on the economy if we leave.
>
> The consequence is that people are starting to feel they are being spun.
>
> The effect of this may be people become switched off, disengaged and don't vote; or they actively believe the crap that it is all an establishment conspiracy and are driven into the arms of Leave.
>
> This does not mean we should back off risk as a core message.
>
> Risk is fundamental to this campaign – and it must be clear in people's minds as they vote. Stephen and Ameet firmly agree.
>
> What we need to consider is our tone.
>
> We almost have the opposite issue to the general election.
>
> Then people thought you didn't want it enough.
>
> Now we look like we want it too much.
>
> So I think we need to tap into your 'statesman' quality more and shift tone a little.

I walk over to North House with Stephen Gilbert for a Stronger In meeting. He's constantly looking over his shoulder, waiting for Michael Crick to doorstep him over a general election campaign issue. The poor guy has too much on his plate, but he's handling it well.

We have a lot to talk about. First on the agenda is the television debates. Several people, including Lucy Thomas, who I have asked to lead on the debates, are worried about Angela Eagle being put up by Labour in the final BBC extravaganza at Wembley Arena. She's too much like Ruth Davidson, who is a far more formidable debater and should definitely be on the team.

I also point out that no one has taken these debates seriously enough, dismissing them as almost irrelevant, and I'm prepared to bet we'll be in a stew on 21 June, wondering if we are going to win, and lamenting the fact we didn't put up our strongest team. Will is reasonable and agrees that he will go back to Labour, but I sense he's struggling to get any traction with a suspicious Leader's office.

I head to the dentist. I've somehow managed to damage a wisdom tooth.

I have an hour-long appointment. A beefy Jewish man in his sixties, with a charming manner – he's very good at what he does. He tells me he is going to give me gas and asks what my tolerance for alcohol is. I say 'pretty good' – and he says he'll take that into account. I feel nothing for a minute or two, then suddenly I am swept in the air and floating several feet above the reclining seat I am lying on.

The sensation is one of complete peace, being only vaguely aware of a man injecting me and tearing away at my jaw.

I float back down to earth – and reality intrudes immediately. The highly respected John Curtice has delivered some bullet points about where the race really is. It echoes what Jim Messina and Ryan Coetzee are saying:

- It's much closer than the headlines.
- Remain probably ahead a bit.
- Tory vote has swung a bit to Remain, but party still badly split.
- Not clear warnings have influenced economic perceptions.
- Economy is a clear Remain issue; migration a wildly Leave issue; security no one's issue. Influence a Remain issue but most people don't care that much.
- Remain and HMG had successfully held the ground on the economic argument. The Leave campaign had never put Remain on the defensive on economy.

A BBC team wants a briefing on what Stronger In is planning going forward. I do my duty, before laying on thick my growing concerns about their coverage. They often strike me as being like a rabbit stuck in the headlights of the Leave campaign approach.

The classic example is the claim that when we leave we can spend the £350 million a week we supposedly save on the NHS. The IFS and ONS have now dismissed the figure as completely wrong and yet there are endless shots of the Leave bus parading round the country with it on, as well as clips done with people standing in front of it. The most senior BBC figure there tells me, 'The problem is – that is their number and they want to use it.' This is absurd – does it mean I can make something up that suits me and assert it?

To be fair they do challenge it in their more discursive programmes, but what I'm concerned about are the mass-market short bulletins and website images that end up being seen by tens of millions.

Their campaign coverage is more about balancing the claims and counter-claims of the two campaigns, instead of a focus on 'due impartiality', reflecting where the weight of expert opinion is. The key word is 'due' – giving contributors the coverage they deserve. I point out I'd be laughed out of the room if I tried to suggest that the BBC should give as much weight to a climate-change denier as they do to all the scientists who believe it's real.

The £350 million for the NHS isn't the only issue. Leave are often allowed to assert that Turkey is about to join the EU, complete with broadcasts showing arrows indicating tens of millions of immigrants flooding into the UK; also that there will be an EU army we will be forced to join, and that the overwhelming majority of our laws are decided by Brussels. None of this is true. The BBC point to the 'Reality Check' strand, but it's not in simple bulletins that are the most watched or listened to, or anywhere near the top of other running orders.

I point out that a simple rebuttal from us to all of this does not suffice – it's automatically discounted, with Leave supporters taking a similar position to Mandy Rice-Davies on claims by Lord Astor that he had never met her. To paraphrase her, 'We would, wouldn't we.' The BBC needs to step up and spell things out. A campaign that is predicated on lies cannot be treated in the same way as one that isn't.

That night, UKIP's Diane James is asked if people will need visas to visit the EU if we leave. She makes what should be the fatal error of saying, 'We just don't know.' All of us spot it and I'm clear we need to weave it into the fabric of our messaging going forward – these guys really haven't got a clue. Leaving really is 'a leap in the dark'.

Friday's papers are the predictable horror show on immigration. DC is mocked up, sticking his fingers in his ears and saying 'la la la' in front of a map of Britain packed to its borders with people.

After a series of calls with the media team, I join a 7.30 a.m. cross-party call chaired by Will Straw. It's designed to catch up with what the In campaigns for the various political parties are doing that day. I want to get across a blunt message: this matters. We failed on immigration yesterday, hardly anyone stuck to our line that we accept it's a problem, but Leave's solution of trashing the economy is no way to deal with it.

I'm beginning to realise – the strength of our campaign that we celebrate (a broad coalition taking in most of the Government, Labour, the Lib Dems, the Greens and the TUC), is also a profound weakness. We can't exercise the fingertip control that we had over messaging in the general election.

Some of the people on the line sound like they are spewing out the equivalent of Ukrainian tractor production results in the Soviet Union – telling us how many places they've been and how positive the reaction is. For the sake of diplomacy and unity, we need to nod along.

I call Ruth Davidson, who sounds like she's in bed. Why wouldn't she be? It's still early by any normal standards. I say we spotted how well she did in the Scottish debates and we need her to do the massive Wembley arena debate at the end of the campaign. She's immediately up for it. When I tell her Angela Eagle is also being considered for the team, she gets straight to the point, 'Angela and I are very similar. Are you sure you want two shovel-faced lesbians?'

Later she says I responded like an embarrassed Hugh Grant, muttering and bumbling. There are worse things to be compared to, but I recall laughing out loud and saying, 'I'm glad you said that. But the Labour party just aren't budging on it.' She accepts this and has a few extra tips. In the Hydro debate in Scotland, she says the noise was so loud, the participants literally couldn't hear what the other side was saying. The Wembley audience is to be six thousand − it's a worry.

Will Straw pulls me to one side and says, 'I've got some news. Sadiq Khan, the new London Mayor, is prepared to be in our final debate.' It means going against the wishes of the Labour leadership, but it suits us, allowing a balanced team for the final debate. Lucy Thomas, who has been pushing for Sadiq, points out the only fear is that the debate will be on the longest day of the year during Ramadan, and he will have been fasting all day long.

Will has less good news with the results on the polling of Labour voters. The analysis he shows me is shocking:

- Labour voters are deeply confused and uncertain about the party's position on the referendum and the position of Jeremy Corbyn.
- Only 47% of voters believe that Labour party politicians are 'mostly in favour' of Remain.

- Only 11% of voters say they have noticed Jeremy Corbyn making a 'persuasive argument' about the referendum over the past week.
- In focus groups in London, Brighton and Ipswich over the past two weeks, voters were uniformly uncertain about whether Labour itself was mostly for Remain. They tend to say one of two things about Jeremy Corbyn: either they don't know what his position is, or he's for Remain but that 'his heart isn't in it.'
- Undecided working class women in Liverpool mostly assumed the Labour party was for leaving the EU.

The conclusion is stark and obvious. We desperately need Jeremy Corbyn and/or other Labour heavy hitters to get onto evening broadcast news. Other coverage is also needed, but without getting him on evening news broadcasts, cutting through to voters is almost impossible.

In a normal campaign you would take this, work up a plan and action it. This isn't a normal campaign, and we need to cajole, nudge and encourage a Labour leadership that is at best in no mood to be lectured, and at worst actively wishes us harm.

By Saturday 28 May, I worry we are now in serious trouble.

It's not that I think we are going to lose, it's more we may not be able to move forward if we win.

I get a call from James McGrory, who says Gove and Boris have written an open letter to the PM criticising him for clinging to his pledge to cut net migration to the tens of thousands. They say he's 'corroding public trust'.

They also warn that the impact of free movement will increase hospital waiting lists and class sizes unless we get out of the EU.

It feels like an act of war.

What makes us flinch is that it's intensely personal. They are effectively accusing the PM of a lack of integrity. It's the kind

of thing we would hesitate to say about a leader of the opposition – let alone someone in our own party. Can the people
behind this be serious about reconciling when this is done – or
are they trying to make it impossible whatever the outcome?

It's also clearly a strategic decision to keep immigration front
and centre by creating the biggest blue-on-blue assault of the
campaign so far.

After a long day of calls and meetings, I'm in my car with
my eldest daughter and three of her friends, having picked them
up from Thorpe Park. They are all understanding and keep
quiet, part fascinated, part bemused as Switch put me on to a
conference call with DC, Graeme and a couple of others. Before
the PM comes on, some are angry that Gove is part of a
Government that has this as its policy, and Boris stood on it as
part of the Conservative manifesto, and yet they are attacking
it. I understand their position, but also think it's like calling men
out for visiting a brothel by saying they are supposed to be
Christians.

DC is clear from the off, 'Just ignore it.' I understand his
sentiment, but a simple 'No comment' isn't going to cut it.
Graeme says our line to take should be, 'destroying our economy
by leaving the single market is no solution.' He's on the right
tracks.

After a bit of discussion, I get to: 'This is a transparent attempt
to distract from the fact that the overwhelming majority of
economists and businesses believe leaving the single market would
be disastrous for jobs, prices and opportunities for people.'

I hang up and make the call. The more I think about it, the
more the Boris/Gove letter seems motivated by an intention to
kill.

Later I send DC the piece Tony Blair has written for the
*Sunday Times*, saying it is good. He agrees, before going on to
say that the Gove/Johnson stuff tomorrow is 'depressing beyond
belief' and 'deeply maddening'. We both believe it suits Leave

to have a Tory war. It's clear that spats like this make Labour, Lib Dem and Green supporters think it's about Conservative infighting – and turnout will be depressed.

I wonder if we have been victims of our own success. No serious economist thinks leaving won't harm us. Leave is reduced to trashing experts and focusing entirely on immigration – something they claimed they'd never do in all their speeches and articles before and in the early stages of the campaign. Have we somehow forced them onto a winning strategy?

Meanwhile, we are sucking up endless punishment, unwilling to hit back in any serious way. We may cross the finish line first – only to find that we are torn apart. Something in my bones tells me no good will come of this. Then there's the possibility we might actually lose this thing.

How many people are confused and irritated by the noise and being left thinking, 'What the hell?' as they flick two fingers at the so-called 'political class'?

# Chapter 23

## Attempted Coup

THERE'S NO WAY round it – the papers on Sunday 29 May are ugly.

The combination of the Gove/Boris immigration letter and Priti Patel saying rich people don't understand the pressures of immigration (she might as well have said, 'I'm talking to you, Cameron and Osborne') feels nasty and brutal.

The BBC doesn't even bother to cover the *Observer* splash, about ninety per cent of economists saying we'll be harmed if we leave the EU, though we are pushing it for all it is worth on social media.

It's a miserable experience.

All of us have feared that Tony Blair will be toxic on *Marr*. In fact he handles himself like a true professional, avoiding all the elephant traps. But that's the problem – he got through it unscathed, when we should be having people putting runs on the board. The lead story on the BBC is still Boris, Gove and Patel attacking the PM.

News comes through that this evening's meeting will be held at the PM's constituency home. It means a ninety-minute drive there and back. He says he will feed us. I try to spend some time with my kids, while tweaking some words for him to look at on the economy and immigration.

Come 5 p.m., I'm driving to the PM's house. The roads are clear and the sun is shining.

His home is in rural Oxfordshire – an idyllic part of the

world. I park and walk round the back, where Kate Fall and he are already surveying the garden. The others are stuck in traffic and won't be here for half an hour.

Someone called Mary, whom DC describes as a long-term family friend, is preparing dinner and offers to make me a cup of tea. DC shows me a barbecue, which looks like an oil barrel that has been cut in half, with a spit above it. The spit is nearly an inch of metal and two chickens are impaled on it.

We go through to the lounge and I sit in the precise place I was just over a year ago, as we watched the general election results programme go out. 'Yes,' says DC, 'we only all gather here in times of complete emergency.'

He says, 'People keep saying they think it will be all right, but I'm very worried.'

The rest of the team arrive. We start by discussing an event where he'll share a platform with Sadiq Khan tomorrow, but all anyone wants to talk about is the Gove/Boris letter. DC seems remarkably clear-headed about it. 'It's the right tactic for them: try to bate us into a blue-on-blue spat, which makes everyone think it's about the Conservative party – and that depresses turnout.'

That, or they want to kill us. Part of me wants to hear him calling them out as despicable before he comes to this conclusion. But he doesn't.

He then runs through all the options we could take in response:

1. be Zen and refuse to rise (as we are now).
2. fight back.
3. call out their strategy. Say we know what they are up to – and we won't fall for it.

He chalks off number two – it just makes things worse. It reminds me of the saying, 'Don't wrestle a pig. The pig likes it and you get covered in shit.'

He also thinks number three doesn't work – because it's too

clever. Which takes us back to number one. The next time they say anything, we call it 'increasingly desperate' and move on.

We turn to polling. Our latest tracker puts us ahead: 53–47. It also finds that fewer people now think Labour politicians are associated with Remain.

DC wants to know what Jim Messina has to say. Stephen Gilbert tells him he thinks it's tight.

We move on to posters – and specifically if we are going to target Boris. As people talk, a penny drops for me: what is the point of having a go at him? Where does it get us? It doesn't further our message and it's just a sub-category of the blue-on-blue argument. DC agrees, 'We should stop going on about posters attacking Boris. It's a trap.'

We head outside for some food. Mary attacks the chickens with her hands and a pair of scissors, lamenting the lack of a sharp knife.

It is still warm enough – and the heat from the barbecue helps.

At quarter past nine, dessert is brought out. DC leans back in his seat. I'm clear if I don't get home now, I'll be knackered. He offers me an espresso to wake me up.

Ameet and Liz get in the car back to London with me. I drive them to Hammersmith. It's dark and we are all tired. The discussion is about what happens after the referendum. I say my threshold for eating crap is low and I don't think we should do contortions to hold onto power, with crazy people holding guns to our heads. If he goes rather than face that, I believe history will look kindly upon him.

We listen to the Radio 4 news and *The Westminster Hour*. More blue-on-blue Conservative ultra-violence, making us feel even more queasy. Ameet asks how many Conservative MPs DC would need in a leadership election for him to survive. He thinks 240 out of 330. I think it would need to be higher.

Needless to say this is worrying talk, but I think we need to prepare. Let's not humiliate ourselves. Better to be dignified.

We've got to win the bloody thing first, though.

Any doubt that the Leave campaign is setting itself up as an alternative Government with alternative policies is dispelled a day later. Leave is briefing they would stop the EU imposing VAT on fuel bills – saving the average consumer £60 a year. We throw out a late-night rebuttal, but wake up the next morning to find it prominent on the BBC news.

There are too many people on the morning media call at 6.15 and I have to tell them to be quiet and speak one at a time.

At first people talk about putting something out in a week, challenging them on all their ridiculous spending claims. It's a hopeless proposal. We need something now. It's suggested Joe Carberry work up a 'dossier' pointing out all their ridiculous spending commitments. But he needs to do it right away.

I then call Norman Smith to say the Leave proposal is another example of 'fantasy economics' and that they've spent double, triple, then quadruple the notional £10 billion they'd get back if we left the EU. Of course, they're forgetting that money wouldn't exist, because our economy would have shrunk.

The 7 a.m. news has our sharper line. I imagine steam is coming out of Joe Carberry's ears as he works up a document showing all of their absurd spending commitments.

While this is all happening, I am standing in my bathroom in front of a bowl of water, hoping to shave before I take a shower. Calls keep coming and I can't start. I wonder if I am ever going to get out of this room – and get into the campaign.

Ed, then George, then the PM . . . then another conference call . . . the pressure is rising. I feel it – and I take a mindful breath.

Joe's document arrives at 7.37 a.m. It suggests they have made

£111 billion of spending commitments. It's in good shape, but I take three minutes to add headlines and quotes about 'fantasy economics'. I've warned Norman Smith to stand by. I fire it back to Joe – and it's out by 7.47 a.m.

The story at the top of the 8 a.m. – most listened to – BBC bulletins is now that the Leave campaign has been attacked for fantasy economics and making outrageous, incredible spending commitments. It feels like a win.

So why do I feel so disconcerted? A pattern is emerging. To deny it would be foolish. This is no longer simply an issue of whether we should remain in or leave the EU. We are at another level. Somewhere we never imagined. The Leave campaign is setting itself up as an alternative Government – complete with their own policies to be enacted should Cameron and Osborne lose and be deposed.

The words 'attempted coup' spring to mind. They seem strange on my lips as I later test them out on other people at No. 10 and ask if I am over-reacting. They don't think it's ridiculous at all. They have had the same thoughts – key figures in Leave advertising themselves as an alternative Government.

The polls are a cause for concern. Ryan Coetzee keeps delivering notes saying we are being badly hit by their claim that £350 million a week will go back into the NHS if we leave the EU – despite it being preposterous. He believes we are likely to see a downturn in our numbers. I'm working on my emails when our daily tracker comes in. It puts us on 55 and them on 45. 'Get in!' I say, despite secretly knowing this is all crap. It's a weird psychological boost – even though we know the polls can't be trusted.

That boost goes when ICM issues separate phone and online polls with the same answer. The Leave campaign is ahead 52–48.

When I look into the detail it's totally confusing, using a series of methods to weight the data, because they don't have faith in the initial sample. The pollster then comes out to explain his methodology, concluding that, despite the result, in the end he thinks Remain will win. I wonder what on earth the point of all this is, when the people behind it come across as so muddled. I suppose at least it spooks people with the prospect we really could leave.

Jim Messina comes in to discuss where we're at. Some paper bags full of Pret a Manger sandwiches, fruit, crisps and Diet Coke are dumped on the table.

He warns we've gone from plus six to tied in the polls, saying, 'It was the same the month before the election. But we made the right choices, kicked ass and won.' He warns, 'Our models get ugly if we don't do enough to boost turnout.'

After endless meetings, I get on the Tube back to No. 10. The 4 p.m. is just starting when I am asked to take a call from Steffen Seibert, one of Angela Merkel's closest aides. There's no doubt who holds the cards in this situation. Steffen tells me what she's going to say about hoping the UK will remain in the EU. She wants to do it in German at a press conference on Thursday. He also wants to do it with Reuters. I keep trying to intervene, but it's a bit like standing on a road trying to talk to the driver of a slowly moving juggernaut.

I manage to get across to him that it's more likely to be covered here if she takes a question from the BBC. He says he will go away and consider.

Straight after this I go to the Chancellor's study, where Will Straw is waiting for a meeting. We head in and sit on the green leather armchairs opposite George on his sofa. I think it's supposed to be a general catch-up, but George wants to iron out the issues we are having attacking the Leave campaign and specifically Boris. Leave seem to have no compunction about finding ways to attack the PM — so why aren't we managing to do anything in return?

The truth is, we're at an impasse. Will Straw says Labour In 'won't do it', asking why they should do our dirty work. That only leaves the option of doing it through the Stronger In campaign. George expresses queasiness about this – knowing the Leave campaign will wind up the right-wing press about No. 10 being at the centre of things and playing the man not the ball.

It's a strange stand-off. Both sides want to score a goal, but no one wants to be accused of putting the ball in the back of the net.

I trudge over to Stronger In. It's increasingly clear that Leave are doing another big immigration story tomorrow. I end up sitting in the sweaty, small meeting room on a conference call trying to work out exactly what it is.

I'm still on a call about 10.20 p.m. after it's emerged Leave has signed up to an Australian points-based system to control immigration. As the minutes tick by and we need to be out there rebutting this, I'm finding our conversation deeply frustrating. Our wonks keep arguing about whether it is fair to say certain things on points of detail the public will never know or care about.

I cut through it. 'I don't want to hear any more! Migration Watch says it doesn't work, Australia has more immigrants per capita than we do. It means leaving the single market. Our response is: it doesn't work, it's likely to increase immigration and it means leaving the single market, which would wreck the economy.'

The BBC breaks the news, which will dominate tomorrow, on its 10 p.m. bulletin. Laura Kuenssberg's live report just runs through how they claim they'd manage immigration with an Australian points-based system. I'm amazed that we have not been approached for a response – or that she has not pointed out the obvious flaws in what they are suggesting, including that doing it would involve leaving the single market. My guess is that the story has been done on a 'no approach' basis, where the people offering the story make it a condition of the journalist getting and running it that they do not approach the other side. I can't help feeling that the role of an editor is to put the story into proper context – not just put one campaign's side.

We seem to be going through a low patch with the BBC, who are lapping up everything on immigration.

We have a big announcement from the TUC tomorrow – confirming their full backing for Remain with a poster highlighting new research that indicates wages will go down if we leave. By all measures, it should get a good show on broadcast.

But the next day ends with a concerned email from the PM: 'No TUC package on the [BBC] ten . . . I am worried. DC.'

He's just watched a bulletin where Leave's supposed solution to immigration dominates, followed by a piece showing Boris driving around the country in a bus shouting the odds, with Michael Gove and Priti Patel the grinning acolytes next to him.

There's a moment where Laura Kuenssberg asks Boris if he is attempting to set up an alternative Government and he looks flustered, turns to Priti Patel and says, 'Priti, you'd better answer that one. But the answer is basically – no.' Surely people can see that's just not good enough?

All day long, George has been incensed by the fact that Leave's immigration story has been dominating the agenda. I try to cut through the frustration and point to what is going on, 'They are running as an alternative Government. It's shocking to us, but that's a good story. We know what we need to do – discredit the immigration story and push them to cover our TUC story.'

The conversation turns to who is best to do our clip on the immigration story. Obviously it is Theresa May, but there's nervousness she won't deliver after her previous intervention misfired. The PM calls her – running through what he thinks she needs to say. It seems to work.

We're looking at pushing the fact that the RSPB is supporting us tomorrow. It's brilliant that they are writing to a million members, but it's too soft for the news. Ameet comes up with the idea of getting the Chancellor to write a letter to Vote Leave saying they are being reckless. I suggest Alistair Darling as a co-signatory.

While all this is going on, I'm worried about the upcoming TV debates. We're in the crazy situation where we and the BBC want Sadiq Khan to be one of our team of three at the Wembley Arena debate. Sadiq wants to do it, but no one (not the Labour people at Stronger In, not the BBC, not Sadiq) wants to tell the Labour Leader's office. I'm clear that the BBC asked, so they need to write formally to Sadiq giving him cover. Others worry, what will Corbyn's office do? Will they throw their toys out of the pram and insist they bigfoot Sadiq? That could mean John McDonnell doing it, or even Jeremy Corbyn. A disaster.

The best possible solution is that we have Amber Rudd, Nicola Sturgeon and Angela Eagle do the ITV debate in a week and Sadiq Khan, Ruth Davidson and a business figure do the BBC Wembley event two days before the vote. Once again, the pain of trying to run a broad coalition is crystal clear. We can suggest things, but we can't demand. Meanwhile the ITV debate is days away.

I race over to No. 10 to meet Bill Knapp, an American consultant who's here to help sharpen lines for the PM's *Question Time* appearances and the wider TV debates. His easy charm belies a razor-sharp brain.

We take him through to the Chancellor's dining room. He's just had a shower at his hotel after an overnight flight from Washington. He says, 'I read your *Daily Mail* today. Jesus – I felt like turning round and getting back on the plane!'

'Yep!' I say – it's hard to believe the sheer intensity of the campaigning against us.

He asks me, Kate and Ed to fill him in. He takes the occasional note before coming out with his thoughts, which feel on the money:

- All the emotion is on the other side. You can't win that choice between the status quo and getting back freedom and control.
- You have to tap into something that's emotional too.
- You have to articulate a negative and positive message.
- They are articulating a positive message. What I get from you is the lack of a disaster.
- You need to say: 'This is the wrong direction and here's why: All the experts say it's going to cost. It's going to prevent us from doing what we need to do to move forward.'

His thoughts are interesting. Almost fact free – appealing to common sense or emotion. He comes up with a few more:

- What is the purpose of the EU? It's the single market. It's about not going to be overrun by China and Russia. So we don't get our lunch eaten.
- This is about building some strength so we can succeed.
- We have to position the other side as quitters. They want to cut and run. We don't quit. Women are the swing voters. We're quitting on our kids' futures. (I like this a lot.)
- They act like the internet and globalisation don't exist. Let's get real and get into the real world and win.
- You're never going to make people feel good about the EU.

And this – for me – is the best one:

- Leaving is rolling the dice on our children's future. What kind of parent does that?

I watch the 1 p.m. news. The TUC story isn't mentioned at all – other than a brief aside at the fag end of the wrap-up two-way with the reporter. I write to James Harding and Katy Searle asking how it can be so unbalanced and am assured all will be well later.

The TUC story just about gets on the six o'clock news – and is nowhere at 10 p.m. Prompting the worried text from the PM.

I feel utterly exhausted. The phoning, texting, emailing and meetings today have been relentless. If the BBC's flagship news bulletin is any kind of indicator, we have got nowhere. Can they really not see how this is wrong? Have they discounted the TUC story out of some misguided sense that we had a hit on another day? If they have, they have missed a good news story and something that is vital to our campaign: demonstrating that this is not just a Tory on Tory war, but that other key parts of the political spectrum are on our side, with news stories that support their case.

How on earth are we going to tell Labour voters that politicians and organisations representing them believe it is in their interests to vote Remain, if the biggest news organisation in the country won't cover one of our biggest moments properly?

I go to bed with nagging doubts. Could we really be beaten?

# JUNE

# Chapter 24

## I Know Waffle When I Hear It

I WAKE UP ON Thursday 2 June to better headlines on the *Today* programme. They begin on the head of the GMB union saying Labour needs to be more passionate in making the case for Remain. It's not a positive story for us, but at least it's a signal to Labour voters. The next story is about Corbyn coming out in favour of Remain – and there are two more that we can chalk up as good for us. Senior sources at the BBC tell me they realise they screwed up, marginalising the TUC coming out for Remain yesterday, and are now attempting to redress the balance.

The papers remain the dark clouds on our horizon. The public relations firm Portland has released a pamphlet on Brexit – it includes a questionable piece by Gove claiming that as Justice Secretary, 'I have experienced the frustration at our inability to refuse entry to those with a criminal record and even some who are suspected of terrorist links.' Many in Government react angrily, saying it's not true and most of the article covers areas that are not even in his remit, but the *Telegraph* splash on it.

When I speak with DC, he's angry with Gove. 'I'm going to lose my temper and unleash one on these people on live TV soon.'

Jim Messina comes in to see the PM in his office. He perches on the edge of the blue couch, knees spread wide, and tells us, 'The thing that keeps me up at night is turnout. We have to increase it.'

The PM asks him to give his opinion on the polls putting

Leave ahead. He says, 'They are massively over-sampling people who did not vote in the last election. Those people favour Brexit by about eighteen per cent.'

DC asks how we can be sure they won't vote this time. The answer is we can't be, though the pattern is they tend not to, believing nothing they do will change anything. He also follows the view – built up across thousands of referenda, including in Scotland – that 'Don't Knows' are likely to hold out until the end before breaking our way.

At the end of the conversation, DC asks which Jim thinks is easier, getting Hillary Clinton elected President, or this? He doesn't even think for a moment and just says, 'Hillary.'

We ask if he thinks we're going to win and he says, 'I'm encouraged, but not over-brimming with confidence.'

As we prep the PM for his Sky News interview and audience Q&A session, news starts to come through that Merkel has intervened. It sounds like a diluted version of what her team had suggested – essentially saying she wants us to stay in, and it'll be hard for the UK to do deals in Europe if we're outside the room.

A senior Downing Street figure reviews what she said and is very disappointed, 'They never deliver the killer blow. They tell you they will, but they just don't say it.' He believes she was squeamish about appearing threatening.

I check on the latest news. Boris is auctioning a cow on my TV screen. I also see an embargoed story for the morning from the Home Affairs select committee. It says that a population the size of a small town (13,000) of foreign criminals who should have been deported is still in British jails. The chairman of the committee, Keith Vaz, who says he is a Remainer but is known for publicity seeking, has said it is a major problem for the Remain campaign. I can't understand it – why do people supposedly on our side keep handing bullets to the opposition?

DC and I get in the car to Osterley for the Sky debate. We

do a bit of light questioning, but I try to keep it nice and easy.

We've just been into the Sky studios to have a look round and are back in the convoy to get some food when I put on the *BBC News at Six* on my iPhone. DC and I try to watch it. As we do, we're suddenly aware of the driver looking confused. We appear to be driving into a bus garage.

The convoy does a U-turn. They can't find the restaurant. I think it's on the left, but they turn right into heavy traffic. They then have to do another U-turn so tight I can't believe they don't scrape the paintwork on a stationary bus.

DC, who is keyed up about the programme tonight, says, 'Come on guys, I'm supposed to be having a relaxing meal before I go on.'

We step out of the car, the PM into traffic and me on the kerb. As we do, the referendum section begins on the news. I boost the sound, and hold the screen close to our faces, with DC leaning in to me to hear. We are now standing by a canal side with people staring. Suddenly we hear a man singing out of tune and very loudly. I look up and see a drunk, unsteady on his feet, earphones plugged in, shouting/singing Bob Dylan's 'Forever Young' into a phone.

We try to focus on the package on Jeremy Corbyn, but the protection team try to move us along. We wander at a snail's pace along the canal – with the man now following us.

We can just about make out what's happening on my tiny screen as we march forward. The singing fades and we make our way into the pub where we have come for dinner.

Jon Ryley, the head of Sky News, is waiting to meet us outside the studio. I let DC and him go ahead, so there's a clean shot of them going in. After thirty seconds I race after. The studio appears to be a pop-up – just 100 seats, with the PM very close to the audience. It's bright and clean, with a sharp yellow-and-blue theme.

We put the PM through his paces to warm him up. There's

a real sense of jeopardy in taking questions from a studio audience. There are legendary moments where politicians have been left flummoxed by blunt questions. The team jokes about the moment in *The Thick of It* when the minister is asked, 'Have you ever had to clean up your own mother's piss?'

Liz Sugg and I walk him down to the studio. He stands in the wings and we make small talk to try to lighten things up.

I jog back up to the green room, where the team has opened some wine.

The first part of the show is an interview by their political editor, Faisal Islam. He starts punchy and gets punchier, asking if DC knows the number of people who have come into the UK since he became PM, and then how many who left. He answers – making clear the net number coming in is 600k plus.

The interview is almost all about immigration. DC's practice has worked, though – he gives a sentence in response, then pivots back to the economy.

A wag on Twitter sums up the experience as:

*Faisal Islam:* Immigration.
*Cameron:* The economy.
(Repeat)

Good. This is a battle – a test. Faisal Islam does well, but at points he's a little too cocky, asking at one stage, 'Which will come first, economic meltdown or World War Three?' The audience laughs. DC does a brave job of defending his speech on the EU and security, pointing out he never talked about WW3. It doesn't matter – when they're laughing and you're explaining, you've lost the round.

There's a commercial break, then DC is standing ready for the audience. He plants his feet wide apart, anchoring himself.

Kay Burley loses control of the PM and the audience from minute one. The audience wants to interact. The problem is there are no boom microphones capable of picking up people who haven't asked a question. DC starts talking back to them – obviously he can hear, and he doesn't know that people watching can't. Kay doesn't assert herself and it feels a bit of a mess.

Then a student called Soraya asks a question. She claims to be a Remainer, but attacks the campaign. She speaks about Turkey and her worries, but says she comes from a family of immigrants. I have no clue what her point is. DC tries to answer. She interrupts him to tell him not to interrupt her. When he tries to give an answer, she says, 'I'm an English Literature student, I know waffle when I hear it.' It feels like she's been practising the line in the mirror all day long. There's a smattering of applause. The hacks go mad on Twitter – relishing the idea that someone has taken on the PM and is speaking truth to power, when in reality she appears to be little more than a confused attention seeker.

DC calms things. And we get to the end of the show with no real scars.

It's dark when we get in the car. As the doors slam, DC wants my run-down. The social media reaction shows that even hostiles think he did well. I can see he feels pretty confident. I show him various tweets as he calls Sam to get some reassurance.

Back in Downing Street, a bunch of people including George and Bill Knapp are in the No. 11 dining room. There's a spread of Moroccan food on the table, and I grab some of the meat and pitta bread. I lean in to George. 'Alright?' He nods. I talk for a bit, but I want to get back to watch the news. I walk out into the warm night air. I wonder how many more times I will leave this building and walk down the street, nodding to the police as I step out onto Whitehall.

Some of the next morning's newspapers are a joke.

The *Telegraph* headline is: 'CAMERON SAVAGED AS VOTERS REVOLT'.

I text Chris Evans, the editor, and Peter Dominiczak, the

political editor, telling them I think it is simply wrong.

Papers that would normally be attacking Soraya for her incoherence and self-regard lionise her. It's another reminder of how we are playing uphill in this referendum. The very same papers that would have been cheering us to the rafters, if the same event had happened in the general election, are making life uncomfortable.

DC calls to say, 'The problem is most people didn't see it, but they're getting their sense of it from the endless press digests on TV and radio, or reading the biased coverage.' Once again it is clear we do not have a champion in the press – and with the broadcasters often, though not always, taking their cue from this kind of coverage, we are always going to struggle.

I fully accept that we took what we could get in the general election – with the *Sun* and the *Telegraph* knocking lumps out of Labour, and the *Guardian* and the *Mirror* knocking lumps out of us. Now we have the *Mail*, *Sun*, *Express* and increasingly the *Telegraph* smashing us, while the other papers that are supposedly pro-Remain either throw their hands up in horror at the brutality of the campaign, or do endlessly reasonable pieces about the other side.

I take a deep breath and tell myself the broadcast media packages major on our economic message, as well as the 'roll the dice' line, and that is how most people will consume this.

After an early morning encounter on *Good Morning Britain*, we shoot through the rush hour to a hotel at St Pancras station. It feels like we are entering a giant and imposing Gothic film set: the ceilings sky high, the lighting dim.

We're here to meet Simon Walters from the *Mail on Sunday* – the one paper that does seem to be really behind us.

The PM says he is ready for action. We've already talked about making the passionate case for Remain. DC delivers, really stepping up, but not crossing the line into a rant.

Simon wants it to be all about DC versus Boris. The PM

doesn't play directly, but he does attack hard, saying Leave know claiming we'll be better off out is 'nonsense on stilts', and it's ridiculous to portray the EU as an 'evil empire', while expecting them to do a good deal if we leave.

DC disappears off to Kent and I stay back to talk to Simon. He says, 'I've never seen him so fired up.' Neither have I. He thinks we've had a rough ride on immigration, but concludes, 'It'll be sixty–forty to you.' God, I hope so.

I get in the cab back to Stronger In. It's not even 9 a.m. and I feel like I've done a full day's work.

As I sit down, the latest tracking poll comes in.

It says we are winning 56–44. I'm confused. Everyone is worried about immigration, but since it has been front and centre, we seem to be improving our position. Less than a week ago our polling put us on 51–49. There's now been a move outside the margin of error. What is going on?

Stephen Gilbert then says we should just ignore all polls. I wonder, why we are doing one then?

I jump back on the Tube to Downing Street. We have a meeting with the Chancellor in the No. 11 Dining Room to go through the grid.

The main thing to come out of it is agreement with my point that we need a story for when the PM does the ITV programme with Farage next week. I'm clear Farage will attack us in the most vicious way – accusing the PM of being a liar.

We need to appeal to all the people who see him as beyond the pale. Something along the lines of: the choice is now clear, between Farage's Britain – with a shrinking economy, fewer jobs and our face turned to the wall, or the people who are prepared to work together to achieve something bigger and better.

It's agreed I should go and work it up.

A few of us head back to Stronger In to watch Gove on Sky. There's a good team atmosphere in the office. The entire press team is there – geared up to leap on everything.

There's no question that Gove is on the ropes for the first seven minutes. He can't name a single serious economic body that supports Leave. Nor businesses. Nor international allies.

He fights back by saying 'people in this country have had enough of experts.' It's a breathtaking moment – perhaps one of the most cynical things I've ever heard a politician say. Michael Gove parades himself as an intellectual who prizes reason, but when his back is against the wall, he's prepared to attack the very people who know what they are talking about.

He then goes on to attack Faisal as part of the establishment.

His strategy is clear – create the idea that the gilded elite are all part of a conspiracy. It's absurd. What is the Lord Chancellor, other than part of the elite?

We are firing out tweets left, right and centre: 'On the ropes' . . . 'No supporters'. But one of the problems we have is that the Leave members of the audience are just a lot noisier. They applaud anything he says.

I text DC, who isn't watching, and say he has been struggling.

George asks to be kept informed, saying, 'I literally can't bring myself to watch it.' It's in these moments that I realise how high the stakes are – and the sense of personal betrayal at the heart of it all.

Joe Carberry spends the whole time bashing away at his keyboard, filtering any shout-outs into a coherent document.

The audience have some tough questions, including accusing Vote Leave of being 'project lie' and another commenting that Gove is like a First World War general, waving his flag and urging everyone to go over the top, without knowing what we'll face on the front line.

The programme rather fizzles out – Gove looks increasingly comfortable, rolling out what are clearly pre-prepared script lines about patriotism and sovereignty.

I go home thinking it is evident he had every bit as tough a time as the PM. Any fair representation would make that clear.

Later, John Rentoul writes a piece on Gove's performance. He describes his 'Red Mike persona as an act constructed for the purposes of debate.' I wonder if he knows quite how well he has hit the nail on the head.

For me, Gove is an actor. He strikes a pose according to circumstances.

Does he really believe any of it?

Leave's pattern of deceit continues the next day with a 2,000-word letter signed by Boris and Gove. It's an attempt to raise the risks of remaining in the EU to counter our constant barrage of stories about the risks of leaving. It's the most deceitful thing they've tried so far − full of claims about Turkey joining the EU and how there'll be 300,000 more jobs if we leave.

I draft the lines to take for our people: 'As any credible expert will tell you, this letter from Leave is reckless nonsense − they are now guilty of actively misleading the British people. The Leave campaign cannot produce a single expert who believes there is any prospect of Turkey joining the EU. The UK retains a full veto over any new member. We have clear guarantees we will not contribute to any bailout and protections against Eurozone integration. If we Leave, we will wreck our economy, people will lose their jobs and families will be worse off. Leaving is too big a risk to take.'

# Chapter 25

## You're Killing Us

IT'S SUNDAY 5 June and I am worried.

This is tighter than we thought it would be. Bloodier than we thought it would be.

I talk to a very senior broadcast journalist. He says, 'I think the Leave campaign just can't believe their luck to still be in it at this stage.' He pauses for a moment, before saying, 'So many of the things they are saying are just wrong. Literally like sand falling through our fingers and yet the public just don't seem to care.'

This really could be a complete disaster. Reports keep coming through of disaffected Labour voters saying they are sick of immigration.

And yet our media team is doing an amazing job – we completely outwit Leave in the Sunday papers. James McGrory has worked with the *Mail on Sunday* on a story about far-right elements infiltrating Leave. They splash with it. It includes an astonishing set of pictures showing a woman with a large swastika tattoo and her Nazi friend working on a Leave stall. There's also a positive write-up of the PM's punchy interview and a great editorial.

I settle down to watch *Marr*, anticipating John Major. I text a friend, 'Strap yourself in.' He texts back, 'I am. God, I hate this referendum.'

Sir John looks like a man doing well to control his cold fury. He wastes no time in saying he believes Leave are 'misleading the

British people', then goes on to describe it as a campaign that is 'verging on the squalid' over immigration. He says Boris appears to have been converted to Leave on 'a day trip to Damascus'.

Marr asks him about the idea that money would be safer after Brexit. He attacks Gove, Boris and IDS, saying, 'The NHS would be as safe in their hands as a pet hamster with a hungry python.'

The next interview with Boris is weak as water. On air, Andrew Marr appears to suggest they have done a deal – he won't interrupt Boris, if his questions aren't met with long speeches. I am shouting at the TV when Boris denies his unbelievably glib comment that the graph of leaving would be like the 'Nike swoosh' (a downturn, before a sharp rise). He did it in *The Times* and was asked about it on his last appearance on *Marr*. He evidently realises it's not a great look to be so blasé about jobs.

Then there's the moment when he is shown a Leave poster saying, 'TURKEY (population 76 million) IS JOINING THE EU'. Boris smirks, knowing it is a lie – and attempts to justify it. The interview was a failure, and what was supposed to be Boris's big day has been hijacked by John Major.

The referendum has boiled down to a straight fight between the economy and immigration. Voices from across the campaign remain confident that we have the right approach – trashing our economy is no way to deal with immigration.

Peter Mandelson writes a long, thoughtful note, arguing, '. . . crystallising the choice between economics and migration will help us. We ought to encourage it. Those who think migration most important will have already decided to vote against us. We are targeting those who are worried about immigration but are susceptible to the argument that dealing with migration by disabling the economy is not right. So let's reinforce this equation.'

He adds that 'the PM has done well in pointing out that free movement isn't a one-way street into the UK, it is allowing millions of Brits to exercise freedom about where they work, live or retire. And from construction and building to our NHS, the everyday reality in the UK is that we often rely on citizens from the rest of the EU to get the work done and the care provided.'

Finally he suggests the PM make a definitive speech on immigration, but he should not leave it to the end, because it will appear desperate.

The core No. 10 team gathers at Downing Street that evening. We, too, have been thinking about immigration. We are less comfortable than Peter Mandelson about simply saying you have to accept unlimited free movement in exchange for a stronger economy. It's also not assured that a major speech on immigration will do much more than poke the hornets' nest. The bottom line is: what can we say on immigration/freedom of movement that will not be met with derision?

We are left with: Leave are confused on immigration and reckless on the economy. On immigration – they won't solve the problem with their plan for an Australian-style points system (as Migration Watch points out). They are lying about Turkey joining, and they also appear to be demanding more immigration from outside the EU.

We agree to get all our people to constantly point out that we have a plan – Leave doesn't have a plan.

It's late as I get in the car home. I call Will Straw. He's supposed to be on *Today* in the morning. He thinks immigration is hurting us. All of us are being brave, but we know it's true.

I go to bed with a hollow feeling in the pit of my stomach and wake up to the BBC leading on claims by the Leave campaign, which are straightforwardly wrong – that we will be on the hook for higher EU budgets and Eurozone bailouts if we stay in.

It's become a theme of this campaign that the BBC thinks they have to give them equal time, regardless of whether what they are saying is true or not. So it's not unusual for them to start the day just running what they say. I send the following text to key editorial figures in the BBC: 'Another example of you leading on a Leave claim that is literally not true.'

I point out that they really should be dismissing it as a story, but given they are running it, they should at least make plain it's nonsense from the start. It's a fact we have a budget veto and don't have to take part in Eurozone bailouts. They need to be a fair referee – not just allow them to assert something that's demonstrably wrong.

I explain it to Norman Smith when he calls me for a comment and he seems to be agreeing with me. But little has changed by 7 a.m. I send another text: 'Still same. You need to actually say EU rules are clear. Otherwise confusing.'

By 8 a.m. it's changed. But it's depressing we have to go round this course so often.

Later, I pick up from senior contacts at the BBC that they have been arguing all day about my intervention suggesting they keep running stories from Leave that are factually incorrect. They say they haven't learned from what happened during the Scottish referendum.

It's the same old thing, they have a serious problem with quality control on morning bulletins. Who is responsible for taking an overview of the morning output that spreads across so many radio stations, TV and online and reaches tens of millions of people? Having worked at the BBC, I know that there's endless focus on the so-called flagship programmes, like *Today* and the *News at Ten*, whereas the shorter bulletins and internet copy are churned out with little oversight.

I'm beginning to realise that this is just a symptom of a wider concern. Serious journalism is struggling to hold to account those who are prepared to go beyond standard campaign hyperbole and stray into straightforward lies. If a campaign has been officially designated as the lead advocate for one side of the debate, and so much of their core message is untrue – how do you report it in straightforward news terms? The reason I focus on the BBC so much is because of their sheer scale in terms of British journalism. They are a leviathan - in TV, radio and online, dwarfing the competition. If they are struggling it's a serious issue, particularly when newspapers are actively campaigning.

At least we are very much on the front foot this morning – holding a major cross-party event, with strong visuals. We've been given a heads-up on Harriet Harman's speech. She wants to directly attack Boris and Gove. Ameet points out this is hopeless – the PM will literally be standing next to her, listening to her attack people in his party. She needs to do it more subtly.

We contact her team and she agrees to pull back.

I rush up the road to see Amber Rudd for her debate prep. I have arranged for us to use CTN in Covent Garden, which is run by the lovely and supportive Stephen Watson, who has a TV studio in his basement.

Amber is one of my favourite politicians, straightforward, clever and fun. But she is a little nervous. I get her to record her opening statement. The first thing she is doing wrong is not looking down the barrel of the camera. She fixes that quickly.

Then I point out that her script just isn't emotional enough. She needs to have more passion. I suggest: 'They are asking you to take a leap in the dark and take a risk with all our futures. And as a mother, I am just not prepared to see that happen.'

We move on to the Q&A. Her presentation style is classic Tory – reasonable, technical and just a little dry. I feel my mind wandering. I tell her she has to be more aggressive. 'Tell them this just isn't good enough. They're asking us to take a leap in the dark. Kick them hard: "Boris, I might come to you for a good joke, but I'm not prepared to entrust you with our children's futures."'

While the team prep her, I go through to the studio gallery to watch the PM event. It is as I hoped – each of the party leaders standing in front of a Mini painted the colour of their party . . . except for Natalie Bennett, who is standing in front of a green Brompton bike. Apparently the collective that runs the party took three meetings to conclude they were prepared to do this.

It looks a little eccentric, but it's a strong image and the bike makes it stand out. Outers in the Conservative party are attacking the PM for standing with our enemies. I hit back hard – Leave are dragging Labour's Gisela Stuart round the country with them, and Chris Grayling was prepared to share a platform with Nigel Farage. I also note that after ages pushing, the BBC are saying straightforwardly that Leave claims today are wrong. It's a small victory after a lot of effort.

As I come out, Kevin Pringle arrives. He is representing the SNP and Nicola Sturgeon. He's no fool – Alex Salmond's former Director of Comms. He leans forward, peering through steel-rimmed glasses and sucking on a carton of juice.

He says, 'Nicola will give the positive case.'

I decide to be straight with him. We wouldn't have chosen Nicola to be on the platform, as she goes down very badly with English voters, but ITV insisted. 'The big worry is that she says something unhelpful and makes it look like we can't even agree amongst ourselves.' He makes some understanding noises. We'll see next week. Once again it is something beyond our control – someone representing our campaign has a separate agenda.

I walk back to Downing Street in the hot summer sun, ready to join the PM for the Jeremy Vine show. We get in the car together and talk about how close it feels. DC laughs and says, 'Half a point will do it for me.'

When we arrive, we end up having to hang around in a lift that won't move. We finally get to the sixth floor. Jeremy comes out and I take a picture of the two of them together, to tweet out that DC is about to be on.

I listen to the burble of Ken Bruce in the background, the middle-of-the-road music and the sunny jingles, and think, this is a so much nicer world than the world we inhabit. I mention this to DC and he laughs, 'Yes, where people are happy!'

The interview is unremarkable. In the car back, I ask him cheekily about what it's like having Gove and now Steve Hilton out there attacking him. It sounds to me as if Gove is destined for a reserved politeness when they are eventually forced to interact, but he really won't have anything more to do with Steve, who has been highly critical on his current book tour. The theory in Downing Street is that Steve never got over the fact that the PM was prepared to let him go so easily. Life had become intolerable, with Steve falling out with civil servants and apparently behind briefings that DC had betrayed their core mission. When he disappeared, the ship settled and we won a general election. Most can't help noticing that every intervention about Downing Street is unhelpful.

I stay back at Stronger In to watch Andrew Neil interview Hilary Benn. It's the most tedious programme I have seen in a long while. At one stage, Will Straw and James McGrory start talking about pet guinea pigs they had as children.

I'm getting into bed and spot an email from DC: 'The more I think about it the more I think we shd call them out over their lies today over bailouts and budgets.'

He says watching the *BBC News at Ten* he spotted four lies the BBC didn't knock down:

1. We are liable for Eurozone bailouts.
2. Our rebate is at risk.

3. The overall budget can be increased without our say-so.

4. We have given up a veto of future treaties.

He says they are all straightforwardly untrue and we should call a press conference calling them out. I reply that I think it is a good idea, but we need to do it quickly and cleanly.

Come the morning call, others are nervous. Will it look panicked?

I just bulldoze through the idea with the PM. Our news story into the morning is yet more independent world experts, all of whom are warning us of the dangers of leaving – and on the other side, we have people who are basing their campaign on lies. The comparison needs to be made urgently. No one is going to do it for us.

We're asking a lot of Liz Sugg. She's patently wondering where the hell she's going to get a venue at short notice. I tell her it needs to be done by 11 a.m., in plenty of time to hit the lunchtime news bulletins. She says she'll try.

I listen to the BBC 8 a.m. news. Despite the fact that we have the head of the World Trade Organization, the chief executive of Hitachi, and the chair of the US Federal Reserve coming out in support of our case today, there isn't a dicky bird about any of them. Instead there's a load of Leave stories. I am annoyed and send a series of texts. They come back with the usual stuff that it is marked 'somewhere on the BBC'.

I've had enough of this and fire back: 'Not on your 8 a.m. Not on your website. WTO, Yellen, Hitachi, former and Current Biz Sec and head of CBI . . . not anywhere I can see. You're killing us.'

A senior figure responds by calling me to try to explain where there have been bits and pieces of economic news. I am calm and tell him it's just not good enough. By any measure, their biggest morning outlets are the website and the 8 a.m. bulletins – and there was nothing on them. I tell him the PM is doing a press conference highlighting experts versus lies, and I had to persuade him not to have a section calling out the BBC. We don't expect them to be cheerleading for us – we just want proper balance in the final stages of the campaign. I don't think it's a deliberate bias, just a combination of the slapdash and the blasé.

Fired up, we draft a punchy statement: 'Today, on the Remain side, we see three significant, trustworthy and totally independent experts give their view.' We quote the chair of the US Federal Reserve, Janet Yellen, saying, 'a UK vote to exit the European Union could have significant economic repercussions'; then Hitachi saying leaving will put jobs at risk and that those who want us to leave 'have no answer to how the UK could negotiate cost-free access to this huge market with a position outside it'; then we quote Roberto Azevêdo, the head of the World Trade Organization, saying it could take 'decades' to disentangle Britain's trading relations with the EU and negotiate replacement deals with the rest of the world – and leaving Europe is 'a high-risk bet'.

These warnings aren't just newsworthy, though they have gone largely ignored this morning – they are vital to understanding what our future would look like outside the EU.

The PM dictates the most powerful side of the statement:

> That is who you have on one side of this debate. And what have we heard from those who want us to leave? Complacency and nonchalance. A casual wave of the hand. They say people 'have had enough of experts'. On the value of our currency, they say 'the pound will go where it will'. And because they don't have any credible experts on their side, what are they reduced to? Telling complete untruths to the British people.

He then goes on to explain them, before concluding:

> So listen to the experts. Don't stand on the sidelines. This matters for you. There are no second chances or re-runs. So register to vote. And vote to remain on 23rd June.

We get in the car without motorcycle outriders, because it is an overtly political event and he is speaking as the effective leader of the Remain campaign and not Head of Government. Traffic is bad. The police get word that there are some protestors in chicken suits at the front of the building. We are struggling and the protection officer in the passenger seat flicks on the lights and puts on the siren. We shoot up a side street, sending tourists who are out in the sunshine scattering to the pavements. We have to do a U-turn on the Strand and then take another side street. Liz is waiting for us. There are no chickens to be seen as we race inside.

We are taken to the top of the building, which is next to the Savoy, and through a large series of rooms with stunning, panoramic views of Westminster and the House of Commons to the west and the City to the east, with the river snaking between.

I go up to the actual roof, where the hacks are enjoying the sunshine and the broadcast engineers are trying to get a line of sight to broadcast back to base. All of them are a little excited about why they've been called here. We tell DC the coast is clear and he delivers the above words. It's a stunning backdrop, and it feels to me that if anyone heard the case he's making – demolishing Leave's claims with asides about 'we've had enough of experts' – they would surely vote Remain.

But are they listening?

That afternoon the Stronger In board meeting isn't in my diary. Stephen Gilbert calls me half an hour before to make sure my presentation is fine. What presentation? I take a deep breath and walk over.

I arrive last and sit at the end of the table – with the projector set up to show some slides shining in my eyes, so that I feel like a captured soldier who is about to be interrogated. Stuart Rose chairs the meeting and goes round the table asking people what their concerns are.

Almost everyone says, 'Diversity of voices,' with the Green

party MP Caroline Lucas being particularly pointed about the amount she is seeing of the PM. We could be truthful and say – the problem is, we clear days for you guys and all that happens is you come up with some wet statements about how great it would be if young people voted; we're also dealing with a Leader of the Opposition whose speeches on Europe border on the incoherent; so forgive us for having to impose some order on this. Of course, we say nothing of the kind.

Most interesting of all is how most of the people around this table feel that this has gone way beyond a battle between two campaigns about whether we remain in or leave the EU. For most people, it feels like a battle for the soul of the country. Many express the view, in different ways, that we are the sensible campaign, Leave the extreme. Some talk about Remain being open to the world, Leave closed.

As I depart, I wonder how much of this is reflected in the country. Are we really two tribes at war – each unable to see the other's point of view? Much of this has become a conversation between the deaf.

Senior figures in the Labour party have been receiving dispatches from MPs in areas outside the big cities. The news is not good – all are despondent.

A coordinator in Yorkshire says she has been picking up a switch to Leave in the last few days in Leeds. She's been working in Headingley, a student and middle-class area where we expect to do well, and people say they were planning to vote Remain, but now are thinking Leave.

Another says she met young digital workers in Manchester, who said the only EU referendum material they were aware of being shared on Facebook was about Turkey joining and £350 million more a week to spend on the NHS. They thought both these things were facts.

Many of them report back that people agree leaving won't make much difference to the level of immigration, because they assume it's another false promise from politicians they don't trust. But that also means they don't believe people saying the economy will be hit.

A note from a senior Labour MP spells it out:

- Our economic message is ebbing and sounding tired. Lack of trust in any of the institutions speaking out (from PM to IMF to big companies) means the message is being discounted.
- Turkey threat is working to make immigration a live issue for swing voters as well as a GOTV [get out the vote] motivator for Leave voters. It is establishing the risk of Remaining.
- £350m for the NHS is really working.
- The anti-establishment message is working.

She concludes: 'Does Remain have any game changer held back in the locker? If so, worth getting it out.'

The answer to that final question is: No.

# Chapter 26

## This Is Giving Me a Heart Attack

DC AND I drive to the studios at the Olympic park for the ITV special programme – the first half of which will involve Nigel Farage being questioned by the audience, the second the PM.

On the way, I call Sarah Wollaston, the Conservative head of the Health Select Committee and a former GP. She's made a name for herself as an independently minded MP, and surprised me when she came out for Leave. She's been in touch saying she's ready to change her mind. She tells me her postal vote sat unopened in the kitchen for several days and as her pen hovered above Leave, she realised she would be worried if the vote went that way.

She's troubled by the nonsense the Leave campaign is spreading about pouring money into the NHS, and speaks touchingly about her father, who worked as a diver in the military after the Second World War. When he was recently rushed into hospital and was about to have an operation, he told her he was worried she was making a mistake and that leaving would betray everything his generation had done to ensure there was peace in Europe. It's a touching story – hitting a strong emotional note. I promise to contact her early tomorrow.

We arrive to see Farage's purple and yellow, open-topped, double-decker bus, which he was driven here in – and I'm reminded of Russell Brand's line that he is a 'pound shop Enoch Powell'. He's standing in the corridor inside. DC shakes his hand and says, 'Hello, Nigel.' There is a little bit of harrumphing and chuckling, but no words.

I am struck by the people he has around him, all of whom look like bouncers in a club that's trying to look respectable – razor-sharp, oiled hair, extreme partings, and shiny suits. There's no need for caricature here.

We are taken into the tiniest of dressing rooms, which has a wet room sectioned off inside it that is bigger than the rest of the available space. DC perches on a strange white stool, decides it's too precarious and then moves to a swivel chair.

I show the PM a Twitter meme that is being bounced around – a picture of Farage looking stupid, with the words 'racist bellend' as the caption. He laughs out loud.

When Farage is on stage, he comes across as tetchy – arguing with the audience when they bring up the fact that the Archbishop of Canterbury has criticised him. He appears thin-skinned and strangely subdued, his usual theatrics muted, only breaking the pattern at one moment to brandish his passport.

As Farage approaches the end, DC looks at me and asks, 'Remind me, why do we do these things?' I just smile. All of us are hating every minute of this.

Farage gets a bit of a rough ride on the economy and DC says, 'I'm going to get this on immigration.'

It's soon time for DC to go. 'Good luck!' I shout and he says, 'Thank you,' and walks away. These are the loneliest of moments for him, completely on his own – and I feel a pang knowing there's nothing more I can do.

Liz appears with a bottle of white wine and pours us all a transparent plastic cup full.

DC is expert at these encounters. He doesn't get riled, determined to be reasonable – even when they are rude to him about when he should go as PM.

The key moment is when a man called Harry Boparai talks to him about his town becoming a 'no go' area and how he

has to have his children three to a bedroom. The point is —
immigration is crushing me. It may or may not be true, but it's
almost impossible to deal with other than sympathetically.

There's another key moment when DC talks about Nigel
Farage's 'Little England'.

The programme ends. Verdict: unscathed. Though a nagging
voice tells me we need to score some goals. On Twitter the
hacks are lamenting how boring it was.

I get the BBC news up on my iPad. It's starting as we jump
in the car. We watch it — a surprisingly full edit. DC clearly
feels he came out OK and I tell him, 'I'd give the night margin-
ally to you, but the truth is, it was pretty boring.'

DC decides he wants a pint. I want my bed. He meets Gavin
Williamson in the House of Commons. We get dropped in the
cool, night air of the courtyard, and I watch him as he marches
inside. It's just over a fortnight until the vote. Not long until
we know our fate.

On Wednesday 9 June, I head to Stronger In. Having thought
about it overnight, I decide we need to get Sarah Wollaston out
there quickly. If we leave it to Friday, she'll get swallowed in
the coverage of the second ITV debate.

I ask her if she would be able to write 800 words for *The
Times* and do a short interview with Laura Kuenssberg from the
BBC. She ponders her diary and says she will move some things
around.

I then call Francis Elliott at *The Times*, and Laura. I say to
Francis that I am worried they will not recognise this for the
gold dust it is — the first defection of the campaign. He reassures
me it's a strong story that will be covered well. He says *The
Times* has been the most supportive of the papers and I joke,
'That's a bit like boasting about being the world's tallest midget.'
He talks to his editorial team and the message comes back that
they like it — and it has a good chance of being the splash.

Laura Kuenssberg likes it, too.

Mid-morning I go into a meeting at Stronger In with Saatchi about the poster campaign. We all agree that we are right to use an image of Boris sitting on the same branch of a tree as Farage, who is in the process of gleefully sawing it off.

They are also pushing a black-and-white image of a hand grenade on a stark white background. There are words next to the pin that say, 'Don't pull out'. My visceral reaction is that it is too much, though I say nothing as I am prepared to hear why they think it works. One says discomfort isn't a bad thing, it shows that the image has landed and that you are engaging with it on an emotional level. I think it's debatable if that engagement is: 'This is bullshit, they're spinning me,' or, 'I don't like it, but maybe I really should worry?'

Ryan tells them the key questions we face are:

- Do people vote for or against their anxieties? (He clearly thinks 'for'.)
- Will this be the first time in a century that the people of this country have voted against their economic interests?

The final poster they show is of a tiny UK in a wide sea, conspicuously cut off from other land masses. I like it, because it highlights the fantasy they are selling, hoping the country can slip anchor and drift off into the mid-Atlantic, pretending that our destiny is not affected by the reality of our geography, regardless of whether we are in or out of the EU.

I go through the next couple of days with the team. We look at what Labour is planning. David Chaplin, who has long been disillusioned by the struggle to engage with the leader's office, says they want their main news line to be a call to have a million conversations with people. I try not to be dismissive when I hear this stuff, but say, 'So they're going to have a quarter of the number of conversations they had in the election, when they failed to get elected.'

This strategy was widely lampooned after the general election – do they really think it has merit this time? It is obvious David is at his wits' end with them – unsure if they are a hopeless operation, failing badly to understand what it needs to do to cut through, or one that wishes us ill. Perhaps it's both.

After a PMQs session where DC is once again untroubled by Corbyn, I walk over to North House for what amounts to the strangest couple of hours I have spent in politics.

We are gathering people from the Conservatives, Labour, and the SNP to plan for the ITV debate. This is the clearest example yet of people who would normally be tearing each other's heads off working together. At first, it is a few people from the campaign, Alastair Campbell, and Kevin Pringle from the SNP.

It takes an eternity for Amber Rudd and then Angela Eagle to arrive. Both have small entourages. Angela is noticeably concerned about entering into an environment where she is surrounded by sworn enemies. We do our best to set her at ease, but we haven't got much time to establish a trusting relationship.

They all settle in and eat the sandwiches David Sainsbury's staff have kindly laid on for us. As they do, I read an email from Andrew Cooper, which knocks me back a bit . . .

From: Andrew Cooper
Date: Wednesday 8 June 2016
Subject: Daily Tracking

Voting intention (adjusted): Remain 51.3%, Leave 48.7%.

Our lead on what is riskier 'for you personally' is at 10%, lowest in the campaign so far. Lead on stronger/weaker in the EU has dropped from 20% to 13% over the last week.

The last two days have shown the highest lead for Leave so far (13% today) in perception that small businesses are on their side, and the lowest lead for Remain as being backed by NHS professionals.

In perceptions of the two campaigns there are some worrying movements:

- On 'winning the argument', we have slipped from a 13% lead for Remain in mid-May to a 1% lead for Leave today.
- In the last two days, Leave has also moved into a 1% lead on 'explaining their arguments clearly'.
- Two weeks ago there was a 6% Remain lead for 'coming across strongly'.

I focus on keeping the rational side of my brain calm. This was always going to be the tough bit. Don't panic. But I can't squash inside me the small, fearful voice, which is taunting me that we are going to lose.

Turning to the debate, I push the pace – acting as the moderator. To my right are Amber Rudd, Angela Eagle and an SNP official acting as Nicola Sturgeon. To my left, Will Straw, Ed de Minckwitz and Adam Atashzai playing Leave. We go through the opening statements. While the politicians on our side sound a little hesitant and lacking in passion, Will, Ed and Adam relish playing Leave, tearing things up with a passionate, bombastic case for getting out of this sclerotic institution. They have studied our opponents and know their arguments backwards. Ed de Minckwitz does a particularly good Boris.

When they are done, I let Alastair Campbell comment first. He gives cautious praise – clearly in favour of not crushing them just yet.

I say my overwhelming sense was of a lack of passion and we really need to work on that. It's apparent to me from the SNP answers that Nicola Sturgeon is determined to do the positive 'Hello birds, hello trees' case – which will have little impact. I tell Angela Eagle that I need to hear her righteous indignation on behalf of working people.

We do the openings again and the best that can be said is that they are a bit better.

We get into some proper debate. I call time quite quickly: 'You keep being sucked into talking about immigration on their terms. Don't unless you have to.' We fire out lines that they write down and I find myself thinking they are nowhere near as across this as we are, or they should be.

The low point is when Angela Eagle tells a fake audience member that the reason his child's class is swamped by foreign children isn't because of immigration, but Tory cuts. 'What?' I say. 'One – you sound like you are fighting amongst yourselves. Two – it isn't credible: the kids are physically in the class because of immigration, not because of cuts.'

The Labour special advisers in the room kick back a little. But it feels hopeless. I don't give a damn about her having a go at us – she just needs to be credible.

We take a break and I gently take Angela Eagle to one side. You need to kick these people – how dare they tell everyone they are the champions of working people?

I go up to Amber Rudd and write the following line for her: 'You are going to hear a lot of numbers flying around in this debate. But it seems to me the only number that matters to Boris is Number Ten. His pursuit of the next big job shouldn't skew this debate, which should be about the jobs and livelihoods of millions of people.' She says she will say this. This is a significant moment. It's a direct attack on Boris from a current Cabinet minister. It will be a story. I think we will need it.

Outside, the sky is bruised. Then comes heavy, raging rain. Thunder rolls and roars. I'm transported back to school and my English teacher explaining that a 'pathetic fallacy' is when the weather and landscape match the emotional mood.

I find myself imploring them, 'Where's the passion? You're supposed to care!'

After another go, I take Adam Atashzai and Ed de Minckwitz to one side and tell them the only way we are going to get through this is if they provide three sides of A4 that simplify every part of this: the economy; immigration; attack lines. Then drill them into their heads.

I walk back to No. 10, feeling more tired than I ever have before.

At the 4 p.m. meeting I'm asked to talk about debate prep. I say I'm concerned and conclude with the line I have written on Boris. Nick Herbert says he doesn't like it – and MPs are worried about blue-on-blue. I snap, 'I really don't care if they're worried. I'm not seeing a lot of evidence of them doing much and I'm sick of the whingeing. One of the reasons we're in this war is because of MPs trying to have it both ways. Don't blame me for having to deal with the consequences.'

I feel bad – I don't think what I said was wrong, but I shouldn't have said it.

Afterwards, Ed, Ameet and Kate all say they sympathise. It's kind, but the reality is that only a few hours' sleep every night is taking its toll on me.

I drag myself over to Cannon Street for the last meetings of the day and to watch George live on Andrew Neil's programme. Neil's approach is to pick at detail, building the pressure until the person crumbles. Ultimately it is a trial of strength. George pushes back, concedes nothing, and by sheer brute force is standing tall at the end. I feel proud of him.

I text Francis Elliott to ask if Sarah Wollaston is their splash. He texts back: 'Part of it, yes.' I am suspicious.

Late on, I learn they have splashed on something that has been around all day – Sir Anthony Bamford, the head of JCB, has written to all his 6,000 staff to say there's nothing to fear from Brexit.

I feel properly let down. We gave them a grade A exclusive and it's been buried – under a story that can only benefit Leave. They could and should have told us it wasn't getting proper treatment and I could have shopped it elsewhere.

Not for the first time, I think we have no champions.

★  ★  ★

Having gone to bed in a fury with *The Times*, I get up on Thursday and cheer the BBC. They are leading with Sarah Wollaston defecting to Remain. She does a full morning round and comes across brilliantly: a sensible woman, who has reflected. Best of all, her message is that the Leave campaign is based on the £350 million lie – and the NHS will suffer, not benefit from Brexit.

I've been working for three hours by the time the 8.30 meeting comes round. Someone is saying how angry they are with Bamford from JCB. They had assumed he would be on our side.

This is proving a painful experience for everyone.

I spend the morning back at North House preparing for the ITV debate. Amber is late. Angela Eagle is even later. I get everyone to stand together at their lecterns and practise their opening statements. The group watching applauds Amber. I almost let it go, but the fact is it just isn't working for me – starting with a not very good anecdote about visiting a factory last week. When I say it, others chip in that they agree. I say, 'It's got to be core message,' and adapt it off the top of my head.

To be fair to her, we're veering back to something we suggested a week ago and changed. She's being incredibly understanding and flexible.

I get her to repeat it several times so that it is in her head.

Angela Eagle makes the standard Labour case and does well. A young woman from the SNP is standing in. She has a draft of what Nicola is planning to say. It includes a line about how all the countries in Europe are 'independent'. It provokes a ten-minute discussion about whether this is a good thing or not. Eventually I say, 'It doesn't work. Everyone is going to be thinking about the fact that you want independence. If we are confused in this room, then others will be, too.'

They promise to go back to her.

We then open things up to a question from the floor. Alastair

Campbell asks, 'What is the number that immigration should be set at to ensure the country isn't full?'

There then follows a truly disturbing moment when Angela Eagle stares at him for a full ten seconds before saying, 'I have no idea how to answer that.'

We have another go, but it's clear no one is sure of the lines. I say, 'OK, stop. This is hopeless. You all need to realise – we shouldn't see this as a debate. It's an opportunity to get our message across. If someone says immigration – you find a way to repeat our lines. If someone says NHS, you clobber them with Sarah Wollaston. At the moment you're like rabbits in the headlights.'

We're hours away from the programme and none of this is working. We haven't even spoken directly to Nicola Sturgeon. I'm worried that we are going to be horribly exposed over the course of two hours of prime-time television.

I then get Ed de Minckwitz and Adam Atashzai to pull out the three sides of A4 I asked them to write and ask Amber and Angela to ensure they have each of them on their lecterns tonight.

We run through it and Angela Eagle announces she has to leave. I apologise for being tough and she is keen to let me know I am one hundred per cent right. She reassures me it will be all right on the night.

Alastair and I talk. He says he thinks Amber will be fine, but he is concerned about Angela. He's sent her an email reminding her, 'This is the biggest thing you have ever done. You need to take it seriously.'

Another Andrew Cooper email comes through. He says that the reporting of the referendum as a blue-on-blue soap opera is reinforcing the idea that the only people really wanting to keep the UK in the EU are the Government faction of a deeply divided Tory party. It is helping create an anti-incumbent vote. The email ends: 'Conclusion obvious.'

The conclusion is indeed obvious – we need to see and hear more of Labour. But how we do that is by no means clear. As Stephen Gilbert puts it: 'We must get strong Labour voices out, but it is clearly a problem that even if they agree to do stuff, and many of them are very keen, they get no cut-through. In some cases this is because Labour Stronger In activity is frankly being undermined by the Labour leader's office.'

He suggests getting Gordon Brown to join Stronger In and do a ten-day, high-profile tour to motivate Labour's vote. He goes on: '. . . if we remove Conservatives from high profile media, there will be nothing from Remain because Labour will fail to deliver – again in my view making it imperative that we get senior Labour people, into and at the head of Stronger In.'

The PM sums it up: 'Agree we have a problem. The difficulty is solving it without leaving field clear for Leave campaign.'

Back at Stronger In, I spot Ryan and Stephen in the tiny meeting room just off the entrance. You can get a maximum of four people in there without them being pushed up against each other. They tell me action is needed to get Labour voices clearly out there making the case. Stephen wants to set up a new campaign, 'Progressives for Britain', where we see the leaders of Labour, the Lib Dems and the Greens together.

He has the right idea – though the execution sounds very North London. The real message we are suggesting is: Save Britain from people who don't have your interests at heart.

Jim Messina fires in an email, saying that he agrees with Stephen, and he ends it: 'Are we having fun yet? :)'

Ryan, Stephen and I remain in the room together and discuss what is to be done. I can help by calling very senior broadcast figures and pointing out they are ignoring decent Labour stories.

Key Conservatives aren't convinced. They believe the story of who is the next PM is vastly more interesting to the media (and rightly so) than hearing from another ex-PM. We need to find a message that works, which can be carried by the people who can get on the news, not hope to carry a message by those who cannot. The trouble is our routes into these people are limited to say the least.

We are facing a stark truth: we have no control over a Labour party run by Corbyn and McDonnell. The sad fact is the senior Labour people on our campaign have had more face time with the Conservative PM than they have with the leader of their own party. To us the Labour leader's office resembles a madhouse, where the patients have taken over the asylum. There's also the real possibility they don't really care if we win or not – the ensuing chaos and our destruction providing opportunities that could deliver power.

I have to go to the South Bank Studios with Lucy Thomas for the ITV debate. We get in an Uber together with a real sense of dread at what might happen.

We find Amber Rudd in an overheated dressing room. She looks remarkably relaxed. I urge her to keep powering on through the two hours and reminding her to get in there early with her remarks.

I walk down with her to make-up – and stand in a long corridor while there's a conference call with the PM and George on how we get Labour to step up.

DC says he will be seeing Jeremy Corbyn at the Queen's ninetieth birthday celebrations tomorrow, 'I will say to him politely and nicely that he needs to step up and we need to find ways of letting him.' The call ends with DC saying, 'We mustn't throw everything up in the air.'

We go to have a look at the set. Nicola Sturgeon is already there. She is wearing a green suit that is the same colour as the backdrop and says she'll change because of it. After a bit of time working out where the cameras are, I suggest to Amber that she take Nicola to one side and have a chat. They're supposed to be on the same side soon in front of the nation – and yet here we are, tip-toeing around.

They go and sit in the front row. Amber looks up at me, suggesting it is OK for me to approach. I edge my way in and sit down and suggest it's crucial to get our points in early and to keep the energy levels up. I also say there's a danger that Leave will look like a team, while we will be divided, not agreeing on why we need to stay in. Nicola looks at a point on the floor in front of my feet. There's the odd nod, and a sound that I take as agreement, but I sense that it is completely toxic for her having anything to do with me, the representative of a Tory prime minister, whom her supporters resent bitterly.

I also realise the craziness of my position: here I am talking to a woman whose main purpose in life is to break up the United Kingdom, hoping she will help us win the referendum.

We go up to the green room. I chat to Angela Eagle about hitting them hard. The three women are called and we sit down to watch the debate. Angela's partner and her two SpAds come in. Nicola's team choose to remain separate.

When the programme starts, Boris seems remarkably subdued, but he's effective in getting his point across – 'take back control'.

Amber nails her opening – I feel myself relax into the large leather sofa. It's almost word for word the script we wrote together this morning.

When it's Angela's turn, I make a point of saying, 'Come on, Angela!' She does well, delivering the passionate case for Labour voters.

The first question is on immigration. They don't freeze – making the point that it is a complex issue. As I'd asked her, Amber delivers the line I wrote for her, 'There are lots of numbers flying around in this debate – but it seems to me the only number Boris cares about is Number Ten.' Twitter erupts. There are cheers in the spin room. Tweet after tweet comes through.

I've done this game long enough to know you need to get in early to frame it and there's nothing the lobby like more than a bit of aggression. Boris looks like he's flinching. Tomorrow the Leave press has a choice of two stories to write, the brilliance of their team, or Boris put on the spot. I want them to go for the second.

Any objective assessment would say the Leave team were coherent and message disciplined. They came back to the same point over and over. Our team sounded like they were coming at it from different angles. But they looked like they believed in it more and had the better moments. This was always my strategy – to make sure there were enough opportunities to hit them hard, and to have moments that clip down well for the news bulletins, where most people will engage with this.

Our best moment is when they gang up to call out the bus with £350 million on the side. Amber says, 'We're going to repaint that bus – and put a leprechaun at one end, a giant pot of gold at the other, and a rainbow in-between.'

Angela's attack is short, blunt and devastating, 'Get that lie off your bus!' There's a world of difference between the shambles of rehearsals, and their passion tonight. I feel proud of them.

At the end of the night, when we are all flagging, Amber unleashes an attack on Boris, which is almost too much. 'Boris – you're the life and soul of the party, but I'm not sure I'd want you driving me home at the end of the night.' To me it feels like a slightly racy joke, but one commentator claims it's a 'date rape metaphor.'

The Leave supporters go wild on social media – we're playing the man and not the ball. I think it's pathetic, given how rough they have been prepared to be. Someone makes a couple of jokes and the poor lambs are crying like babies. This from Boris supporters, who cheered when he suggested the PM was 'demented' and then 'corrupt' over his engagement with the FTSE 250 company, Serco, and the referendum.

The team come up. I give Amber a hug and Angela a kiss. They did bloody well. Nicola Sturgeon waves and disappears down the corridor.

In the cab back, I watch the BBC 10 p.m. edit. They went for all our lines. ITV seemed even better. More people will watch the coverage of the debate rather than the actual thing – and we look better.

DC calls me a few times. He's heard we kept accepting immigration is a complex problem and didn't like it. I thought it was great. I tell him to make sure he sees the BBC and ITV edit. He calls a quarter of an hour later. 'It worked – the edits were good.'

Seven hours ago, it felt like we were flirting with disaster.

DC ends the call by saying, 'The whole thing is giving me a heart attack.'

# Chapter 27

## We Need a Fluke to Win This Now

I HOPE FRIDAY 10 June is a low point.

The No. 10 team gathers for another meeting to discuss again what to do about Labour. It takes DC a while to come on, so I ask George about the pictures of him with Ruth Davidson on a farm yesterday. One is a low-down shot of both of them literally shovelling shit. I say that's what my life feels like at the moment. George says they also stood next to a bull with a broken penis – prompting Ruth to shout, 'Let's call him Boris!'

The meeting starts with Ed saying he's worried by their message clarity, while we seem to make a range of points.

Stephen and I try to be patient. I spent many hours yesterday trying to get the SNP, the Labour party, and a representative of the Conservative Government to work as a team. Of course Leave had a core message. So do we – 'We're stronger, safer and better off in the EU' and 'Leaving is a leap in the dark'. But getting people in a group as diverse as ours to sing in harmony just isn't going to happen. Instead we keep reminding people how extraordinary it is that people who normally disagree violently are prepared to come together.

Others want to make the positive case for being in the EU.

I pull them up short, 'I'm sorry. I'm totally confused. We've just all been talking about our message being about risk and the economy, how we need to keep hammering it – and now we are talking about handing over one of our last days to the positive case for the EU. We're trying to win over the "Hearts versus Heads" people and the "Disengaged Middle", who we know don't respond to that.'

Someone makes the case that the two aren't mutually exclusive. 'I'm sorry, they are,' I say. 'The reporting of this won't be both – it's one or the other. News doesn't operate in double messages and it makes it look as if we can't make our mind up. Of course, you can have the positive case in what you say, it just shouldn't be what we push as the news headline. Either our core message is risk, or it's positive. We all seem to agree it's risk – so why are we using one of our precious last days talking about the positive case on the news?'

There's real pushback, but I am convinced. We cannot try to ride two horses. Way back at the beginning of all of this, we decided we needed to win over people who wanted to leave the EU in their hearts, but could be persuaded to stay when they realised it was a risk to their pocket and their future. That has been the core of our thinking and we need to hold our nerve.

I look round the room and think several people look sick. But I am sure we cannot let internal debate be reflected in external arguments.

George ends the meeting saying, 'Everyone slags off negative campaigning, but it's the only consistent message that's working for us. Britain has a great future – don't risk it.'

After shooing everyone out of the PM's office for an interview with the *Observer*, I head to the Chancellor's dining room to talk more about how on earth we get the Labour party to score some runs. Stephen comes in, having had long conversations with the Labour element of Stronger In.

The message coming back is that Gordon Brown wants to do more, but he has a whole series of grudges and fears. Apparently he is saying, 'They've done this to me before. They've stabbed me in the back.' He was furious that a day he was supposed to be leading ended with George warning from the Tokyo summit that house prices would fall and taking the news.

A couple of very senior figures in the Labour party have told us they're willing to talk through back channels, but their job could be at risk if we let it be known. There really is fear and loathing there.

It's obvious what Labour need to do – spell out that if we vote to leave the EU, there'll be an agenda that actively harms working people. Ameet makes me laugh when he says, 'Yeah – if you thought George Osborne was an arsehole, wait until you see these guys!' To his credit, George thinks it's funny, too.

The truth is we have no power over Labour and no confidence they can deliver. Their message is weak – and they appear to have little concept of what a news story actually is. We are merely going round in circles.

Late tonight, I feel like I'm hitting a wall. I keep having to recharge my phones because I'm taking and making so many calls. The campaign is making me ill – my chest is wheezy and I have the early symptoms of an ulcer.

By any standards, the media team is doing an amazing job. We have a steady stream of experts explaining why they back Remain – and the BBC is leading on thirteen Nobel scientists talking about why it would be a disaster for Britain if we left.

We're also working hard on spelling out why we'd have to seriously review our finances if we left, given that the independent Institute for Fiscal Studies says there could be a £40 billion black hole.

This is the central push of what we are giving to the Sundays – the *Observer* interview, as well as a *Telegraph* Op-Ed. There'll be good stuff in the *Mail on Sunday*, too – including the Archbishop of Canterbury saying we should Remain, and Boris allegedly being caught plotting when asking an MP if he thinks they have fifty signatures yet to spark a leadership contest.

The main thing that's worrying me is a *Sunday Times* story claiming we are secretly trying to negotiate visa-free access to the UK for a million Turks. They have a series of 'Diptels' from our embassy in Ankara from May this year. I'm convinced we need to hit it hard.

This involves trying to get a number of civil servants on a conference call. A couple of them are seemingly treating 'Purdah' as a holiday and don't come on.

I dictate a line that needs fleshing out with a few facts that I want to get to the *Sunday Times* – I also suggest it comes as a joint statement from the Home and Foreign Secretaries. While it is being drafted, I call Tim Shipman, the newspaper's political editor. I tell him it is selectively leaked in order to make something appear true that isn't, 'You're also doing Leave's bidding.'

He is indignant, 'What am I supposed to do? It's not coming from Leave.'

'Don't treat me like an idiot. This may not have come direct from them, but it's plainly being done "hands free", or at least pushed by someone trying to help.'

I also call the editor, Martin Ivens. He says he isn't aware of the story and I talk him through why it is wrong – finally emailing him the following:

> These are selectively leaked quotes from diplomatic telegrams designed to give a completely false impression that the UK is considering granting visa liberalisation to some Turkish citizens. This is completely untrue.
>
> The Government's policy is, and will remain, to maintain current visa requirements for all Turkish nationals wishing to visit the UK, regardless of what arrangements other member states in the Schengen area may make with Turkey. Schengen visas do not give anyone the right to access the UK.
>
> The purpose of Diplomatic Telegrams is for our embassies around the world to feed back information on the position and

views of foreign governments. They are reports from our diplomatic posts, not statements of British Government policy.

As a full reading of these diplomatic telegrams shows, our overriding focus has been on working with the Turkish authorities to tackle illegal immigration via Turkey, because that is in our national interest. And it has been successful, with boat crossings from Turkey to Greece having fallen dramatically since the EU–Turkey deal was implemented.

I hope the takedown is as comprehensive as it is devastating. But I have little doubt they will run the story anyway.

Will Straw has been talking to Gordon Brown. My heart sinks at what is coming back. He wants to lead the Labour charge by challenging David Cameron to adopt a positive agenda for Europe. This would be some combination of a reduction in fuel bills through coordination on energy, more action on tax havens, support from the EU for communities with growing populations from immigration, coordination to tackle terrorism, and defending workers' rights.

I don't know where to start on how bad this is. It makes Remain look disunited, with different wings arguing against each other. Rather than send a clear message to Labour voters that they will lose out if we leave, it will introduce new and confusing arguments.

I hate being negative – Will is doing everything he can to try to make this work, but the Labour leadership and Gordon Brown aren't helping. I send the following email:

Let's do the call. Sorry, but I think this is pretty hopeless really. In my old job I would be saying, this is a news programme, Gordon Brown repeating his weak and confusing lines on Europe is not news. It feels lacking in urgency, too. Craig.

Will, Ameet, Ryan and I join the call. There's a lot of discussion about Gordon Brown's message. I chip in, 'I'm sorry to be blunt.

But this just isn't big news. We need to give them a line that works credibly as a headline. He can do all the detail he wants, but if it doesn't have a sharp newsline that works for us, it'll just be Gordon Brown makes a lame intervention – and will get next to zero cut-through.'

Peter Mandelson joins the call. We end up spending at least forty-five minutes describing the positive policy agenda Gordon Brown wants to put forward. It includes the assertion that if we stay in, there will be a million more jobs created. I am scathing about this – 'How many focus groups do we have to do that tell us the public don't trust numbers that appear to have been plucked out of thin air?'

Peter hits back, 'What are people voting for, if it is not an institution that creates jobs?' But Ryan agrees with me, specific numbers sound made up and are the surest way to stop people listening.

Brown also includes a line on having a fund for areas that are particularly pressured on immigration. I roll my eyes – with two weeks to go, are we seriously about to go out there with a brand new policy on immigration? 'We are way off the point here. The message we need to bash Labour voters over the head with is: If you vote Leave, you are letting people who do not have your interests at heart take over. You and the people you care about will be worse off.'

Peter tells me, 'You need to be exposed to hard-core Labour voters in Hartlepool and Doncaster, who think we have nothing to offer them on immigration. If we don't do this, we will have problems.'

'I simply don't accept that. I am well aware that's a serious issue. But I also know that you can't fatten a pig on market day. We know what we want to get across – we need to hammer that.'

Later Peter agrees they need to persuade Gordon Brown to make the main story on Monday that Gordon Brown leads the fightback, spelling out Labour voters have the most to gain from remaining, and the most to lose from Leave politicians taking control.

The next morning I am genuinely shocked by the *Sunday Times* splash: 'Leaked UK plan to open doors for 1m Turks.'

The sub-heading is: 'Proposal under wraps until after EU vote.'

The story's first witness is Iain Duncan Smith, who accuses the PM of being 'in cahoots' with the commission to perpetrate 'an appalling deceit' on the British public. I knew they would do it, but this is beyond the pale given we have been clear none of this will happen.

You have to turn to the bottom of page three and the very end of the article before you get our statement, which destroys the story.

I've worked hard on the broadcasters to say they cannot cover something that is conclusively not Government policy in any way – and to their credit, they don't touch it.

The story is a classic of its kind – magnify and amplify certain points, diminish key details that knock it down, and defend it to the hilt as the truth. I am determined to stay Zen about it all, but there's something maddening about how a newspaper can lend credence to a campaign that is doing all it can to mislead people.

I drive to New Broadcasting House to meet the PM for the Marr interview. As I park, I look in my rearview mirror and I see the flashing blue lights of the motorcycle outriders coming towards me.

I meet the PM in the rather miserable canteen. It's window-less and humid. The back wall looks like a microwave showroom – with at least a dozen for people to heat up their food. It feels like the set of a dystopian movie.

At these moments, we work on lines we hope will appear on the news. 'I want you to be consciously warning people of the risks. When you think you've said it one too many times – say it again.' The point is ensuring we have a clip that works on the news.

We watch Nigel Farage from our green room. I notice that when he's asked about sterling falling he says if it drops a few percentage points, 'So what?' I am immediately onto it – getting Stronger In to work up a whole load of social media. I also drill it into the PM's head, telling him he must launch an attack on him, saying, 'So what? I'll tell you so what . . .'

Farage is still on air when we walk through to the studio, being asked about his appalling remarks about HIV+ people coming to this country for treatment. 'How do you know if someone coming to this country is HIV-positive?' He seems to just 'Harrumph!' in response.

DC is calm and measured throughout the interview – repeatedly warning of risk. He also lands the Farage assault. I feel pretty good about it all. He never really feels under serious pressure. The feedback is good from others, too.

The rest of the day is lost in calls.

I get in my car and drive in for an evening meeting at No. 10. The streets around Whitehall are closed for the Queen's birthday, so the final half mile seems to take an eternity.

I arrive for a pre-meet, which finds Kate, Stephen, Andrew Cooper (here for the polling), Liz and Ameet already in there. I'm a little late, so they bring me up to speed: how much should the PM and Chancellor be doing in the run-up to the day?

All of our inclinations are the same – not very much. We need to clear space for Labour and that means not trumping them.

The PM and George come in at 7 p.m. They both seem to agree with the approach. But I know this is the definition of stress for them, being asked not to fight too hard for their own futures.

Andrew says he thinks the slip in our fortunes appeared to

have bottomed out on Thursday – and we should take some confidence from that.

Next on the list is the fact Labour is being allowed to take centre stage. George sums up our fears, saying, 'It's crazy to absent yourself from the field of battle in the hope that some non-existent army is going to turn up.'

I get home late and have to watch the news on delay. As I am watching the lead story, I get an anguished text from the PM: 'Are you watching the BBC? How is this balance? It was my Marr day, unbelievable.'

As I come to the referendum coverage, I see there is one weak clip from the PM on how pensions will be at risk if we leave, followed by what feels like a shamelessly helpful piece for Gove, taking him to his parents' house in Aberdeen, and discussing how his father's business went to the wall. It irritates me that in it, he is simply allowed to assert that Turkey will join the EU without challenge.

DC calls, and again is understandably outraged.

A call comes through from a senior figure at the BBC. They are emollient – and so am I. He explains that he has kept the dodgy *Sunday Times* Turkey story off the news all day long, when they could have done a separate piece on it, but didn't. This is fair enough, but I also point out that the *Ten* is the BBC's showcase programme, it should be an accurate representation of the day.

Monday 13 June is the worst day of the campaign so far. The overwhelming sense is one of ground rush. Not long until we hit land and everything seems faster, more threatening.

Amid the blur of taking dozens of decisions an hour, I have a moment of clarity:

- We have the right message – we must not wreck our economy. It's coming across loud and clear with a regular drumbeat of businesses coming out and warning of the consequences – 'rolling thunder' as the PM calls it.

- But there is a simple truth, that we are also defending something that most people find unacceptable. The EU insists we accept freedom of movement, with potentially unlimited immigration, in exchange for access to the single market. I am as metropolitan and liberal on immigration as they come, but even I think that's concerning. So what do we do?

Today we have cleared the stage for Gordon Brown to go out and make the case. He gets into spats all day long on immigration.

After several meetings, I whizz over to the CTN studio in Covent Garden, where I'm meeting Ruth Davidson to prep her for the Wembley debate. She is bang up for it and will do well.

She immediately tries out a Boris zinger on me, 'You've already been sacked twice for lying. Why are you doing it again?' I tell her it's too much, but she's definitely been thinking.

She also has an idea to appeal to the 'Don't Knows', saying, 'If you don't know, don't go.'

When it comes to talking about Stuart Rose screwing up about wages rising if we leave the EU, she says, 'This isn't just any gaffe. This is an M&S gaffe.'

Halfway through, I have to pull out to have a conference call to work through news stories for the next few days. It's slow progress, feeling like torture.

Later on, I notice that Twitter is going wild about the ICM poll that is due out at 5 p.m. Apparently it has been delayed a couple of hours and the conspiracy theorists say it's because the markets are closed.

I text Andrew Cooper. He tells me he's heard it's a four-point lead to Leave. Actually, when it comes out it's a six-point lead. I feel a little sick.

Late in the evening, another poll drops. This time it is for YouGov. Leave has a seven-point lead. It's starting to feel as if the bottom is dropping out of our world. The hacks are all going mad. It's hard to believe we faced this kind of thing in the election not that long ago.

I want to get some sleep. I'm just turning in when Peter Mandelson calls me. 'What did you think of the ten o'clock news?'

'I suppose it was good to see Gordon Brown out there. But his message felt a bit mushy.' I don't want to push it too hard, we argued at the weekend.

'I suppose that's better than nothing.' He goes on to say, 'We need some kind of spectacular luck or fluke to win this now.'

We begin to discuss if we should make a bold move on immigration. He thinks we need to say something, to be given permission to be heard. The call goes on for some time.

I have gone from sleepy and depressed to wide awake.

A few hours later, I draft an email to the PM:

I had a moment of clarity today.

We are asking people to accept something that is wrong: the unreasonable position of the EU that there should be no limit to freedom of movement. They have acted like any big institution – intransigence in the face of early revolt.

Long term their position is unsustainable and it may take us leaving the EU to break the deadlock. So where does that leave us?

You could give a speech saying:

- I have listened.
- The British people are right to be worried about immigration and the impact it has on our public services.
- Much of that immigration is good. But we have had too much of a good thing.

- I am also clear that trashing our economy is no way to deal with immigration
- and given a straight choice between our economy and controlling immigration, I believe we should choose our economy. It is the foundation of everything from jobs to opportunity.
- But I no longer believe there should be that straight choice.
- We should vote to remain in the EU AND impose limits on immigration. I will do that by x, y and z . . .

I know this is tough and rough and some is unworkable . . . but is there something in this? Of course there are downsides – and maybe we just need to hold our nerve, but a lot of people feel they are being confronted by an unfair choice.

I decide not to send it tonight – and go back to bed. Five minutes later I am still wide awake, I sit up and press send.

I wake up to a series of texts sent late at night. They are summed up by this one from Robert Peston: 'Can you do anything to regain the initiative?'

DC responds to my late-night email: 'Spot on. Always been my worry. We shouldn't be asking people to choose between immigration levels they don't want and an EU they don't love.'

I show this exchange to Will Straw, who says he completely agrees – there is a huge amount of anecdotal evidence that we are in trouble on the doorstep.

I feel I am on a journey on this – as I jump on the Tube to Westminster, three hours after my day has started.

It's packed with commuters. I try to think my way through this. This is where I get to:

Is this real? It's definitely the case there has been a shift to Leave, but has it been decisive?
If it is real, in the sense that they are riding a wave that is in

danger of taking them over the line, do we make a grand gesture or do we hold our nerve?

If we do that people will say we have panicked.

Can we have credible voices from Europe who will support us if we do? And if we do, will anyone believe that they are any more than panicked sailors urging us to join them on a sinking ship?

I talk this through with Ameet and Graeme at my table in my No. 10 office. Both are worried and think we should not do anything rash. Ameet says one of our biggest issues has been the idea that they need us more than we need them. This has the danger of making it look like only when the British people held their feet to the fire were they prepared to listen – and so we should vote out to get more.

For Graeme it's simple. A big promise now simply won't look credible.

There's a brief 8.30 meeting at Downing Street. As I walk through, I run into a series of ministers, including Patrick McLoughlin, Anna Soubry and Sajid Javid, all of whom have turned up for a non-existent political cabinet. They are all clearly on hot bricks. Anna is saying how bad it is on the doorstep. Sajid thinks we'll be all right.

I go through for a meeting with the PM, George, Ed and Kate. DC isn't quite ready for us. I slump down on the sofa outside his office next to George, who is sniggering as he looks through a piece on his phone. It's by Matthew Parris and has six reasons to vote Remain. His final one is the personality of those supporting Leave:

Michael Gove is someone you'll not hear a word against, because we all like him, respect his intelligence and believe him to be a fundamentally good man. But when he grows eloquent, I cannot quite banish from my nostrils the smell of burning witches. These people do not make a government. There are too many there that you'd want for your lively dinner party, but would hesitate to leave in charge of your goldfish.

George and I are unable to stop laughing.

Inside the meeting, DC reads out the email I sent him last night. I then feel bad putting the other side of the argument: we'd need to be damn sure we have rock-solid support in Europe if we go forward, and the likelihood has to be that we won't.

DC laughs and says, 'This is evidence that you can be very persuasive whichever side you argue.' I think it's meant as a compliment. I feel trapped – understanding the need for radical surgery, but now thinking it might kill the patient.

There's some discussion about saying that freedom of movement would be on the agenda at the first European Council meeting after the referendum. This sounds like a total non-starter – 'Don't worry guys, we're going to have a chat about it after you vote!' There is zero credibility in that option.

We come to the conclusion that we should not throw everything up in the air. Instead, we should make sure we have several moments where the PM levels with the nation – 'We are on the verge of making a catastrophic mistake, where the future of your family is at stake. Don't risk it.'

All the way through this we have held to one core belief: telling people they will be poorer if they leave the EU trumps controlling immigration. Late in the day, none of us are quite so sure of that any more, particularly when people are being told they can control immigration and improve public services. But after walking through the arguments, it's evident we can't shift now.

A call has been set up with Angela Merkel. It now seems pointless. The idea was to test the water with her to see if we can agree to make plain that much more will be done on immigration, but as the time approaches, we realise it's a fool's errand.

Even supposing a magical plan can be set in train – and it certainly isn't – it will look desperate.

Angela Merkel comes on the line. DC explains the situation and that he has now decided this is not the moment to ask for more – though it will obviously need to be revisited if we win.

# Chapter 28

## Nigel, You're No Fisherman's Friend

B Y WEDNESDAY 15 June I feel certain: whatever the outcome of the referendum – we'll be out of No. 10 quite quickly. I don't see how the PM can survive.

I mention this to Kate Fall, who doesn't even blink. 'Oh, yes . . . this is the burning of Moscow stage.'

DC disagrees – he is sure that we will be able to steady the ship and continue. A win, combined with a strong will, is going to see us through.

George is doing his emergency budget today – it's already top of the news and it is very specific. It warns that he'll have to increase income tax by 2p and reduce spending on the NHS.

He talks it through on the early call – explaining the pressures he will face, with questions like, 'You passed a law saying you wouldn't raise tax . . . you made a series of promises based on an economic plan . . . why are you breaking that?'

His answer is that 'I made those promises on the basis of a properly planned economy – not the idea we'd back Brexit . . . and my role as Chancellor is to warn about risk.'

The phone rings as soon as I've hung up. This time it's Norman Smith asking if I have seen the letter from fifty Tory MPs saying they would refuse to support any such budget. It's a clever response – it drags it into a blue-on-blue process row.

My phone lights up on the way to the Tube. This is catnip to hacks – the Chancellor being told his job would be untenable in the event that he suggested such a budget.

As I am walking down Devonshire Road in the early morning sunshine, I call George. He hasn't yet heard about the letter. I say he needs to emphasise the point that someone would have to deal with the massive black hole that the IFS say would exist. He says OK, but I can hear that he's taken aback. Thinking about it, it feels more and more that he's acting like he is prepared to sacrifice himself. He's forced it back onto the economy, but at what personal cost? And nagging at the back of my mind is this question: has this misfired? Should we have been so specific – suggesting such horrific solutions? Could he not have had more impact with less, simply saying there's going to have to be an emergency budget, and none of the options are palatable?

At the 8.30 meeting, the Chief Whip and Gavin Williamson are both worried, knowing there will be blood come what may. All of us can see the emergency budget news is going down like a cup of cold sick with MPs.

Later that morning, as I arrive in DC's Commons office, he's obviously concerned PMQs will be a bit of a nightmare, with Conservative MPs waiting to stick the knife in over what's being called George's 'punishment budget'.

My old friend, Oliver Dowden, now an MP, is sitting opposite me. He says, 'The MPs have gone "potty pots" about it!' He has a wonderfully nursery-school way of putting things, which makes everything seem even more absurd.

As we are talking, the daily tracker comes through. It puts us on 52.7 against 47.3 for Leave. That counts as good news at the moment.

DC is antsy – he doesn't really see the point in having practice questions fired at him and decides to go down to the Commons to 'soak up the atmosphere'.

Corbyn is surprisingly helpful in his approach – pointing out how repugnantly disingenuous the Leavers are being by claiming to be on the side of working people and the NHS. It doesn't really matter. The whole of Westminster is focused on something going on outside the chamber. Nigel Farage is on the Thames with his flotilla of fishermen complaining about the EU, while being comprehensively trolled by Bob Geldof shouting, 'Nigel – you are no fisherman's friend.' Geldof has the advantage, because he brought a PA system. Farage is clearly incensed.

I look back at the TV covering PMQs and think: if someone had told us two years ago we'd be in a position where Corbyn and the SNP's Angus Robertson would be supporting us while our MPs remained silent – and Bob Geldof was screaming abuse at Nigel Farage on the Thames . . .

How did it come to be this surreal, through-the-looking-glass, topsy-turvy madness?

I get back to Stronger In in time to watch the six o'clock news. Completely against my advice, Theresa May has done an interview with Laura Kuenssberg. Whether it's by accident or design, she has reopened the debate about if we need to do more about freedom of movement.

I find the interview frustrating – it's not clear what point is being made. It would be better if she had stuck to her submarine strategy.

The calls start to flood in. I do my best to smooth it over with Francis Elliott. But it's clear he is having none of it. I am short with him. You know we aren't reopening this before the referendum – you know this wasn't a deliberate attempt to do that. Talk to the Home Office.

I call Liz Sanderson, who is one of Theresa's SpAds. It seems to be news to her that this is starting to spin badly out of control, with the Home Secretary and Chancellor looking at odds. I ask her to get on it.

I call the BBC and ask them to change their online page, which headlines a stark statement that doesn't really reflect her view. They agree. But the genie is out of the bottle.

Next up is Peter Dominiczak of the *Telegraph*, eager to compare her words to George's earlier, which the Home Secretary seems to contradict.

I call one of the Home Office's senior civil servants, focused on media, and point out an intervention that I was told was meant to be helpful is having the opposite effect. He keeps telling me he cannot be fired for acting in this, when he is supposed to be an impartial civil servant. I tell him bluntly that what I am asking of him as a grown-up at the Home Office is to recognise there is a problem here and get someone to deal with it.

It's all happening while Gove is on *Question Time*. Adam Atashzai is marching up and down the office shouting things for people to tweet. I intervene at one point – Gove's just said there will be 'bumps in the road' if we leave, we need to hammer him on that.

I feel knackered. We are being knocked about by indiscipline from all sides in this ramshackle coalition. More to the point – I am worried by the extent to which Gove and Leave are running an anti-expert, anti-establishment, anti-sense strategy that is gaining traction.

As I go to bed, Graeme texts me the results of the Ipsos MORI poll that is to come out tomorrow and in the *Evening Standard*: 'Usual terms: Standard poll – Leave 53, Remain 47.'

This is very bad news.

One of the key points of comfort – in the general, confusing muddle of different voting poll numbers – had been the fact that phone polls, which we believed to be more accurate, had consistently shown us in the lead.

Thursday 16 June begins with a pre-6 a.m. call from James Chapman, George's director of communications. It's a *cri de coeur*. The BBC is leading on IDS, Nigel Lawson, Michael Howard and Norman Lamont criticising the Treasury and the Bank of England for 'peddling phoney forecasts' to scare people into voting to stay in the EU.

The BBC seems to be just running it straight. Have they stopped to deconstruct what is going on here? It's being claimed that our central bank, set up to ensure economic stability, is part of a conspiracy to keep us in the EU regardless of the harm it causes to the people of this country. I find myself questioning if I really understand what is and isn't acceptable any more. Surely the BBC should be properly taking this to task in their bulletins, running the story as outrage at such an irresponsible claim?

James wants us to make it as uncomfortable for them as they are making it for us, saying, 'George really went for it yesterday – and win or lose, he's going to have to live with this for years.' I agree.

I call the PM, having drafted some tweets. I suggest, 'It's deeply concerning that the Leave campaign is criticising the independent Bank of England,' and, 'We should listen to experts when they warn us of the danger to our economy of leaving the European Union.'

The *Standard* poll drops, and you can almost hear the Westminster village take a sharp intake of breath. Ben Page, the chief executive of Ipsos MORI, is tweeting that the reason for the huge swing is purely and simply down to immigration.

There's a small group meeting with the PM. I've just heard it's been confirmed that Corbyn is replacing Alan Johnson on *Marr* this weekend. Stephen says, 'It'll be a rough ride and we will all be sitting on the edge of our sofas,' but we agree it's probably the right thing to do.

At the end of the meeting, we hear about some more of Jim Messina's modelling. He reckons it is currently 51–49 to us.

I have a fifteen-minute break before the PM does an interview with the *Sunday Times*. I've talked DC through what I suggest he should say and I decide to write it out, instead of print it, because I can't use No. 10 computers for campaigning:

1. Make a big deal of 'there is no turning back' if we decide to

leave. It's final. Make clear that getting this point across is 'mission critical' to the final days of this campaign. We are talking to people who don't realise it is final.

2. Make a meal of your 'deep concern' about how experts are being trashed. If a mechanic said to you, 'I wouldn't go on the motorway with my family in that car – the brakes are faulty and it's leaking oil,' you wouldn't do it. So why don't we listen to the 'independent experts' who tell us jobs are at risk, prices will rise, the economy will shrink, putting pressure on public services?

3. Key message – tell him, 'It's your family's future. Don't risk it.'

I place the hand-written piece of paper on his desk and run my fingers along my words saying them aloud in case he cannot read my handwriting.

He picks up the piece of paper and places it beside him, as Tim Shipman comes in with a photographer. DC is very 'hail fellow, well met' with him, talking about his wife, who is now a key member of the events team, despite having been furious about last week's front-page splash, claiming there's a secret plan to let a million Turks into the UK.

DC goes for it in the interview. The most telling moment is when he specifically names Gove for his 'bumps in the road' comment and does a riff – 'Lost jobs, a bump in the road. Bang! Higher prices? Bang! Another bump.'

Almost as soon as we are done, we go on to a call with Martin Ivens. We've heard the *Sunday Times* is on a knife edge as far as which way it'll declare – Remain or Leave.

DC has a go, but Ivens is cagey. Instead of making clear which way he'll jump, he asks, 'What are the messages out of Berlin?' It seems an odd question. I think he'll do a massively equivocal editorial, but who knows on which side of the line it will fall.

Back at Stronger In we discuss what our best approach is in the dying days. Ryan is clearly wound up by what we're dealing with. He looks at me and says with real despair, 'A revolution of idiocy is happening across the Western world and it's landing in Britain on Thursday.'

The office is crowded round the monitor above my desk to watch the England *vs* Wales match in Euro 2016 and I go for a coffee with Lucy Thomas to wake myself up and get some space.

As I'm ordering, Lucy gets a call from Simon Darvill, who is our youth coordinator. He's heard that Jo Cox has been stabbed at a Leave rally. We pause for a moment in shock. It's curious that she would have been at a Leave rally, but coming from a news background, I've learned to be cautious about first reports and head back to the office to see if we can find out more.

It looks as if there will be nothing but uncertainty for a while. I feel physically sick – the combination of this news and the campaign catching up with me makes me feel that if I don't lie down soon, something bad will happen. I walk back up the road towards the flat I've been allowed to use. Sir Alan Parker, the chairman of Brunswick, calls for a general chat about the campaign. As I talk to him, I lie down on the bed. My other phone is going wild.

I don't want to be rude, but I really need to attend to this.

It's more news on Jo Cox. The Labour party has decided to suspend campaigning. Will wants us to do that, too. The PM is on a plane to Gibraltar, where he is due to talk to a few thousand people. I want to be able to have the conversation with him, because he's going to have to turn the plane round. But I realise that's not going to work – and I agree there should be no more from the campaign.

I drag myself up and walk back down to the office.

There is a conference call as the PM lands in Gibraltar. We are brought up to speed with the latest. Jo Cox has died. It will be announced when the family has had a chance to deal with the news. The police are making raids.

All of us are shocked.

To many, it feels like a moment may be crystallising in the campaign. This morning Farage launched a poster with a crowd of brown-faced men looking like they are filing into this country with the words, 'BREAKING POINT' and 'The EU has failed us all'. The image is in fact Syrian refugees being transported across the Slovenia/Croatia border and had nothing to do with free movement. It has been condemned as overtly racist, because the original picture had white faces in it, which have now been obscured.

Now it's reported that the killer shouted, 'Britain first!' as he attacked Jo Cox. There are questions about links to the far right.

The football has finished and the campaign office is in a post-match torpor. I wave to Will Straw and pull him into the meeting room, filling him in on all the detail. There's not much either of us can say.

At the back of each of our minds is a thought that makes each of us uncomfortable – what impact will this have on the referendum?

I have to disappear to go and see Justin King, the former head of Sainsburys, about an appearance at the BBC Wembley debate next week. It seems to take us forever to get across London to a discreet, uber-modern business club.

It's odd trying to brief him, thinking of everything that's just happened.

As he whizzes off to another meeting, I stay back to catch the six o'clock news with the debate team. It is heartbreaking. An image of a vivacious, talented, caring, campaigning MP, who was also a mother of two, is plain to see. What did she do to deserve this?

In another pathetic fallacy, it starts to hammer down with rain as I get an Uber ride home. I can't face going back to the office and there's nothing I can't do on the phone.

When the PM lands back at 8.45 p.m., we talk on a conference call. He is tired and saddened at the end of a long and tragic day. Next to grief, the overwhelming sense is that we must not allow anyone to politicise her death.

The suspension of campaigning is already having an impact. The IMF has knocked back its planned story on the impact on the economy by twenty-four hours. The *Sunday Times* interview we did a few hours ago is now hopelessly out of date.

I slump on my sofa. Ameet calls – he says all of this has made him ask the same question that's been rattling round my brain like a stone in an oil drum for some time, 'What kind of country do we live in?' Jo Cox's killing may not be related to the campaign, but the violence and shock of it, in the midst of what has been a bruising period, seems to put everything in sharp relief. Both of us feel the country is incredibly divided – and that is saddening.

This has gone way beyond winning and losing on the EU – it feels like a Battle for Britain. Part of it is wondering what the hell is going on in terms of challenges to the PM, which seem more to do with gaining power than about Europe. Another part is how our opponents can be so mendacious. We are confronted by the willingness of supposedly thoughtful, educated people to manipulate, deceive, and try to kick away the foundations of sensible political debate – trashing experts, refusing to have a plan, telling people things they know not to be true.

Alex Massie writes a piece for the *Spectator* blog saying no one can be blamed for the murder of Jo Cox but her killer, but speaks of a feeling of profound discomfort at a world where Nigel Farage can release the 'Breaking Point' poster. He concludes: 'I cannot recall ever feeling worse about this country and its politics than is the case right now.'

I have rarely been so tired and confused – or been in the middle of something that feels so important.

# Chapter 29

## A Voice of Compassion

I WAKE UP ON Friday 17 June and feel a moment of peace. Then a thought enters my head like bacteria: we do live in a country where an MP as good as Jo Cox can be killed on our streets. The bacteria divides and divides – until my mind is full . . .

A week today, we will know the result of the referendum, but campaigning has been suspended for who knows how long.

I settle on my sofa, bracing myself before being immersed in the horrifying coverage. Some reports focus on the killer's mental health. Others react by saying that if there was any suspicion that he was an Islamist, who had slipped into the country from Europe, we would never hear the end of it. I don't know what to think.

I have an overwhelming sense that we must rise to this moment. I want to talk to DC separately to the others. It's just after 6 a.m. and I text him suggesting he calls me when he is ready.

He comes through ten minutes later, just as I am standing at my sink, ready to shave (calls covered in shaving foam have become a staple of my day).

We talk about the expectation that he leads in this moment. We are all reticent about it, because we don't want to be accused of being political, but we need to find a way and a moment to speak about the horror of what has happened.

Before the 8.30 meeting, I have a conference call with Will,

Ryan, and Stephen. All of us are agreed that we need to find a way to respond properly to all of this.

I have been looking at Jo's social media – and the pinned tweet at the top of her Twitter feed is an article for the *Yorkshire Post* saying it's not racist to be worried about immigration, but we need to be thoughtful about how we deal with it – and wrecking our economy is not the answer.

One suggestion is to get Andrew Mitchell, whom she knew from his days as International Development Secretary, to call on the Leave campaign to withdraw its poster suggesting Turkey is about to join the EU. This seems a little randomly political to me.

Graeme Wilson comes in and suggests a religious figure needs to speak. I wonder if Archbishop John Sentamu would do it.

I try to lift the conversation. Should the PM give a speech? Should he visit the scene?

I have to leave the call to go to a meeting with the PM. DC is already in with George, Ed, Kate and Simon Case. I pull up a chair and talk through where the campaign is getting to – thinking he should visit the scene.

The conversation is long. There's a lot of discussion of how this reminds us about what is precious in our politics – and what needs to be banished from politics.

Simon Case is sent from the office to see if he can make contact with Corbyn's team. Apparently he is on a train to Jo Cox's constituency and we are struggling to contact him. 'Surely someone on his team must have a mobile phone,' says the PM.

We return to what he wants to say. DC stands up, gets some paper and a sharpie pen. He starts to write it down.

Some want him to make an angry speech where he calls out the lies and nastiness of the Leave campaign. This is not the country we are or should be. I can tell DC is moved, but it's just too inflammatory – sounding like we are linking the two for political ends, even though that's not what people really want to do.

We seem trapped in the Prime Minister's office. I'm convinced we just need to get up to Jo Cox's constituency. We start finding the right words. Simon says it's possible Corbyn will visit with him.

David Cameron finds his voice and dictates the following words:

The first time I met Jo Cox was in 2006 in Darfur. She was working, as she always did, in the most dangerous parts of the world, fighting for the lives of refugees. And today we come here to commemorate a life lost.

Two children have lost a mother; a husband has lost a loving wife; and Parliament has lost an amazing person – a voice of compassion, who epitomised the importance of serving others.

This has profoundly shocked our nation. And I think it's important we stand back and think about three things:

First: that we should value and treasure our democracy, and the fact that MPs are rightly out there with the public, accountable and accessible. Jo died doing exactly that – she died doing her job.

Second: that politics is about serving others. There are passionate debates. We may not agree with what politicians say. But fundamentally, we should remember why they're in public life: to serve the national interest and improve people's lives.

Third: that our democracy here on these islands is a remarkable and precious thing. We have peace and stability, underpinned by tolerance. So where we find hatred, intolerance and division, we should banish them from our politics and from our communities.

The values Jo fought for were community, tolerance and service. The best way to honour her memory is to redouble our commitment to them.

★　★　★

It's time to get up to Yorkshire. As we leave, news comes through that Jeremy Corbyn will share a platform with us. George has been speaking to the Leader's office through Labour's Deputy, Tom Watson. It's been agreed there will be no campaigning in the coming days, including no street stalls tomorrow. That makes little sense to me, but we're rushing so much, I don't have time to think about it.

Instead of getting into the usual Government Jaguar, the cops take us in a Land Rover. As we shoot along the road towards Northolt, I read Andrew Cooper's latest polling analysis. It is tight:

> Today's headline voting intention: Remain 50.8%, Leave 49.2%.
> I reiterate what I said yesterday: we are, within margins of error, 50/50.
> About 20% of voters are either completely undecided, or giving a vote intention but also saying they may still change their mind and vote the other way.

Now we have left Downing Street, messages come flooding in. Some say DC needs to up the anger in his statement; others that it needs to be calmer. He just ignores it all, 'We're in the right place and I have to learn it. I've only just got yesterday's Gibraltar speech out of my head.'

The calls come in thick and fast on the helicopter flight, which is due to take forty-five minutes – I manage to take some, shouting above the noise. The rumour mill that we are on our way up is in full flow.

Ameet wants us to go through what is happening for Sunday. Liz pours me a cup of tea in a painfully thin paper cup. DC learns his script.

We land at a police field in Yorkshire. They also keep police dogs here and they bark angrily as we walk to a two-floor Portakabin, where a lovely lady makes us more tea.

DC has written a condolence card. I put on the 1 p.m. news,

with Jane Hill rather tongue-tied as she tries to ad-lib the links between packages at the scene where we are heading.

I sit in the support car driven by Sean with a large bunch of flowers on my lap. He tells me he has driven here very fast. I ask him how he thinks it's going. All his ex-army friends are voting Out. I wonder if he thinks the death of Jo Cox will have an influence. He tells me that he's been talking to some people who think it is all part of a conspiracy.

Seriously? Apparently so.

We arrive in the town. It is tourist-board Yorkshire, the houses on steep streets and rolling countryside on the outskirts.

I walk out with the flowers. Hilary Benn is there with Jeremy Corbyn, who stands notebook in hand attempting to memorise the script he's planning to deliver. I can see down a steep hill the media and people surrounding a memorial covered in flowers.

Hilary Benn is incredibly friendly. He strikes me as a kind and decent man, as we talk about what has happened.

After a while I make a point of going up to Jeremy Corbyn. I shake his hand and thank him for agreeing to do this today. He says he is glad to. I ask him if he has seen the family – he hasn't, they are in Reading, but he has spoken to Brendan Cox on the phone. Apparently he has spent the morning telling his three-year-old and five-year-old that their mother has died. 'How do you do that?' he asks me and I shake my head. There is no sensible answer to that question.

Jeremy Corbyn enquires if I know where the Speaker of the House of Commons, John Bercow, is. I hadn't realised he was coming, but as I look round, I see him arriving in a car with a No. 10 press officer.

I walk down the hill with Corbyn's press officer. We stop at a spot just in front of a phalanx of cameras. I crouch down on the damp, stone ground. I look up the hill and see the politicians coming down bearing flowers. The PM leads them as, each in turn, they lay them at the memorial. Then they walk over to the cameras.

DC is no more than a couple of feet away. He looks down at me, then at a reporter who asks him a pre-prepared question. He delivers his words well. Jeremy Corbyn is a little rambling, but I hear a clear soundbite from him about rejecting hatred. As he talks, I am aware of John Bercow moving in from the background before saying a few words.

I let them walk away, but they are caught by people who understandably just want to talk. I move so as not to get cut off from them. A woman puts her hand on my shoulder. Another shakes my hand. She thanks me, I thank her – though we are not sure why, it feels the right thing, the human thing to do.

I walk next to the PM as we move up to the cars. Lots of people are saying, 'Thank you for coming here.' There is no awkwardness – just people searching for ways to show they care. I find myself holding back tears.

The next stop is the parish church. The politicians are there to sign the book and light a candle. I chat to the local vicar, who says he's not sure if two or two thousand people will come – it doesn't matter, he's happy to provide a place that's open if they want it.

It's time to go and the PM is swept outside. This is normally my cue to run. But at that moment Jeremy Corbyn calls me over, 'Craig. Thank you for today. And will you thank everyone at Number Ten for what they've done? I'd really like you to do that. It has meant a lot to me.' It takes him a long time to say. I don't mind – he is utterly sincere. For all our differences, like most politicians, he is a decent man whose heart is in the right place.

I look down the long church path and see the PM standing at his car with the door open. He's obviously wondering what we're discussing that is so important. Later he jokes about all the new best friends I've been making along the way.

The sun is shining as we fly to the PM's constituency. I race through some emails and end up falling asleep.

On landing, the PM wants to walk back to his house. I don't blame him. It feels like we are in a world of pastoral bliss. A ewe is standing by a fence making a lot of noise. I ask whose house we are passing, 'That's Chadders' [Peter Chadlington], my spiritual father.'

He says Sam ran into Michael at the school gates. I ask him what he thinks Gove makes of it all. 'I don't know – embarrassed, I guess.'

I say, 'I can't help feeling angry with him. The supposedly great intellectual rubbishing experts and getting himself wrapped up in a nasty, immigration-focused campaign.' DC agrees, thinking he may be wondering how on earth he ended up here.

We turn the corner into his drive and the debate prep team are there waiting for us. DC says they should have gone inside.

We sit in his living room and I take the seat that seems to be mine whenever I'm here. DC wants us to make a list of all the things he has to get across on Sunday's *Question Time* programme.

It's pretty easy. The briefing team are young, smart and on it – and it's good to hear them in action. By this stage, we can all recite it word for word.

I step outside into the sunshine. The air is thick with dandelion fluff floating on the wind. I call some commentators to brief them. All of them think we are going to win, but it's going to be tight. Most of them rail against the angry, mendacious nature of Leave's campaign.

Ryan sends me the following email about debate prep:

Circumstances have obviously changed over the past 24 hours. But I think there are some clear takeaways from the track and focus groups over the past week: No blue-on-blue. No personal attacks. Make a case about the economy, our place in the world and the sort of country we want to be.

DC is due to have a call with Gordon Brown. He wants to persuade him to do an event involving both of them, Tony Blair and John Major.

Word is, Gordon isn't up for it.

He is gruff and blunt when he comes on this line. But he makes a good case – he is appealing to a different audience, who don't believe in the establishment. He sums it up best when he says, 'You're appealing to a group who are secure, who might become insecure. I'm trying to appeal to a group that is insecure, by telling them they might become more secure by remaining in the EU.'

DC says he thinks we need a 'shock factor' for the undecideds, and what better way than all the surviving PMs think it is a bad idea if we leave.

'We had the shock factor yesterday,' says Gordon. 'I don't think it will work.' It's plain to me this isn't going to happen. Brown says there are too many people who feel they have nothing to lose. When we talk to them about risk they say there's nothing to risk. In his view, there's not a greater sign of the establishment than four prime ministers.

As I'm driven back to London, I get a text from John Witherow at *The Times*: 'The Times declares tomorrow, I think you will be ●.' The emoticon he has chosen has come out as a big black spot. I assume it is meant to be a smiley face, but I call him to check. He thinks we will win.

I buy the team a drink in a pub in Chiswick and as I walk home I get a call from Peter Mandelson. He is irritable, 'Who agreed that there should be no campaigning this week?' I tell him there was an agreement between Tom Watson and senior Downing Street figures. He tells me, 'You have been taken for an enormous ride. This suits the leadership down to the ground. They never wanted to campaign – and they only did because they were forced into it. Now they have the perfect excuse not to do anything. I am furious!'

He goes on to say, 'Corbyn and Watson want us to lose this referendum. Everyone needs to wake up.'

The next morning I wake up to a stark message from him: 'We are headed for disaster.'

I'm not sure how I am supposed to respond.

There is anxiety everywhere. Lord Guthrie has taken it upon himself to switch sides and tell the *Daily Telegraph* that he now wants to leave the EU, because of the threat of an EU army. There is no prospect of an EU army.

I read the papers thoroughly, wondering why I need to know that Kelvin MacKenzie says the first of his ten reasons to leave the EU is: 'Those two posh boys in Downing street will be out of a job'.

There is one ray of hope. An online poll by BMG puts us 11 points behind, but they have also done a phone poll that puts us 7 points ahead. Andrew Cooper has pointed out consistently that the failure to sample enough time-poor, busy professional people was shown to be one of the biggest reasons why the voting polls had been wrong at the general election. So this poll, which has made efforts to include such people, ought to be among the most accurate.

I go for a run to clear my head, get home to take a few calls and hear the 'news notification' going off on my phone. I am standing by my desk and the message imprints itself on my brain.

'Thomas Mair, charged with MP Jo Cox's murder, gives his name as "Death to traitors, freedom for Britain".'

The significance of this is immediately clear – even though I am hit by a torrent of emotions, ranging from disgust to anger.

I call a few people, including Peter Mandelson, whose reaction to the news seems to be one of relief and a hope it will give people pause for thought.

The PM takes a while to get back to me. He has been walking down Chipping Norton High Street. I am buying some lunch in M&S when he calls. He tells me he is feeling much more positive. People are coming up to him and wishing him well, from all walks of life. He can feel it moving.

A leading Sunday newspaper journalist texts me, 'It's over. You've won.'

The rest of the day is a blizzard of calls – working hard on shaping the papers for tomorrow. The most significant conversation I have is with Tim Shipman to find out where they are in terms of who they will support.

He says it's been a tough day at the *Sunday Times* – with the editor, Martin Ivens, saying the paper is going to recommend that we leave the EU. Interestingly, the splash will be a line from our interview: 'Cameron warns there's no turning back if we leave.'

Late on I have a conference call with the team. The papers are landing well for us. I tell them how proud I am of them.

As things stand – I think we are going to win.

# Chapter 30

## This Truly Is a Leap in the Dark

I T'S CLEAR THE Jo Cox killing has dampened the Leave campaign, to the extent that Gove's headline in the *Telegraph* is the assertion that there won't be a recession if we leave. That fails on two levels:

- They're playing on our turf (the economy) because they can't play on their own (immigration).
- Using the word 'recession', even to deny it, should make people worry.

The daily tracker poll gives more reasons to be cheerful:

> Today's headline voting figures: Remain 52.0%, Leave 48.0%. That's a slow but steady and unmistakable reopening of a lead for Remain. This is consistent with the published polls.
>
> The YouGov poll indicates that the move back towards Remain started before the murder of Jo Cox.

I watch Corbyn on *Marr*, who by accident or design is utterly hopeless as far as persuading people to vote Remain goes. He says some warm words about Jo Cox, but completely fails to say anything that would be helpful for the campaign, before actively harming it by stating freedom of movement does not need reform. He is completely at odds with the views of traditional Labour voters, but seems blind to it. No wonder many of his MPs fear losing the north of England, the way they lost Scotland.

Alastair Campbell sends me a text: 'Jesus God almighty.'

It arrives just as I am sending one to Ryan and Will, saying: 'Oh God.'

Will makes a general point about all politicians failing on immigration throughout this campaign. I respond – maybe, but this is a key interview and some of us are managing to give the right line. (The *Sunday Times* splash has been described as 'a thing of beauty' by Ryan Coetzee, because it nails the crucial 'no going back' point.)

I watch Gove. He is typically articulate, rattling out perfectly formed sentences like a debating machine. He claims to have 'shuddered' when he saw the Farage 'Breaking Point' poster. But when asked if he still stuck by the Vote Leave statement claiming a million Turks would be here within a few years and we should be careful because of their high birth and crime rates, he says he does. My jaw drops. I feel genuine anger listening to him, as he stands by something so inflammatory.

DC calls me to get my estimation of what's gone on. I tell him there's no point varnishing it, Corbyn was hopeless. I also tell him Gove was a disgrace.

I race out to pick up my kids to have a Father's Day brunch, before getting in a car to Euston. I have a train to catch at 12.40. There's no way we'll make it. I ask the driver to turn the car round and drive me to Milton Keynes instead. Inevitably we end up talking a bit more about the referendum. He's for Out. He's a decent enough bloke, but it's staggering how much Leave propaganda he's swallowed without question. I take him through why each bit is wrong. He wants to listen.

We pull up to some lights and I spot a Remain campaigner. I wave him over and take one of his stickers, placing it on the headrest of the passenger seat. He takes it in good heart.

He gets me there on time and I shake his hand. He's precisely the kind of person who should be concerned about leaving – the shrinking economy countless experts warn about, impacting his trade and the opportunities of his children. He says he'll think hard, but I doubt I converted him.

We're rehearsing in a hotel that is twenty minutes outside Milton Keynes and has seen better days. The decor is tired and the rooms feel municipal.

As I walk in the door, DC arrives. He asks me to go up to his room and not the conference room where we will be rehearsing. He tells me he thinks he's landed Baroness Warsi, the former co-Chair of the Conservative Party – defecting from the Leave camp.

He calls her and as he speaks, I survey a giant platter of fruit. I stab the tiny pomegranate seeds with a black, plastic pick. DC tells Sayeeda Warsi that he has always thought this is where she'd end up – and that she couldn't go with Leave. He tells her I will call with a media plan in ten minutes.

When he hangs up he leans forward and does a downward fist pump.

I walk outside the hotel – telling Francis Elliott of *The Times* that I want to give him a chance to redeem himself, having buried the Sarah Wollaston story.

I call Sayeeda. She tells me she watched the morning political programmes, hoping that the change in tone of the campaign would continue after the murder of Jo Cox, but she was shocked to see Farage and Gove out there, 'doing it all again'.

She is incensed, telling me she is horrified by the xenophobia and lying.

An hour later she calls me saying she has spoken to *The Times*. I also ask her to talk to the BBC.

The prep for tonight's *Question Time* event takes place in a room with an overly large table. There are several bowls of fruit chews on the white table cloth.

The key thing to get straight is how DC deals with the inevitable Jo Cox question.

I think he needs to sum up the horror, pay tribute to her

values, and then move on to the horrible nature of the UKIP poster and the motives behind it. We have several stabs at this before he gets it right. It's clear he is walking a tightrope.

We spend a lot of time finding ways to get 'Don't risk it' and 'No going back' into his answers. I emphasise that the objective of tonight's exercise is to put doubt into the heads of people who consider themselves to be wavering.

After about an hour we get restless and stare out of the windows at a wedding party gathering in the sunshine below.

DC decides he wants to go for a walk. A group of us join him – there's plenty of gallows humour about what the hell we thought we were doing calling this referendum, and who has been the most obnoxious on the Brexit side. Priti Patel is a popular choice.

I travel with DC to the MK Dons stadium for a brief look at the set. It's a unit in the middle of a vast, windowless room.

The podium DC is to stand on is a giant 'Q' and I worry it is a trip hazard. David Dimbleby has been positioned with his back to the audience and in the PM's eyeline, so that he can intervene when he wants.

We are taken to a room in the adjoining Hilton hotel. There are two giant plates of biscuits and a bed. He's got half an hour to get his mind straight, so Ed, Kate and I go for a drink.

I'm reminded of the line in *Paradise Lost*, 'They found no end in wandering mazes lost', as we walk along an endless corridor that seems to stretch into infinity. We finally find reception, where we are pointed to an empty bar, with a TV tuned to the BBC News Channel. All of us agree, 'This is such a campaign experience,' lost in an anonymous hotel, which could be anywhere in the country, waiting, part-bored, part-anxious, part-desperate to be put out of our misery.

I am so exhausted now that I don't even feel tired. Each new task feels like a mountain to climb and I steel myself to do it.

We go back to meet the PM and take him into make-up. Unusually for him, he is showing his nerves. We run through his key points.

With a few minutes to go, Liz and I walk the PM to the programme – into the great dark room, with the set like a beacon in the centre of it all.

We stand in the wings. It feels as if a lot is riding on this. Liz and I make banal remarks in an attempt to ease the tension. 'Tie all right?' he asks and we make a show of checking, though of course it is fine. The music strikes up and he strides on to audience applause. He is alone. We've done all we can. Only he can do it.

Liz goes back to the dressing room. I watch from the wings – somehow feeling better about seeing it in the flesh.

David Dimbleby introduces the programme. He says the first question is from Jo Cox. My brain tries to calculate this. How on earth have they picked someone with the same name? Why would they be so crass? Of course, it's the question that is about Jo Cox. He apologises – saying it is a terrible thing to say.

DC follows the script of making sure he gets his tribute across, before raising the 'Breaking Point' poster. He uses one of our pre-scripted lines, suggesting you have to question the motivation behind that poster.

Dimbleby skilfully moves it to questioning our motivations for certain actions. Was it right that John Major referred to the Leave campaign as 'squalid'? Surely it was wrong to say ISIS would be cheering Brexit. DC deals with it well enough.

I am standing just a few feet from a man in the audience with a bushy beard and red Converse shoes. Any time anybody says anything that vaguely supports Brexit, he cheers and claps, before thrusting his hand in the air hoping for a question.

The audience is full of people keen to assert themselves. One man declares that we should not listen to experts, before declaring himself to be one.

The programme moves on to immigration. There's no doubt that DC is on the ropes, tripping over his lines on the 'tens of thousands' migration target. I watch – nerveless, like a trainer in the corner, realising his fighter could go down or he could twist off the ropes and start punching back.

The key moment comes when an angry, older Brexiteer accuses DC of being Neville Chamberlain. Something snaps in the PM – outraged by being compared to an appeaser. I wonder if this will lead to triumph or disaster. He tells them his desk in Downing Street is two yards from the Cabinet Room where Churchill made the decision to fight on in the Second World War. He makes the point that Churchill wanted the support of the French and the Poles, which wasn't available to him – but he didn't give up on European democracy. It sounds barnstorming. The audience claps and cheers. It's clear so many people want their leaders to show some fight.

The programme glides into landing.

DC is visibly rattled when he comes off. I tell him he did well and I'm sure it will clip down well on the news. He asks me if I am sure. As he gets into the car, I put my hand on his forearm, 'It was better than all right – it was really good. You will see on the news.'

Before we get back to London, I have a call from him asking again how it went. He really is troubled by the skirmishes on immigration.

I call an Uber from No. 10 and share it home with Kate. She's worried that if and when we win, there are votes on the Finance Bill that the Brexiteers will use to hold us to ransom as soon as next week. Both of us express our hatred for this situation – and disbelief that it all came to this.

Everyone I run into asks how on earth we came to call a referendum. The truth is it was unavoidable. The reality is we are in the trenches, out of ammunition, bayonets fixed, ready for yet more hand-to-hand conflict if we survive this skirmish.

We are nearly there. We have no clue where we will land.
This truly is a leap in the dark.

The next day the Sayeeda Warsi story lands well. It's the splash
in *The Times* and the lead on the BBC – calling out the xenophobia and hatred, with a special kicking for Gove. Leave are
claiming they didn't even realise she was supposed to be one of
theirs. This is garbage. She was clearly associated with them.

This morning we're doing an interview with the *Sun*. It
feels like a gamble, because they've attacked us so hard for so
long.

I get in a car to No. 10. It is pouring with rain. Standing by
the road is a solitary Stronger In supporter, holding up a sign.
I want to get out of the car and give him a hug for caring so
much.

I link up with the PM and we get in the car. He's feeling
upbeat about Sayeeda. He's also seen that *Question Time* did clip
down well for him.

We meet Harriet Harman and huddle under an awning
watching the rain, while the events team sort things out. There's
a bit of an awkward conversation, before they settle into talking
about Jo Cox.

On the train, I mention to the PM how rattled Boris appears
to be that he is getting so much criticism for the Leave campaign
going so hard on immigration. He's been on stage talking about
supporting an amnesty for illegal immigrants. We are the liberal
ones on this, but neither of us is convinced about creating a
magnet for illegal immigration.

Tony Gallagher and Tom Newton Dunn from the *Sun* squeeze
into the seats opposite the PM as the train leaves and I sit next
to him. Tony is saying how odd *The Times* splash on Sayeeda
is – we don't want to tell him how delighted we are.

The interview is fine. We give them a line on petrol prices
rising and a line on how reform isn't over. It feels like everyone

is sticking to the deal that they'll do it straight. I watch them dash through the rain for shelter at the next station.

I get in the car with DC and we talk about the lie of the land. He's not sure of victory, but says, 'Hypocritically, Leave MPs now want me to stay.'

Some Brexit people have asked to see him at 10 p.m. on Thursday. It's plain this is just drama and he should avoid it. I wonder what he thinks will happen in the party. He suspects there won't only be people saying we stole it if they lose, 'There'll be plenty of people who feel it's been dragged away from them by Boris, who has been a Johnny-come-lately in all of this.'

We consider a message sent from Andrew Cooper: 'Encouraging new poll out tonight: 'Remain 53%, Leave 47%. It will have a lot of credibility with the media, because it's from John Curtice.'

Today we are to be followed around by Laura Kuenssberg. The idea is that we visit a series of factories to show the supply chain – and how a small part, the moulding around the buttons in the door of a Mini, moves through a number of factories, employing a lot of people and resulting in us being able to sell a lot of cars, tariff free, into Europe.

We arrive at the final factory, where the Mini is assembled. The PM leads a small press group, including Laura Kuenssberg, around the production line. It's an impressive sight – almost like seeing a jigsaw puzzle being put together. The PM looks like he's bordering on the eccentric, as he goes along the line doing his own piece to camera, designed to tell the story.

As he carries on, Laura asks me how it's going. I tell her and ask her the same question. She tells me it's all been very un-edifying on both sides. I try not to be too pissed off, because I just don't accept we're even close to what Leave is doing. My main point though is, 'When will journalists take responsibility for their role in this?' They want clean, simple, preferably con-frontational stories – and reject stories they consider too subtle or nuanced. It makes political organisations of all stripes be more hyperbolic, just to get on the news in the hope we will be heard.

She seems never to have considered this. Something that seems so clear to us is far from obvious.

Filming done, we race back to Parliament, where the PM is to join the statements about the death of Jo Cox.

I'd like to see them. But I have to go to North House for the preparations for the Wembley debate.

When I arrive, things are already in progress. Sadiq Khan, Ruth Davidson and Frances O'Grady, the General Secretary of the TUC, are at their lecterns, with the Stronger In rebuttal team playing Boris, Gisela Stuart, and Andrea Leadsom, the Energy minister.

I sit in the front row, with Alastair Campbell behind me.

Our team is wordy, leaden and slow. They take forever to get warmed up – eventually stumbling on the right lines. They should be killing on the economy, but they are being killed. And immigration is a mess. The key question is put once again: does the panel agree there should be a limit to the level of immigration? Frances stumbles, then crumbles. She doesn't know the answer. Ruth has a confident stab, then falls flat on her face, saying, 'Oh bollocks!'

I press pause several times and give them the basics – passionate attacks about Leave not having a plan; pointing out they are all over the shop on immigration (and that we need to get out of our defensive crouch and start fighting back).

They're also poor on sovereignty – knocked back by claims of how much laws are forced on us by Brussels. It's a revelation to some that this is rubbish and that we have total sovereignty on defence, setting taxes, schools, hospitals, and so on. Just as in the last debate, I tell them they need to call them out and attack.

All of them are engaged and want to listen. But this is the

last time I will see Frances before the night. This is a frightening prospect – I fear she really could blow up. Lucy Thomas has been playing Andrea Leadsom and points out how easy her case is, beginning each answer with, 'As a mother . . . ,' repeatedly asserting, 'We have a bright future ahead as the fifth largest economy . . . ,' and the answer to any problem being, 'Vote Leave, take back control.' It's rubbish, of course – but effective rubbish. By contrast, our answers involve patient explanation.

I take Ruth and Sadiq to one side and tell them that a lot of the weight of this will rest on them. They need to write down their answers, learn them and attack.

I get on a roasting Tube to Wembley to go and see the set with the Stronger In team, Ruth and Frances.

We're taken in through a back route, walking down long, narrow windowless corridors with exposed wires. It reminds me of the bowels of a ship. Ruth sees it as 'the kind of place the Teenage Mutant Ninja Turtles would hang out.'

We're shown the vast stage. Frances looks a little spooked.

Everyone is hot and irritable – wondering if we are strapped to a rocket that could land anywhere. I'm dehydrated, needing some water, but there's none around. There's a debate about whether we go against the blue or the yellow backdrop. Then there's the fact no one seems to have settled on the precise format, despite the negotiations having gone on forever.

Graeme Wilson calls to tell me the piece on the Mini on the BBC worked well, but it was preceded by a piece about how Nigel Farage was claiming the PM and George were exploiting Jo Cox's murder for political ends. He has no evidence, so why is it worthy of such a prominent position?

Suddenly I am not feeling hugely confident as I head for home.

# Chapter 31

## It's Supposed to be About Europe

WE PICK UP that Steve Hilton is briefing that he attended a meeting in 2012 where civil servants told the PM he had zero chance of hitting the tens of thousands immigration target.

He's doing a piece for the *Mail*. An attempt to get the PM to engage is met with, 'Don't engage.' His strategy is not making them feel they've got a rise out of us. The problem is that we don't have an answer when others approach. I suggest we at least say, 'We don't recognise his version of events.'

DC fires back, 'Yes, good. He's so desperate for Brexit, he will say anything.'

My main question is: why is Steve Hilton being given so much attention? Someone the public have barely heard of claiming something for which he offers no evidence.

I'm only half amazed when I hear the BBC is actually leading on this. In their news values, Steve Hilton beats the billionaire investor George Soros and a bunch of supermarket chiefs, who say prices will rise if we leave the EU. I dig out the papers from that meeting. The civil service were in fact advising it was entirely possible to reach an immigration target of the tens of thousands.

The newspapers are the usual horror show, with the odd delight. A couple of dozen French companies have taken out full-page ads asking the UK to Remain in the EU. There's also a full-page ad from Richard Branson backing us.

Set against that is the *Telegraph* coming out for Brexit. I was told that they were going to do it last night, but not to worry, it wouldn't be the splash. The top third of the front page has written in red ink: 'If the choice is between hope and fear, we choose hope.'

It's an absurd device. Set up a false choice and then go with the one that suits you. I send a text to the editor saying, 'Which would you go for if it was a choice between fantasy and reality?'

For weeks we've had in our grid the Four PMs moment. It's been sunk by Gordon Brown. So it has now been replaced with DC coming out into Downing Street to give a speech. It should be a straightforward affair, which I have insisted should be no more than six minutes. What is before us is a portentous speech that spends forever banging on about security and our role in the world. I feel frustrated – where is our core message? Where is the clip we want on the news? DC asks what I want. I reel off the core message, 'There's nothing more positive than having a strong economy with all the jobs and opportunities that come with it. Don't risk it by leaving the EU, because there's no turning back. Vote Remain.'

I go on to say, 'You need to tell them you are going to tell them it. Tell them it. Tell them you've told them it.'

Ameet starts getting restless in his chair and starts making irritable points about how we need to build an argument before we get to that point. Lots of people back him up. I snap, 'I'm sorry. This is not going to be watched by millions of people. The best we can hope for is a couple of clips on the news and for some people to watch the first fifteen seconds on social media. All this portentousness is hopeless. We know the security argument doesn't work – and yet it's the first half of the speech.'

DC says I am right. I leave the room to take a call. It's obvious when I come back in that they have been talking about me being a bit intense. I pride myself on being calm, but I'm exhausted and fed up. I feel bad.

Next up we have three fifteen-minute newspaper interviews.

First in are Lionel Barber and George Parker from the *Financial Times*. Lionel does the whole interview. He sits on the edge of the Chancellor's chair and asks about the PM's future. He appears to be conducting the whole thing like a chat-show host, looking at me with a smile occasionally to see if I have clocked what he's doing.

Anushka Asthana and Heather Stewart come in from the *Guardian* – and ask all about what country we want to be.

Peter Dominiczak comes from the *Telegraph* – for him it's all about, 'Haven't you effectively written off all our readers as small-minded?' The answer is we respect them, but want them to know why we worry.

I race over to North House for debate prep. As I do, I look at the daily tracker:

Headline voting intention: Remain 53.7%, Leave 46.3%. Remain lead: 7.4%.

Underlying attitudes clearly moving towards Remain over the last few days. The moves on 'irresponsible' and 'scaremongering' are significant – the biggest in these areas in 54 days of polling. It's believed they are clear evidence that Jo Cox's murder has made an impact.

I find Sadiq Khan and Ruth Davidson ready to go for it.

We patiently take them through what they should say and when – furnishing them with a series of quotes and scripts to deliver in various circumstances.

My big point to them is: these people are literally making it up; you need to be angry about that, because people's jobs and rights are at stake. You need to challenge them on everything – fight back on everything. Ask them difficult questions.

At one point Sadiq Khan brings out a Leave leaflet that suggests Syria and Iraq will also be joining the EU. It's an outrage, and he ends his point by saying, 'I'm beginning to think you've all got something against brown people.'

I know Ruth will be good and I think Sadiq will be. I am extremely nervous about Frances not being here. I take Will to one side and say we must get through to her some more suggested lines.

It's time to get to Wembley. It's hot and sweaty on the Tube. We arrive and walk to a side street where our bus is parked. It's an odd moment watching it slowly fill with our strange bed-fellows united in a common purpose: Ruth, Sadiq, Sarah Wollaston, Tim Farron, Justin King . . . it's a surreal day trip to who knows where.

It seems to take an eternity to drive the few streets to Wembley Arena. I send some encouraging news through to the PM and George:

- The PM's personal texts and calls to David Beckham have worked and he's come out for Remain. Michael Gove responded by saying John Barnes supported Leave. In fact it isn't true and Barnes has done an angry interview condemning them for their immigration frenzy.
- Leave has accepted a £600k donation from a former member of the BNP.
- Brendan Cox, Jo's husband, has done an interview.
- Some polls coming out tonight put us ahead and there's this rather weird and rather specific 'Bing Predicts' note Andrew Cooper has forwarded me: 57.62% to Remain and 42.38% to Leave.

George calls me – he wants me to ram the BNP donation down their throat, saying in politics you should always pay if you accept questionable money.

He is in a thoughtful mood – believing this would not have been close were it not for Boris's popularity and Gove's ability to influence News UK and Associated Newspapers.

We arrive at the venue. There is a crowd of people trying to get in. A helicopter buzzes overhead. We line our people up to get off the bus and be greeted. After a few seconds, I walk in and I sidestep a reporter hoping to doorstep me. A few people text to say they saw it on TV.

We are taken straight to the stage for checks and meet Frances O'Grady there. There's a bit of cheering and booing from the people already seated. It sounds like it could be a bit of a rabble. Robbie Gibb, the editor of all BBC TV's political programmes, is running around saying they will be told to be calm.

I step down off the stage to take a call from DC. He's just done an interview with a local BBC station. 'Yet again, it was all about immigration. I wanted to tell them, "This is not the immigration referendum. It's supposed to be about Europe."'

Our debaters retire to their dressing rooms. I am asked if I'd like to take part in the coin toss for who opens the debate and who closes it.

It's weird running into people like Paul Stephenson and Will Walden – special advisers who have joined the other side. We're friendly and shake hands and chat amicably enough.

We are marched into a room for the coin toss. I make a joke about Robbie doing it, saying I always believed he was a great tosser. Leave say they'd be happy to forfeit the coin toss and let us choose. I say we should just go ahead and they should call. They call 'heads' and choose to go first. That's fine, because I'm happy it means we have the final word.

I'm taken to a large room that is filling up with various people associated with our team. I chat to Liz Truss and Amber and also Labour figures like Chuka Umunna and Chris Bryant.

It's all broken up by calls with Simon Case and the Palace. It sounds like the press want to leap on a story about the Queen allegedly asking dinner guests to give her three good reasons to stay in the EU. I get through to the duty press officer at the Palace, who doesn't seem alive to the danger. Simon Case is on to the Private Secretary. I can feel this one slipping away, just as 'The Queen Backs Brexit' did – once it's out the door, it's out the door and trying to put it back afterwards is no use.

I sit on the edge of a sofa next to Chris Bryant, dozens of Remain people surrounding us.

The team comes out swinging on the economy – pressing them on the lies of their campaign. The debate is absurdly partisan and it's evident that anything anyone says will be applauded from the off.

Boris and his team seem lacklustre. Ruth, Sadiq and Frances are passionate and energised. They nail them on their lack of plan. Come the immigration question, I am nervous. But by some miracle we win and Frances O'Grady, who has been nervous until now, is a star, landing a blow by asking if they want to cut immigration or not? Amazingly, they fail to give an answer. All of them look hypocritically squeamish on the issue. Twitter thinks Ruth is the star – summing up Boris's attitude as 'Just not good enough'.

Ryan, Lucy and I look at each other across the room and are amazed that all the lines we gave them are landing with passion and force.

Towards the end, Chuka wants briefing for the spin room afterwards. Will Straw and I tell him he should hammer: they have no plan on the economy and tonight it was clear they have no plan on immigration.

I go back to the sofa to watch the end. For some reason Ruth is asked to give our closing statement first. This was not what was agreed at the coin toss.

Boris goes last. He gives a speech that concludes that we should declare 23rd June Independence Day. He gets a standing ovation from his supporters.

I head to the corridor where the dressing rooms are to go and tell the team how great they were.

The first person who piles down it is Boris. I say hello and he squeezes past me saying, 'Independence day, Craig!' He's definitely on a high. We go into Sadiq's dressing room and I give Ruth and Frances a hug. I tell them they were brilliant and they should feel proud that they won it. Proud that such different people came together for something we believe in. Proud that the emptiness of Leave's promises were exposed. We talk for a while, but there isn't much more to say.

In the spin room the hacks are in agreement – they believe we won.

DC calls to say how well it clipped on the news. I don't think we changed many votes, but our campaign feels buoyant at the moment – and Leave look confused and on the back foot.

The morning of Wednesday 22 June brings debate analysis. The only soundbites used are on immigration. I can see why the PM feels worn down by it.

But most of the reviews are good.

I look through the papers and think Gove has totally lost the plot. He doubles down on his claim that we've had enough of experts with a comment that the economists warning of the dangers of Brexit are like the Nazi propagandists who condemned Einstein. Is he losing it?

The PM has had enough and attacks Gove on the record:

> To hear the Leave campaign comparing independent experts and economists to Nazi sympathisers – I think they have rather lost it.
>
> These people are independent – economists who have won Nobel prizes, business leaders responsible for creating thousands of jobs, institutions that were set up after the war to try to provide independent advice. It is right to listen.

Late in the day Gove gives an immaculately constructed and delivered apology. Surely he must be wondering how he got to this place – seen as having gone way beyond the pale by those he supported as modern, compassionate Conservatives, while ranting about Nazis and attempting to justify the reactionary campaign he leads.

I spend the morning at Stronger In, working through how we're going to handle the voices speaking for us as the polls close and the results come in. Tony Blair comes in to address the office, introduced by Will as 'the most electorally successful person alive'.

Blair speaks a lot of sense: 'We have come together for a set of values that go to the core of what this country should be.'

He tells us he is sure we are going to be successful, before going on to put his finger on one of the problems of this campaign, 'The more outrageous people are prepared to be, the more they can catch an agenda.'

In the Q&A he says, 'There are only so many times you can put an issue as weighty as this before the British people.'

'You're telling me!' I say in a stage whisper and he laughs. I have a good chat with him at the end and he tells me he thinks the PM has led this well. What he doesn't say, but he has remarked upon before, is that there is an increasing clash in this country that has gone beyond left and right, and is now about open and closed – those who see our future as one of constructive engagement with a big, complex world, and those who want to seal themselves off and walk away.

Our tracker poll comes through as he leaves, putting us on 54.3 and them 45.7.

There's another conversation around the desk about what we say when this is done. Ryan points out that forty-six per cent of people who want to leave the EU believe this referendum will be rigged. How do you find a way to speak to them? Many others responded to polls saying they trust no one. How do political campaigns engage with people who have got to that stage – other than what Leave has done: telling them they are right, there is a conspiracy and we are all being lied to by a powerful elite, who don't have their interests at heart?

I dutifully hang about into the evening, watching all the

bulletins and filling the PM in on how his whistle-stop tour of the country is going.

Later on, there's a call from Labour's Yvette Cooper – she's asking me to brief her for the last debate. I'm happy to help. The truth is I feel I have a lot more in common with her at this moment than half the people in my own party.

I walk out into the late evening sunshine. It feels balmy and cosmopolitan, as if I shouldn't have a care in the world.

I finally think we've done it. We are going to win.

It will feel like the greatest relief of my life if I am right.

# Chapter 32

## Referendum Day

THURSDAY 23 JUNE: Referendum Day. I feel a real sense of calm. I don't know why, but something tells me we are going to be OK. Everyone, everything points to us winning.

I manage to get a lie-in, which means up by 7 a.m. My mind just won't let me go beyond that.

Westminster is throbbing. There are Stronger In people everywhere handing out stickers that are going like hotcakes. I'm not foolish enough to think this is exactly representative of the country.

The morning meeting starts at 9 a.m.

Stephen Gilbert tells us turnout has been high. The main concern is that the Remain strongholds will be indifferent, so all energies are going into getting out our voters. We have a brief chat about what the PM should say tomorrow. My view is that the PM should declare, 'At the general election, I spoke of one nation. Today I want to do all I can to ensure one party.' DC likes this and wants to work it in.

We go through who should do the media from when the polls are closed. I have a stock of loyal Cabinet ministers lined up, including Nicky Morgan, Amber Rudd, Liz Truss, Stephen Crabb and Ruth Davidson. Nicky texts me:

Craig – you may already know this, but Labour's line tonight will be that in the course of this campaign the Tory party has imposed its own divisions on the rest of the country, leading to further intolerance, hatred etc. – so normal service resumes after 10 p.m. and important we get tone right. Nicky.

The meeting thins right down to the PM, George, Ed, Kate, me, and Oliver Letwin, the PM's senior policy adviser in the Cabinet Office. DC wants to talk through the options if we lose:

1. Resign, hanging on until the Conservative party has managed to find itself a new leader.
2. He says he will stay on to steady the ship, but won't be able to see it to its destination. This involves not giving a specific date for going and creating a negotiating team, made up of a number of leading Brexiteers (he names Boris, Gove and Whittingdale, as well as George Osborne).

Oliver Letwin speaks first. He makes the powerful case for Option 2. He believes we should do this because it is clearly what is right for the country. Going will cause a great shock that could make things worse.

The PM invites me to speak next.

'We tell ourselves that a win is a win, allowing us to do what we want. But we also need to understand that a loss is a loss. My main concern is you – and I want you to be able to go with dignity. If you lose and stay on, you will be fighting reality. The combination of the right-wing press and hardcore Brexit MPs will want to eject you from the system like a virus. They'll say you're clinging on. And don't forget the narrative will be that this is a vote against the establishment, with you looking like a key representative of that establishment trying to go against the result. You won't be able to withstand the pressure – you'll look undignified and you will go.'

I can see DC nodding along with this. I know he has already made up his mind, probably even before this discussion.

George comes in next, 'I've been fighting with two irreconcilable thoughts.' The first is what I have just argued. The second is that history is littered with examples of governments that have been through torrid times, only to survive. DC laughs, saying, 'Prime Ministers also resign.' Kate joins in supporting George's case.

No one is aggressive. No one feels they need to prove others wrong. This is a group of people who care very deeply about David Cameron and the country and want to do the right thing. Each of us would happily be proven wrong.

I have another go. 'We seem to be discounting any sense of the countervailing forces. We often speak of moments where everyone sets their hair on fire and runs around screaming about one event or another. This is going to be the mother of those moments – and I just don't think you could survive it.'

There is some pushing back and forth. I feel tears welling in my eyes at one moment. I hear the point about doing what is right for the country.

My other fear is that it will sound like, 'The people can be trusted with democracy – until they make a mistake.' DC goes out to the loo. As he does, I remind everyone of the Knight in *Monty Python and the Holy Grail*, taking hit after hit, having limbs sliced off – yet still urging people to come on and try to beat him, claiming 'It's only a flesh wound.' In other words, he doesn't know when he's beaten.

Oliver Letwin moves on to what would happen in a Conservative leadership election. He thinks it would include Theresa May, Boris and Gove and it would be a competition on who could be the most 'Leavist', with Gove the only one who really believed it.

Someone questions whether Gove could cope. I think his latest comments on Nazis are an example of him feeling the pressure. DC says what we know is that Gove is prone to 'infarctions'. I suspect he knows just about enough about himself to realise he couldn't cope with it all – and that he's done some kind of deal with Boris to make him DPM and Home Secretary, or perhaps even Chancellor of the Exchequer.

Next the conversation moves on to when there should be a reshuffle if we win. DC's feeling is we should take the heat out of everything and leave it to September. I suspect that's the right thing, but we need to realise it will create a vacuum that will result in every newspaper running endless reshuffle demands. DC says he understands that, shrugs and says we can ultimately withstand it.

Interestingly it is Kate who raises the prospect of us winning, only for them to still demand George's head. DC's view is that they can 'get stuffed'. Everyone feels protective of George, who has given his all and left himself exposed throughout this fight.

Once again I am left thinking – it's over, even if we win. No one else thinks that is the case.

Late in the afternoon, the skies open. I am fielding a stream of, 'What's happening?' calls, with journalists hoping I can throw them a morsel of insight. I look out towards St James's Park, which is little more than a slate-grey blur, how Monet might have painted it.

I have described at the beginning of this book the torment of results night. The sense of everyone persuading us we were on a path to safety, only to fall into quicksand, and coming with it the slow descent, realising that nothing and no one would save us.

It was painful to write.

I am back in No. 10 to watch David Dimbleby call it formally on the BBC at 4.39 a.m. He says, 'The decision taken in 1975 by this country to join the Common Market has been reversed by this referendum . . . there is absolutely no way that the Remain side can win.'

I feel strangely calm.

The pound is dropping to its lowest level since 1985.

I find a group of people gathered just inside the door to No. 11: Laurence Mann, Gabby Bertin and Liz Sugg. All of them have red eyes from crying. I give each of them a hug and ask, 'What are you doing here?' They shrug as if to say, it's as good a place as any. They are discussing whether DC should go. Liz worries people will hold it against him, because he kept saying he was going to stay on in the circumstances. As gently as possible, I argue that I am willing to be wrong, but it's not right for him, it wouldn't work anyway, his heart isn't in it – and worse, it isn't right for the country.

A small voice inside me is also saying: they broke it, they own it.

I walk into No. 11 and into George's study. He is sitting alone, watching a tiny television. I put my hand on his shoulder and say, 'Hi.' I am suddenly aware that I have put back on a Remain T-shirt.

I ask him how he thinks Gove and Boris feel. My hope is that they feel real pain, wondering what on earth they have done. George pricks that bubble, simply saying, 'Cock-a-hoop. In politics you always believe you'll be better than those who went before you.' I wonder. I still suspect Boris and Gove never thought this would really happen – hoping to be the valiant losers who stood up for justice, without ever having to pick up the pieces. Now they have to.

A small group gathers in the PM's office. I am getting texts pressurising me to say he will speak before the markets open. There's no chance of that: he's upstairs with his family and none of us are going to impose on that.

My phone goes – a conference call is being set up with Philip Hammond. I wonder if he is so eager now to face the music. I take the call back at my desk phone, with dear Adam Atashzai, still enthusiastic to do the best job he can, even in defeat.

When Philip Hammond comes through, he says, 'Are you going to say to me what another person at Number Ten just said?'

'What's that?'

'You're on your own!'

I burst out laughing, 'Oh, come on! He didn't say that!'

'He did!'

'Well, you're not on your own. We're here to talk it through.'

We agree he needs to be calm and conciliatory – the British people have given us an instruction and it is our duty to do our best. He seems to accept this. I'm not sure it really matters, it will dissolve in the tsunami of news.

There's a fair amount of sitting around and waiting for DC to come down.

My eldest daughter, Maya, wakes up and sends me a WhatsApp message: 'daddy I just heard that we left, it's so bad I'm so annoyed but you did really well and I'm sure there's nothing you could have done. Love you xxx'.

She follows up: 'I'm really proud of you X'.

I send her back: 'Thanks darling. I'm ok. I love you very much xx'.

For the first time I don't think I'm going to stop myself crying. I walk through to the bathroom opposite the private office to take a moment.

DC arrives around 7 a.m., trying to have a sense of humour about it all: 'Well, that didn't go to plan!' He goes on, 'We haven't got much to complain about. It was a seventy-two per cent turnout.'

There are quite a few of us now in the room. DC reads through his farewell speech. The room thins out. DC is planning to make a number of calls. The most important of which is with Michael Gove, the chairman of the Leave campaign.

Switch patches me in.

Gove comes on and says, 'Hi.'

DC takes charge immediately, 'I wanted to call you to formally concede and to congratulate you on a stunning victory.'

'Thank you, PM.'

'From here on, I'm keen to provide stability.'

'There are some particular things we should talk about regarding how the negotiations proceed.'

DC cuts him off at the pass, he sounds ultra-polite and friendly, though I detect some cold brutality here, 'Well, I'll make a statement shortly. It'll really just say: result received and accepted and it must be delivered.'

There's a long pause.

'All right, take care.' I can hear uncertainty in Michael Gove's voice – what is DC planning?

The conversation lasts no longer than a minute. They have been typically British and polite, but there is no love lost here. Others who listened to the call are incensed, 'Did you hear him – as if he was the PM dictating terms?' I think he's not aware of what is about to hit him.

The next call is to Sir John Major. He's kept waiting a bit too long while DC sorts himself out, but he is very kind when he comes on, 'I'm so sorry. I think the world has gone mad. You did all you can.'

DC tells him that he has come to the conclusion that the only right answer is to resign and that he hopes he won't be perceived as cutting and running. Sir John Major is clear, 'I hate saying that you are right – but the alternative situation would be impossible and undignified.'

The final call before he faces the world is to Nicola Sturgeon. There is some elaborate felicitation before he tells her he felt she was part of a strong campaign and that he is personally disappointed. He wants her to be involved in any negotiations.

She tells him she appreciates that and she will seek to protect Scotland's involvement in the single market. Of course, she is saying that she will take a diametrically opposite view to the Brexiteers who are negotiating.

It's just after 8 a.m. DC is ready to go out. He asks the Duty Clerk for the 'plastic fantastic', in other words, a folder where each bit of paper in his statement can be slid into a plastic pocket, to stop it flying away.

I turn up the TV, which is now showing an image of the No. 10 door. I'm suddenly aware that the private office is now full of people. George stands next to me. Kate is in tears. I put my arm around her shoulder as we watch.

It's obvious from the moment he walks out of the front door that he is resigning. Sam wouldn't be there if he wasn't going. He looks at his calm authoritative best. When it comes to the section of his speech saying he will steady the ship, but he can't be the captain who sails to the next port, a big banner flashes up on the bottom of the screen: 'Cameron Resigns'. He gets to the final sentences about loving his country and he begins to choke up, just about getting to the end without crying. He turns, takes Sam's hand and walks inside.

Thirty seconds later, they are back in the private office. There's a spontaneous round of applause that goes on for well over a minute. DC makes his way to the door of his office. He is standing eighteen inches away from me. He waves his hands to silence people and it takes a long moment for them to stop.

He makes a small speech about this being the best team he could hope to have and how we have all done an amazing job. He turns to go into his room and Sam follows. The door closes.

They come out a few minutes later and I stand up. He gives me a big hug and I feel the tears well up in my eyes. I think it's the first time there has been meaningful physical contact between us. Sam comes and gives me a hug, too, 'Craig . . . ,' she says – and there's no need to fill in the blank.

Kate suggests a few of us go over to Inn the Park in St James's

Park for some breakfast and we troop across. The sun is shining. Squirrels are darting around. Tourists are oblivious, as they take selfies. The world is still turning . . .

I check in with the Stronger In team. They are in a pub in Smithfield. I suggest to the group who have had most to do with them that we head over.

It's a tiny pub, with most people spilled out into the sunshine. Will is wearing a hoodie. Others are still in yesterday's clothes. I hug them and commiserate one by one. Most are well on the way to being pissed. I buy a round. It's a cash-only pub, so I run across to a cashpoint. The barman is a sweet, but almost comic character. At least three times in my ninety minutes there, he attempts to carry a stack of glasses and drops them on the floor – each time emerging with a massive dustpan and brush to sweep it up.

I feel I don't want to hang around too long. People will start to get morose. I've also just had a maximum of ten minutes' sleep. If I drink anything, I will collapse.

As I am about to leave, Gisela Stuart, Boris Johnson and Michael Gove hold a press conference. I stay to watch Boris. It looks more like a funeral to me than a celebration. Someone says, 'They've been caught with their pants down.' I walk out before Gove speaks – I don't think I can stand to see his elaborate and fatuous nonsense. I cling to a sense that they are regretting what they have done, and that surely Boris wishes he had a time machine to go back to the point where he wobbled and go the other way.

I get an Uber back to No. 10. Sturgeon is giving a press conference. She is straight out of the traps saying a second independence referendum should be on the table, adding menacingly, 'And it is on the table.' I find myself thinking she now has a compelling case – the rest of the UK has taken a decision that Scotland rejected. That decision will have a demonstrable impact on Scotland and its place in the world. Of course, she is going to struggle now with questions over Scotland's deficit, would they really want to join the Euro, and should there now be a 'hard border' between Scotland and England – but she's spotted her opportunity.

I pop into No. 10, but there's not much more to do. A call comes through from Merkel. I notice there's very little addressing the sadness of the situation. Perhaps she doesn't know what to say. The closest she gets is, 'What is painful to me is that young people failed to turn out in numbers to vote.' Quite.

I think I will collapse if I don't get some sleep. I grab a couple of hours and then make my way to pick up my kids.

Life goes on.

I feel sad and sanguine. I've been fighting for a long time – a big part of me feels released.

DC texts:

> Couldn't really put into words today how much I appreciate all you have done. Would have lost it. Be proud and strong. We were fighting a good fight. All love dc.

I text back:

> Thank you. Not just for saying that – but for an amazing few years. I was happy to fight for and with you time after time. Craig.

AFTER

# Chapter 33

## Like Jokers at an Auction

I'M INUNDATED WITH supportive texts. It's lovely to know that people care. Most are of the 'can't believe that just happened, hope you are OK' variety. My standard response is: 'I'm fine. Pretty sanguine. It appears we don't live in the country I thought we did.'

Over the weekend, I reflect a little with the PM. He clearly believes there was little more we could have done: 'I failed fighting for something I believed in.'

He also thinks that he miscalculated – believing that 'reasonable sceptics' would be for In. He is staggered by the number of people who never argued for exit but then took up the cause.

Stephen Gilbert calls. He sounds very down. All I want to let him know is that he fought valiantly. He obviously wonders what on earth he nearly killed himself for. Both of us say we were noticing that it was starting to affect our health.

I text a few people to ask if they are OK. Most come back saying they feel very sad.

I have bad moments, but there's the compensation of relief. At least it is over.

After the ground rush of the previous few days, the week passes in slow motion.

There's a sense of the leading Brexiteers fleeing the scene of the crime. Some make clear the £350 million claim was never really serious. Boris's weekly column seems an exercise in pure denial. He asserts the referendum wasn't really about immigration. He also suggests we can have access to the free market, without any need to follow the rules or have free movement.

Janan Ganesh describes Michael Gove and Boris Johnson as looking like 'jokers at an auction whose playfully exorbitant bid for a vase had just been accepted with a chilling smash of the gavel.'

The Vote Leave campaign seems to disappear in a puff of smoke. No one is around to answer questions about what they did or what happens next.

Our 8.30 meetings continue – though a little more sparsely attended than before. Plans are made to ensure machinery is in place for Brexit. The PM is clear the decisions are for his successor, but there's a duty to make sure they have the advice they need from the outset. He asks the Cabinet Secretary to move immediately to set up a new team, drawing on the Cabinet Office, the Foreign Office, the Treasury and the Department of Business. This team will need to be led by and staffed by the civil service's best and brightest.

DC remains as good-humoured as ever. He reads out one of the many notes he has received. It's from a rabbi, who says the section of the Torah that Jews are being directed to at present is the time when Moses is rejected by his people. DC puts on an affectionate accent and quotes, 'Against Moses!' And then, 'You are a true mensch . . . it is the fate of leaders not to be valued and not to be thanked.'

It's time to go through to Cabinet. I walk into the room and look across at Michael Gove. His face is crimson, looking like he may be about to have a coronary. Once again, he seems to be engaged in the most elaborate performance as events take place around him. He grabs his pen with excessive vigour, scribbles and underlines ferociously. When he turns the page he takes the fabric bookmark and lays it down along the spine of the notebook with excessive care. Occasionally he places his elbows on the table, his palms pressed against each other, and drums his fingers together, varying the tempo. No one else is so fidgety or seems to draw this much attention to themselves.

DC rattles through some points:

- clear instruction from people.
- no Brexiteers or Remainers any more, just one Government.
- the machinery he plans to set up and how it will report to Cabinet straight away.
- we still have a mandate and manifesto we should deliver on.
- people think the party conference is a natural break for the new leader to be in place (some think longer, some shorter, 'I'm not particularly fussed!').

Chris Grayling is the first to speak. He does not pay tribute to the PM, instead saying there must be no perception of a vacuum. He dispirits the room by saying it's imperative the Cabinet meets throughout the summer.

Philip Hammond is next. His main point is that we should use the debate about when we trigger Article 50 (the formal process for leaving the EU) as a major bargaining chip. He says there is fear in Europe – particularly among the Poles, who believe they will be made to pay as now being the largest non-Euro country.

George is the first to praise the PM for his 'good sense and dignity'. He says, 'Conservatives deal with the world as it is, rather than how they want it to be.' He says there is an 'economic adjustment' underway as the more exposed FTSE 250 has fallen dramatically. There will be hiring and investment freezes.

Gove writes all of this down. Especially when George says, 'We need to brace ourselves for ongoing volatility.'

He concludes, 'There will be damage and people will see it. But can you imagine the situation if we had not taken the action on the economy we have done?'

Theresa May notably does not pay tribute either. She speaks in her usual no-nonsense way about the need to 'competently and practically' get the best result.

Jeremy Hunt shows real grace and emotional intelligence. 'You have done your country proud and we are all very proud of you.'

Do I detect a little shame on the faces of others who have failed to pay tribute?

The person next to me nudges and asks, 'Is Gove going to speak?' He certainly hasn't indicated he wants to.

Justine Greening, the International Development Secretary, makes the rather good, but sensitive point, 'This was a Government that was elected under the "Competence versus Chaos" strapline.' She believes our international standing is at stake and we should get on with having a new leader soon, rather than having 'myopic discussions'.

It's only when Michael Fallon is speaking that Gove finally puts up his pen to speak. Again it is in an overly emphatic way, pinching the end between thumb and forefinger, so that all of it is held aloft. There are still a few left before it gets to him.

Sajid Javid makes an alarming intervention. Yesterday he raised eyebrows with a Pollyanna-ish approach on *Marr*. Today he is blunt. 'I've been talking to business non-stop since Friday and I am not going to sugar coat it. The situation is very bad. Confidence is bad. Many companies will announce the freezing of recruitment and redundancies. Fresh produce is likely to rise in price by three to four per cent. Inward investment deals will collapse.' He repeats, 'It is not right to sugar coat this.'

Gove raises his eyebrows rather theatrically. Finally Sajid warns about universities in chaos, not knowing what the situation is around foreign students.

Michael Gove is finally invited to speak. He gives an effusive tribute, saying history will be generous to DC. He goes on to acknowledge the divisions in our society – saying nearly half the population will have felt robbed and 'we need to be unified in stopping those who seek hate and division.' There's then some guff about needing to work together. Anyone hoping for some flesh on the bones will be disappointed. He looks to me like a seagull holding a fish in its beak that is too big to swallow – eager to keep hold of it, but also not sure it can carry the burden.

I go over to the House for the PM's statement. Politics feels like it is in utter chaos. A prime minister going, no opposition. Dozens of Labour MPs are making clear that Jeremy Corbyn is no longer acceptable. He has to keep appointing new people to his shadow cabinet, and even they feel they have to resign soon after.

We hear that the new MP for Tooting is being introduced to the house. Someone says, 'I'd advise her to keep her mobile phone on – she might end up in the shadow cabinet at this rate.' DC uses the line during his statement and brings the house down.

Corbyn chides his backbenchers. Some of them shout 'Resign!' back at him.

A friend of mine who has a senior job in media in the United States comes into No. 10 for a coffee that ends up being a three-hour chat.

She tells me she has watched the referendum campaign with interest and is currently wrestling with how she is going to deal with Trump *vs* Clinton in the race to become President of the United States. She sees that there are direct parallels between Trump and the Leave campaign:

- Both with official status (the Leave campaign given the stamp of approval by the Electoral Commission; Trump to be the Republican party nominee).

- Both prepared to say extreme and outrageous things that are deeply misleading and often straightforwardly wrong as a matter of fact.

Covering that as an impartial journalist reporting on a campaign is tough. I reflect on how important the BBC's role was – especially when parts of the press were campaigning so vigorously for Leave – and how they struggled to get it right in a heavily regulated environment where balance is a requirement.

It was certainly hard for them and I would not have expected them to be anything other than impartial. But ultimately they should have done better. The BBC is such a key player in terms of scale and influence and they fell short.

So how could it have been different? Too often the BBC led on stories that were simply wrong – particularly on its morning and online output. Senior editorial figures needed to step in and say, 'Yes, we will do this story, but we will make clear that it is factually inaccurate from the outset.' Too often the Remain campaign's rebuttal, which was inevitably seen as partial and therefore suspect, was tagged on as an afterthought, when BBC editors should have been stamping their own, independent authority and analysis on the output. Again, the key phrase is 'due impartiality' – people and organisations should get the impartiality that they are 'due' and have earned.

Similarly, it took them too long to realise that reporting two sides of an argument is hopeless if you can't help people to understand where the weight of opinion lies. As Paul Johnson, the Director of the Institute for Fiscal Studies put it in a recent article in *The Times*, 'We really will find that we have "had enough of experts" . . . if all we are presented with is spurious disagreement from which we cannot disentangle what the experts are actually saying, and why.'

Finally, the BBC did not do enough to set the agenda themselves. Looking back, I am shocked by the number of times they took their stories – particularly on morning bulletins – from newspapers with an axe to grind, sometimes on things that even those papers didn't consider worthy of putting up in lights.

They could, for example, have done some proper journalism on why the university sector felt it would be badly damaged, providing stories that could and should have been at the top of the news.

In short, if you are the biggest beast in the media jungle – and the BBC is by a mile – it is incumbent on you to confront a serious issue. It's not as if the referendum presented a new problem for the BBC. As Paul Johnson pointed out in the same *Times* article, a review of the use of statistics, commissioned by the BBC and written before the referendum, but published after it, found a huge frustration in experts and the audience at being presented with rival claims, with no guidance on which has more merit.

It recommended, 'the BBC needs to get better and braver in interpreting and explaining rival statistics and guiding the audience.'

The BBC needs to recognise it is an issue and address it.

# Chapter 34

## What Went Wrong?

ON THE TUESDAY after the vote, we head to Brussels for the PM's final European Council.

On the flight over he says, 'My strategy is going to be to get them not to kick off. I'll read them a few home truths on immigration. And say it might have all been different if there'd been an emergency brake.'

The common view is that the pivot point in all of this was in October 2014, when Merkel made clear that the simple, obvious solution, an emergency brake on the number of migrants, could never work and would never be given. A journalist from the *Daily Mail* has told me they honestly don't believe the paper would have campaigned for leaving if that emergency brake had been granted. What became obvious is that the European Union has as its core belief that the freedoms of moving goods, services, money and people are inextricably linked as a package. They thought the UK benefited massively from the first three – so it should and could cope with the fourth.

DC says, 'We got things in renegotiation that in years to come we will bitterly regret not having. Making sure the pound was protected and ensuring it was clear it's a multi-currency union was crucial. They fought hard against it.' It's true, but the kind of thing that just didn't translate as a serious advantage to typical voters.

We go in to the UKREP offices, and laugh at the sign outside saying, 'From the magma of chaos, order is restored time after time.' I always thought it was a crap quote – and I'm convinced now.

There is a lot of hanging around.

Merkel comes to see him for a one-on-one. He calls me, Ed and Simon Case in when he is done.

The headline from the meeting is clear. Merkel was adamant, 'There could never have been an emergency brake on the number of migrants.' The fear is that history will write that we should have got more from the renegotiation. It's evident that was not true. DC takes comfort from knowing this. He could not have achieved more.

The Prime Minister's official spokeswoman, Helen Bower, and I head over for dinner with the lobby while the PM is with the other leaders. I tell her to stab me in the leg with a fork if I end up in an argument, but the truth is they're all rather morose, not quite sure how the hell we got here.

After very little sleep, I arrive at North House for a board meeting.

The agenda is essentially two items:

- what went wrong?
- where, if anywhere, do we go from here?

David Sainsbury has, as ever, been generous. There are pots of tea and coffee and platters full of sausage and bacon rolls.

Exhausted after little sleep, I grab some coffee and two rolls, which I smear with brown sauce, and take a seat at the end of the table.

I say, 'Hello,' to Peter Mandelson, whose body language could not be more obvious, his torso is twisted away from me and he only grunts grudgingly.

I sense something is up.

Andrew Cooper is not here. This seems unusual, but his wife has a hospital appointment.

Stuart Rose calls the meeting to order and Will is invited to sum things up. He was at the Stronger In wrap party last night and his voice is rough.

He has had an update from Andrew Cooper and this forms the basis of his initial remarks.

We had believed that a high turnout would work for us, but it didn't: 'There was a large number of angry people who hadn't voted for a long time that came out – and that was fatal for us.'

He also believes that we did not have a credible answer on immigration – arguing that the Conservatives were hamstrung by their commitment to bringing net migration down to the tens of thousands – and Labour faced criticism for allowing vast numbers of people in from the 'accession countries' – the Poles and other eastern Europeans.

He goes on that we had believed that undecideds would naturally swing to us, but the evidence is that they were prepared to choose less immigration and 'more control' over a stronger economy.

There's been a lot of argument about why we weren't more positive, but he says we discovered time and again positive stories just didn't cut through with the media, or work with crucial swing voters.

He points out that Leave spent way more money than we did, specifically referring to the wrap around the London *Metro* in the last few days of the campaign, funded by the Northern Irish Democratic Unionist Party. Why was it done in their name? Moreover, Arron Banks spent £11 million without putting a penny into Leave.

Most interestingly, he says, 'We have not reflected on quite how poor Labour's leadership was.' He points out that in a recent poll there was a twenty-one per cent net support among members for sharing a platform with other political parties – yet the leadership refused. He then points out the problems of not getting them to be part of our grid – and when we allowed them days, they simply did not deliver.

Finally he argues, 'Their campaign has disappeared in a puff of smoke. They are the campaign that got away with talking nonsense, because for them, there was no return to the political fray where they would have to live with their claims.' He concludes, 'Legislators need to think about the regulation of referendums.'

Stephen Gilbert is invited to speak next. He underlines that we wrongly assumed the undecideds would turn to the status quo.

All of us assumed this would happen. It had been the case at the general election and the pattern of the vast majority of referenda around the world. The reason for this is that the status quo is almost invariably the less risky option – the alternative, in our words, 'a leap in the dark.'

So why didn't that happen in this case, especially as we held a lead among voters as a whole of eight per cent at the end of the campaign on whether Leave or Remain was riskier for them personally?

Among the two key swing segments – 'Heads *vs* Hearts' and the 'Disengaged Middle', whose decisions were always going to decide the referendum – a narrow majority thought that remaining was more risky. They believed that staying in the EU meant continued uncontrolled immigration and spending £350 million a week on the EU, not the NHS.

Stephen is also certain that we were right to focus on economic risk.

I had not intended to speak much. But Stuart Rose indicates to me a number of times that he will be seeking my view.

I hastily scribble some notes, before making a few points, starting with a tribute to the Stronger In team, who I believe handled themselves and the campaign with great skill. I go on:

- We called a referendum on a complex issue that many didn't fully understand and as David Cameron said to me, it became about 'immigration levels they didn't want and an EU they didn't love.'

- As a result, the referendum became a proxy for so many other issues. So immigration, general anger at 'the way things are' and the opportunity to give the establishment a kick all proved crucial.

- No one has done any effective public relations for the EU for a generation and so we were left trying to undo all the nonsense from bendy bananas to claims they make all of our laws, in a few short months.

- Our great strength was also our great weakness – we were a grand coalition of parties, each with a different agenda and emphasis. The backbone of any effective campaign is finding a message and sticking to it remorselessly. We did our best, but it was impossible to control all our constituent parts. The SNP and the Labour party always made clear they were not bought in to Stronger In. There will always remain a question about how many senior figures in the Labour leadership actually wanted us to win. Leave were a small group with a core message they stuck to.

- Leave also ran a mendacious campaign based on a series of lies: £350 million; Turkey; EU army; the scale on which Brussels interferes in our daily lives. And that was just the air war. The leaflets and social media interventions were infinitely worse.

- Finally, our reading of the polling was the economy would trump immigration. It didn't – at least not in the way we thought it would. Many found the big government numbers too big and too specific to be believable. We deployed a parade of experts, which should, in a rational world, have been more than enough to make the economic case for remain and against leaving. But it obviously wasn't. It is hard to think of how else we could have made the argument: these people really know what they are talking about, and they all see leaving as a risk.

As I say all of these things, I am aware of nodding around the table from the likes of Brendan Barber and June Sarpong.

At this point Peter Mandelson spins to me, his face no more than eighteen inches from mine, and says, 'That is a heck of a statement – saying our polling was completely wrong.'

'I didn't say that,' I point out, but allow the conversation to continue.

Mandelson has his attack sorted and I can feel it coming. He praises the campaign as doing everything right. This is his way of intimating that he is blameless. He then goes on, 'But the politics were not right.' His point is that we should have realised that the economic argument was not landing properly and shifted. He makes the same point about immigration. 'We should have asked ourselves: why is this not landing?' His conclusion is that, 'There was an exclusive, not an inclusive discussion at Number Ten.'

It's not even coded – David Cameron and George Osborne (and their pathetic lackeys) should have turned to him. They didn't and now everyone is paying a very heavy price. He says, 'We should have asked ourselves why it wasn't working. We should have discussed it and we didn't.'

I feel my hackles rise. I raise my hand so that Stuart might ask me to speak after.

Peter Mandelson is in his element now – he says the campaign did have a core message that it kept hitting, how can I say that it didn't?

When he is finished I say that I could play a blame game, too – saying that the Labour party was useless and he and others completely failed to exert any influence on them. My point about the message was that every time Labour went out, they tried to say something different – Gordon Brown's first intervention was stillborn, because his top line was about dealing with tax avoidance.

He keeps trying to interrupt me – and repeats a couple of his points. Not for the first time I tell him, 'I don't accept anything that you say on this. We discussed all of this endlessly – including meetings between you and the Chancellor – and each time we all concluded we had a strategy that we needed to stick to, because changing the campaign would be disastrous.'

What makes me angry about this is that he never said any of this during the campaign and did not do me the courtesy of saying it privately before he launched this attack. When I cool down, I realise he needs it to be someone's fault – and he will calm. We all will.

The conversation opens up. Roland Rudd says he was booed every time he went round the country and mentioned the renegotiation. He also says they were 'nasty bastards' – coming up with slogans that were effective:

- project fear
- punishment budget
- take back control

He believes we should have nailed them on the money sooner, and nailed them on their Turkey poster, which in its way was as bad as Farage's. I don't disagree, but when we forced it, no one would bite.

The most significant point he makes is that people told him, 'The UK may be richer in the EU, but Britain is not richer.'

I feel real affection for Sir Brendan Barber as he speaks. He is a good man whose heart is in the right place. He believes that we were the victim of a narrative that has built up over years: 'Don't trust politicians.' He, too, warns about the real feeling of alienation out there.

Brendan believes 'Project Fear' was overdone and the emergency budget backfired badly, saying, 'The Chancellor and Alistair Darling were undoubtedly happy with it, but it came across as bullying and threats.'

He also says that the cross-party involvement of Labour was a disaster. 'They made a clear strategic decision that they weren't going to do much at a top level.'

There are then a series of interventions about how bad it was in the north and Wales, and how we never seemed to deal with that. Someone worries about the way the BBC dealt with it all. 'I was told that all their online stuff is now written so that it can be read on a smartphone. That means you are often reading the rebuttal before you've heard the argument.'

The Green MP, Caroline Lucas, says, 'We won on the facts, but we lost on the emotional appeal . . . There were too many people who felt they had nothing to risk or lose.' She goes on, 'And I'm sorry to say this, but we have an electoral system that focuses on a small number of swing voters in marginal seats — that means people arc going to feel ignored for years.' Her point is, it's no wonder they bit back.

Richard Reed concludes, 'We were too politically correct. We went quiet on their strengths. We should have talked relentlessly about "Project Lie", because we fought a good fight with honour and they fought a bad fight with dishonour.'

# Chapter 35

## The Last One Standing

THE POWER HAS drained from No. 10. The energy that normally pulses through the building has gone – like a speaker that has been blasting music at full volume, which has suddenly had the plug pulled.

The 8.30 a.m. meetings are taken up with questions about a likely leaving date – and what will be expected of DC in the meantime. Also the election of a new Conservative leader – and therefore Prime Minister – the candidates announcing, then the whittling of them down through a number of votes to a final two, who will then campaign around the country.

At one meeting, Oliver Letwin says, 'There are currently a lot of MPs having a conversation with themselves in the mirror – and the reflection is telling them it is their destiny to lead this great nation.'

The expectation is that this process will take until early September, though many want it finished sooner, arguing the country needs leadership.

The current PM does not mind – wanting to do whatever ensures a sensible process. We will watch from the sidelines of No. 10. Some find this process torturous – others declare that they will buy in some popcorn and remain glued to the news channels.

Boris is expected to be in the final two, though there are signs his campaign is in a mess. Most assume this is just another facet of the cavalier approach that has carried him so far. But then Sarah Vine writes a column suggesting that 'we' – herself and her husband, Michael Gove – are responsible for delivering Brexit for the 17 million people who voted for it. It seems a curious claim. Then an email from her is apparently sent by accident to someone, who then forwards it to a journalist.

It includes the lines, 'One simple message: you MUST have SPECIFIC from Boris OTHERWISE you cannot guarantee your support. The details can be worked out later on, but without that you have no leverage.'

Conspiracy theorists do not think it was an accident that it has emerged.

On Thursday 30 June, a few of us gather for a morning meeting, chaired by George Osborne as the PM has an engagement. Gavin Williamson, the Parliamentary Private Secretary to the PM, now working to ensure Theresa May is elected, says there are rumours that Gove is going to dump Boris and stand himself as leader. Gavin knows every bit of gossip in Westminster – most of which is nonsense. No one can quite believe that between now and when nominations for the leadership close in a few hours' time, there will be such a bloody and dramatic turn of events.

A few of the team, including Ameet and Graeme, gather in my office in No. 10 to watch Boris's speech, where he is expected to announce he is a candidate. If something dramatic is going to happen, no journalists appear to have picked it up.

Boris is late. His chosen location is flat and uninspiring and so is his speech. We wonder if these are the words of a man who really wants to be PM. Towards the end, I sit up. He's hinting a twist is coming. He tells his audience he has concluded he cannot be leader. There are gasps. It is clear that MPs who had come to support him, including Nadine Dorries, did not have a clue what was coming.

There's an eruption in No. 10, too. Someone texts, 'OMFG!'

I walk towards the PM's office. He is on the way out of the

building to an event. As ever in these situations, he is the calmest person. He assumes Gove is going to come out and stand. I tell him that if he does it will be disastrous for him. Surely Gove is capable of seeing that?

He isn't – and does indeed announce he is standing. Depending how you look at it, it's an act of extraordinary chutzpah, or reveals a basic failure to understand that people will be horrified by his behaviour. The man who told everyone he believed in Boris enough to be his campaign manager, now effectively saying it was a terrible misjudgement. And not only that – having told people countless times he did not have the skills to be PM, now asserting that he is the best person for the job.

So what went on? I'm told key MPs supporting Boris were gathered that morning to be asked to switch sides. Most did and that was communicated to Boris. A couple made clear they felt it would be dishonourable. As has been reported, that morning Gove spoke to Lynton Crosby, who had been helping Boris, telling him he was going to run, but did not speak direct to Boris, despite Lynton urging him to.

Other, well-placed sources have told me that Gove had made a series of demands that Boris found too much. He wanted to be Chancellor of the Exchequer, to run the Brexit negotiations, be Deputy Prime Minister, and – crucially – to have Dominic Cummings as a very senior figure inside Boris's No. 10. In other words, Boris would be the front man for a Gove government.

As Boris prepared his speech that morning, his world must have felt as if it was crumbling around him. But it still seems to me his decision to stand down immediately was extraordinary. He had the support of a healthy number of MPs; he could have called out Gove; and most importantly – there would have been no more ignominy in being knocked out of the next ballot than going now. He might have survived. My guess is that he would have found it all too humiliating.

We watch Gove announce that he is standing – and see him getting a rough ride. At one point, he is asked if Dominic Cummings will have a role at No. 10 if he is PM and without flinching, he says, 'No.' That feels an extraordinary response given the closeness of their relationship and that he had apparently been demanding of Boris that Cummings be at the centre of things.

When Gove is knocked out, we appear to be settling in for a summer battle between Theresa May and Andrea Leadsom. On paper Theresa should walk it. Andrea is inexperienced. The big thing in her favour, though, is that she is the darling of the Brexiteers and that should play well with the Tory grassroots.

Then Andrea makes a huge error. She appears to suggest she would be a better leader because she has children and Theresa May does not. The pressure on her is intense – and she cracks, announcing that she doesn't think she wants to be the leader after all.

Theresa May will be Prime Minister. We must leave No. 10 – and soon.

A senior journalist tells me it is as if it had been pre-ordained. I see his point. Amid the murder and betrayal, one figure stayed very still at the centre of it all – Theresa May. Now she is the last one standing.

It would be tempting to think that she had foreseen how it would play out. Of course, it is more complicated than that – a lot of skill, a lot of luck.

The skill was in understanding that in a Parliamentary Conservative Party that was split down the middle, the most attractive candidate was always going to be the one that both Remainers and Leavers could stomach after all the bloodletting. Theresa May backed Remain, but she did it in a way that made clear that for her, it was a finely balanced decision.

Her few interventions during the campaign were always calibrated to suggest she was fifty-one per cent for Remain and forty-nine per cent for Leave. Moreover, despite being the minister responsible for immigration, her submarine tactics – disappearing from view for long periods – meant that she was never questioned about it too much.

The luck was that no one could have predicted that the Gove/Boris relationship would detonate with such spectacular results, or that Boris would drop out so quickly. Had it been a straight fight between May and Boris, who knows what the result would have been?

Of course, the key question for Theresa May is how Brexit will be settled. It's surprising the number of people who think it may never happen. I cannot see the circumstances in which any politician could or should amass the political capital to go against the democratic will of the British people, or take on the sheer intensity of the campaign they would face.

For now, Theresa May tells everyone, 'Brexit means Brexit.' Of course, what Brexit means to dyed-in-the-wool Outers in the Parliamentary Conservative Party, large enough in number to overturn her tiny overall majority at will, and the others who want to have as much access to Europe as is possible, are worlds apart.

There will come a moment where the current Prime Minister is faced by the irresistible force of those who want complete control of immigration and an end to free movement, and the immoveable object of business and the vast majority of MPs that supported Remain, who demand as much access to the single market as possible.

Both cannot happen.

Compromise is inevitable. And that will lead to cries of betrayal.

# Epilogue

## 'And so . . . ?'

E D LLEWELLYN, WHO was the Chief of Staff at No. 10, liked to tell an anecdote about when Lord Carrington was Foreign Secretary. He sat around a large table with the best the Foreign Office had to offer, considering a thorny problem.

Each person who spoke seemed to have an even more insightful and eloquent exposition of the problem than the last.

When they had finished, Lord Carrington asked a devastating, two-word question, 'And so . . . ?'

His point was that the highly intelligent aides could describe the problem, but were acting like the proverbial person who, when asked directions, said, 'Well, I wouldn't have started here!' What was needed were ideas on what was to be done.

The Westminster village was crammed full of people who could spot that Europe had become an insurmountable issue – not just for the Conservative party, but increasingly for the country. David Cameron was the prime minister who knew he had to deal with it.

He was prepared to answer the 'And so . . . ?' question with a renegotiation of the UK's role in Europe followed by a referendum. Had he fudged the issue, the pressure would have mounted to such a degree that he would have been sacked by his party and replaced by someone who would deliver – or made to do it anyway.

Of course, he and the Stronger In campaign failed to convince the country that enough had been done to stay in. Most of the reasons given at the final board meeting I have described are important, but with the benefit of a few months' hindsight, only a few issues seem decisive to me.

Some have said Boris choosing to be a key figure in Leave was what did for us. It was certainly a major blow. He was – as Andrew Feldman, the former Chairman of the Conservative Party, put it – 'a rock star politician' for whom the rules seemed different. He was able to shrug off the criticisms and humiliations that would have been fatal to others, and to energise Leave's message in a way that enabled them to reach parts of the elect-orate that were beyond us.

He was important. But I now realise Michael Gove was crucial to their victory – mixing an intoxicating cocktail that was a blend of brilliance and poison.

He chaired a Leave campaign that succeeded in making their immigration argument about the economy and public services – and not just about the number of people coming to the UK. That was the force of the utterly dishonest claim that leaving the EU would save us £350 million a week that could be spent on the National Health Service. The Remain campaign was left noting how strongly it was cutting through, but never came up with a way to neutralise it, other than pointing out that all independent opinion agreed that the number was false and there would be less money to spend, not more, because the economy would shrink if we left the EU.

In a rational world that should have been enough to kill it. It wasn't. Other politicians might have abandoned it – as well as claims that millions of Turks were coming to this country – realising experts saw them as dishonest. He didn't. As Boris looked queasy, particularly on immigration, the campaign Gove chaired doubled down.

In the Tory leadership campaign that followed the referendum, many finally saw the personal ambition and willingness to deceive they had not spotted in Gove before.

It is clear that after the Christmas holidays his wife, Sarah Vine, had left David Cameron with the impression that he would not support the Leave campaign. When that turned out not to be the case, he then insisted he would not play a prominent role, only making the odd speech or publishing an article or two. Within days of saying that, he became the chairman of a campaign that was prepared to attack the people he called friends in ways that were as brutal as they were uncompromising.

He also appears to have played a decisive role in securing Boris, who at the time was reported as describing himself as veering all over the place like a wonky shopping trolley.

In pure political terms, Gove's moves were audacious and brilliant. He was instrumental in providing the bullets for the campaign, and consequently the right-wing press, to fire. He was prepared to see Government policies he had championed, such as the National Living Wage and our stewardship of the NHS, trashed. However, as a supposed intellectual, his wholesale dismissal of experts and his description of economists as the equivalent of Nazi propagandists was shameful.

Of course, it is only right that people stand up for the things they believe in – and Gove had a long track record of being a Eurosceptic. But this does not mean that treating relationships with people he had built up over years with such casual abandon was acceptable. They understandably felt he had betrayed the modern, compassionate Conservative values he claimed to stand for as a politician – embracing UKIP's worldview because he thought it could win – while also betraying them.

The view that David Cameron had dealt with him shabbily, by moving him from Education Secretary to Chief Whip, is a red herring. In fact, the PM felt he was going out of his way to protect a friend, with a plan to promote him again, while other powerful voices were calling for Gove to be simply fired.

Michael Gove was on the record as telling people who asked him about his personal leadership ambitions that he did not have the range of skills or the temperament for the job. He may not have believed what he was saying at the time, as a ruse to get him through uncomfortable interviews, but many came to see the truth in what he said the moment he cut Boris Johnson off at the knees on the morning he was due to launch his leadership bid. Until that moment, Gove had been his campaign manager.

He went on to claim that, contrary to everything he had always said, he *did* now think he could and should be Prime Minister. Crucially, he failed to realise that in acting as a political suicide bomber, one of his first victims would be himself.

Gove is a tragic figure in the Shakespearean sense. In many ways he is a brilliant man, capable of vision, witty and charming, and with a verbal dexterity second to none. But his fatal flaw was to be driven by a vaulting ambition and a preparedness to mislead. He let others down in a way that ultimately crushed himself.

When he appeared on the Andrew Marr programme on the Sunday after he announced he was running for the leadership, the normally polite and generous Marr accused him of being 'a political serial killer', his victims being David Cameron, George Osborne and Boris Johnson. He then suggested he turn to camera and say something sinister in the style of Francis Urquhart/Frank Underwood, the lead, Machiavellian character in *House of Cards*. It felt devastating. I wonder how Gove will ever live it down. He is a deeply talented man who could do so much good for this country – but that will involve setting aside all the destructive game-playing.

For all of that, we have to face the fact that having realised the inevitability of a referendum, we failed to secure Boris Johnson or enough newspaper support. We were risking everything – with too many conditions set against us.

More to the point, the closest thing to a law in politics, 'It's the economy, stupid!' turned out to be wrong for the first time in decades. Our destruction of the Leave campaign over the economy was complete – with international bodies, the Governor of the Bank of England and the overwhelming majority of independent economists warning repeatedly of the dangers of leaving. In the early stages of the campaign, it was almost alarming to see Leave fail to describe what life would look like outside the EU. Realising they had no answer, they bought into Nigel Farage's UKIP agenda – something they always said they would never do. They were also prepared to mislead the public – refusing to let go of the claim that money that was never sent to the EU could be poured into the NHS, telling people millions of Turks would overrun this country, and claiming we'd be forced to join an EU army.

Boris at least had the decency to try to distance himself from some of this nonsense. Gove, whom we should never forget had a picture of Lenin on his office wall, showed no such discomfort. Like Lenin, he believed the ends justified the means.

Having worked with him for a number of years now, I'm not sure what he really believes. A senior Conservative once said of him, 'The thing you've got to understand about Michael is that he is in love with rhetoric. He just loves arguing – he loves the idea of making a case . . . it could be anything.' Having seen and heard him say and do so many things that seem so contradictory, I am still left with one simple question: Would the real Michael Gove please stand up?

Finally, perhaps the most significant issue of all needs to be confronted.

We made assumptions that were wrong about the type of country we live in and how people would react.

We have all seen how the areas outside London, Scotland and Northern Ireland voted to Leave. Closer analysis of the results surprised me.

There have been contradictory accounts about the level of

turnout among young people. Analysis has settled on it being below forty per cent. In fact, turnout increased among every age-group except 18–24s: the group with the most to gain from remaining in the EU. Remain had a sophisticated, widespread and witty campaign that covered all fronts with the young – no one can say that why they needed to vote wasn't made clear. And yet they did not turn out in big enough numbers. If 18–24 year-olds had voted in the same proportions as 35–44 year-olds, Remain would have won.

Results were announced at a local authority, not constituency, level. I asked Andrew Cooper if it was possible to be specific to particular areas. He did some modelling for me. Breaking the results down to a constituency level, here is how the seats around the Nissan car plant, built largely to trade with Europe, voted:

Washington & Sunderland West – Remain 32%, Leave 68%
Houghton & Sunderland South – Remain 33%, Leave 67%

The seat of Jo Cox, who had campaigned so passionately for Remain before she was killed, voted:

Batley & Spen – Remain 38%, Leave 62%

And the seat that contains the Tata steel plant, which many believed would not be rescued if we left the EU, voted:

Aberavon – Remain 38%, Leave 62%

It seems to make no sense for Sunderland and Aberavon to have voted Leave. Doing so threatened the economic livelihood of their area – and therefore the life chances of the people who live there. So why did they do it?

Remain not having enough of an answer on immigration was certainly a major part of the problem. Tough controls on the welfare payments that European migrants could receive on coming into the UK were an achievement in the renegotiation.

It meant that in some cases people would be losing a thousand pounds a month – a major disincentive to coming here. And yet even I, who am as metropolitan and liberal on immigration as they come, questioned being part of an organisation that insists on having unlimited freedom of movement to work. It seems to me it is an unsustainable situation that countries with such varying economies can continue with this system.

In the face of the first rebellion against it, in the form of our renegotiation, the EU's response was to pull up the drawbridge and resist. In 2014 Angela Merkel warned us there could not be an emergency brake on numbers – and even after Britain had voted to leave, she insisted that could never have been on the table. Her roots in Eastern Europe told – when the Iron Curtain came down, she and tens of millions of others were reassured they need never be second-class citizens again. That meant freedom of movement.

For the popular press, the issue was simple: David Cameron said, 'I will not take no for an answer,' in his 2014 conference speech on immigration and the renegotiation. Our belief and claim that we had been true to that statement simply was not accepted and was widely ridiculed.

Despite that, we continued to have faith in the view that our relentless campaign on the economy would see us through. It didn't.

Since the vote, Peter Mandelson has pointed out that he argued for a major intervention on immigration – including a speech by the PM – in the final fortnight of the campaign. The idea was widely rejected, because it would have simply acted as another mechanism to highlight that we could not give people what they wanted.

A more important point is that no one believed that a section of society, which in many cases had not engaged in the political process since Tony Blair was first elected, would turn out in such great numbers.

Turnout for the referendum was 72.2 per cent – up six per cent on the 2015 general election. But turnout in the three counting regions to vote Remain increased by much less than in the nine that voted Leave (where it increased by an average of 7.5 per cent).

The increased turnout equates to about 2.8 million people who didn't vote in the general election, but did vote in the referendum. Ironically, if the demographic profile of these extra voters had been more or less the same as that of the 2015 general election voters, Remain would have won by about 52.5 to 47.5. Most polls, which have to take some view on who will actually vote, made precisely this assumption. That explains why so many got it wrong, and crucially, why most people thought we would win.

Those extra 2.8 million voters backed Leave overwhelmingly – and by more than enough to take them over the line to victory.

On the night, Nick Robinson provided anecdotal evidence from Sunderland of lots of people there who hadn't voted since the 1980s and were all turning out to vote Leave.

So what inspired them to do so?

When I was a child, my parents would pack me, my brother and sister into a VW camper van and take us on the twelve-hour drive to Torry in Aberdeen, where my grandparents lived. Their home was a tenement flat on a steep brae (hill) with a tiny bathroom, a kitchenette (where my grandmother would cook mince and tatties that I would struggle to eat) and two other rooms. The first of these rooms was kept special for when the church minister came. He rarely did. The second room was where they lived. It reminded me of *Charlie and the Chocolate Factory*, because it contained their bed, a table to eat at, two armchairs and a TV.

They were at the bottom – struggling to survive. But they also believed they had a stake in society. My grandpa, who moved from job to job, often in shops, made a point of reading the paper every day and made sure that everything stopped when the news came on. They always voted – believing it was their duty and they should have their say.

They were no different from others in their community. But somewhere along the line, people like them became disconnected from the political process. They felt betrayed – that politicians had feathered their own nests while they struggled. The world changed around them at an often alarming pace, with their communities feeling worse than they had in the past. TV programmes and social media showed the lifestyles of the rich and famous, which were a stark contrast to their own lives that felt insecure and a grind.

Anyone who has been to focus groups is familiar with people who feel angry about all of this. They are like the narrator of Joseph Heller's brilliant but utterly pessimistic novel, *Something Happened*, struggling to put their finger on what changed, what went wrong, and looking for an answer.

I suspect that for many of them the referendum was more than a straightforward question of whether or not it made sense to remain in the European Union. Instead it was a cipher that, encouraged by a cynical Leave campaign, allowed them to put whatever was worrying or angering them on the ballot paper: immigration, feeling let down, ignored, betrayed, a life that didn't turn out as it should have done . . .

Leave were ruthless in the exploitation of that with the slogan 'Take back control', which was powerful and vague enough to mean whatever you wanted it to. If we asked people who moderated the focus groups, 'Surely they don't believe what Leave are claiming . . . that we'll be able to slip anchor, and float away from Europe, turning ourselves into the land of milk and honey . . . ,' they would respond, 'Some do. Many don't. But they're sending a message.'

The feeling in that group was too powerful. It persuaded

them that for once it was worth voting, and they overwhelmed those who asked, 'Don't you realise, things will be worse not just for us, but for you, too, if we leave?'

We didn't do enough to understand them. Will politics find a way to properly engage them – rather than play cynical games, attempting to confirm their worst fears about the world? This question will and should trouble us in the coming years.

In the weeks that have passed since the referendum, I have done a number of interviews and events on what happened and the reality of Brexit. There are a lot of despondent people out there who question, why did David Cameron have to call a referendum? Surely he should have left it? Can there be another one?

I remind them that the question of our membership of the EU had been a slow train coming – with pressure not just from within the Conservative party, but UKIP and the popular press. That pressure had reached breaking point – and if David Cameron hadn't dealt with it, someone would have come along who was prepared to take action.

I go on to point out that you have to be around sixty to have been able to vote in the last referendum on Europe – and the mandate plainly needed renewing.

David Cameron listened to the analysis of the problem, but then had the guts to answer the crucial 'And so . . . ?' question by calling a referendum. It didn't work out for him, but he showed real leadership in facing up to an issue and being prepared to deal with it.

Two days before he left No. 10, David Cameron held a dinner for those who had been closest to him. Friends going back over the decades were there, so too were MPs who first supported his leadership bid, whom he said at one stage could all fit into the back of a black cab.

In his trademark casual clothing of jeans and an untucked navy-blue shirt, he toured the giant table in the state dining room – still joking, caring that his staff find ways to land on their feet. I felt proud to have worked for a man who had always been able to take anything in his stride – and as Kipling put it:

> . . . meet with Triumph and Disaster
> And treat those two impostors just the same

It fell to Kate Fall to make a touching speech about how much he meant to us all and then George Osborne to speak of his legacy. He described David Cameron as a 'quiet revolutionary' – a man who had been prepared to make the big offer of a coalition government that would provide the stability necessary to rescue our failing economy. He pointed out his education reforms, giving parents and teachers control so that pupils could have more of a chance in life; how he was prepared to reform welfare to make work pay and help give people a purpose.

Then he spoke of allowing gay people to marry for the first time – helping people who loved each other to show the commitment that had been denied them . . . two and a half million people more in work . . . millions of apprentices . . . keeping his promise to the poor people of the world, by maintaining our international aid budget, despite the most intense pressure . . .

I'd have added making the Conservative party electable again.

Two days later, his closest team gathered in his study in Downing Street and we talked about the thousands of meetings we'd held here. Larry the cat wandered in, stretched nonchalantly and then found a place on the sofa to settle. Then came Sam and their children, who clambered onto his chair and insisted on writing a note to Theresa May and her husband on the pristine piece of blotting paper that had been put in place just an hour or two before.

Someone came in and told us it was time to go. I walked out into the corridor with Ed, Kate and Graeme, surprised to see a couple of hundred civil servants lining the route. They

began to applaud and cheer. I told them he wasn't coming yet
– but they kept going.

We joined the end of the line – and DC, Sam and the kids
came out a few moments later. Having toured the building
saying emotional goodbyes earlier he was in a more ebullient
mood, high-fiving a few people as he went by.

His team watched his farewell speech from outside the door
of No. 11.

When he was done, he and his family got in the cars that
would take them out of Downing Street for the last time, and
he turned to wave to us.

I thought, I hope history will be kind to you.

# Acknowledgements

The No. 10 media and strategy team.
Back row: Richard Chew, Ramsay Jones,
Graeme Wilson, Caroline Preston
Front row: Giles Kenningham, Adam Atashzai,
Craig Oliver, Ameet Gill

*Unleashing Demons* could not have been written without the help of many people.

Colleagues who became close friends at No. 10 and Stronger In took the time and effort to read the manuscript and offer constructive criticism. Ameet Gill, Graeme Wilson, Lucy Thomas and Adam Atashzai were particularly helpful. All the opinions and any mistakes or misunderstandings are mine and not theirs.

Andrew Cooper, the pollster for Stronger In, was enormously helpful with the sections of the book dealing with polling. He also helped me to break down the results into digestible form.

I would also like to thank the rest of the political media team at No. 10, Giles Kenningham and Caroline Preston, and the comms team at Stronger In, including Joe Carberry, Amy Richards, James McGrory and David Chaplin – all of whom set aside party differences to work for a common cause we all believed in.

My agent, Sheila Crowley, has been supportive and encouraging throughout.

Rupert Lancaster took a huge gamble commissioning this book. We had never met before and I had never written a book – let alone one that needed to be completed so quickly. He was kind, generous and insightful. He also led a great team at Hodder including Maddy Price, Karen Geary, Jason Bartholemew and Juliet Brightmore, all of whom were prepared to crash a busy schedule in order to get the book published in time.

The unsung heroes of this book are the civil servants with whom I worked so closely in the run-up to the final month of the campaign, when I effectively resigned to join Stronger In. They are the backbone of Government, whatever its political stripe. I am in their debt.

# Index

# Picture Acknowledgements

© AP/Press Association Images: 1 above/photo Frank Augstein, 6 above left/Kaname Muto, 8 below/Kirsty Wigglesworth. © Daily Mail/Solo Syndication: 2 below right. © Getty Images: 1 below/AFP/Niklas Halle'n, 3 above and 7 above/AFP/Stefan Rousseau, 4 above left/Matt Cardy, 4 below right/Carl Court, 5 above/Jack Taylor, 5 below/AFP/Oli Scarff, 6 above right/ Rob Stothard, 6 below right/Dan Kitwood, Courtesy of Felicity Kane: 4 above right. © News Syndication: 2 above left, 3 below/ Peter Brookes, 6 below left. © Andrew Parsons/i-Images: 4 below left. © REX/Shutterstock: 8 above/Jonathan Hordle. Courtesy of Sky News: 7 below.

### An invitation from the publisher

Join us at www.hodder.co.uk, or follow us
on Twitter @hodderbooks to be a part of
our community of people who love the very
best in books and reading.

Whether you want to discover more about a book
or an author, watch trailers and interviews, have the
chance to win early limited editions, or simply browse
our expert readers' selection of the very best books,
we think you'll find what you're looking for.

And if you don't, that's the place to tell us what's missing.

**We love what we do, and we'd love you to be a part of it.**

www.hodder.co.uk

 @hodderbooks

 HodderBooks

 HodderBooks